KATE CHOPIN

KATE CHOPIN

An Annotated Bibliography of Critical Works

Suzanne Disheroon Green and David J. Caudle

Bibliographies and Indexes in Women's Studies,
Number 28

GREENWOOD PRESS
Westport, Connecticut • London

016.813
C54g

Library of Congress Cataloging-in-Publication Data

Green, Suzanne Disheroon, 1963–
    Kate Chopin : an annotated bibliography of critical works   /
Suzanne Disheroon Green and David J. Caudle.
        p.   cm.—(Bibliographies and indexes in women's studies.
ISSN 0742-6941 ; no. 28)
    Includes bibliographical references and index.
    ISBN 0-313-30424-6 (alk. paper)
    1. Chopin, Kate, 1851–1904—Bibliography.   2. Women and
literature—United States—Bibliography.   I. Caudle, David J.,
1956–   . II. Title.   III. Series.
Z8168.19.G74   1999
[PS1294.C63]
016.813′4—dc21   99–11306

British Library Cataloguing in Publication Data is available.

Library of Congress Catalog Card Number: 99–11306
ISBN: 0-313-30424-6
ISSN: 0742-6941

First published in 1999

Greenwood Press, 88 Post Road West, Westport, CT 06881
An imprint of Greenwood Publishing Group, Inc.
www.greenwood.com

Printed in the United States of America

JK

The paper used in this book complies with the
Permanent Paper Standard issued by the National
Information Standards Organization (Z39.48–1984).

10 9 8 7 6 5 4 3 2 1

Dedicated to the furtherance of collaborative research in the Humanities

Contents

Preface ix

Acknowledgments xiii

Abbreviations xv

Kate Chopin's Life and Literary Career
  Emily Toth 1

Where Are We Going? Where Have We Been? Twenty Years of Chopin
Criticism
  Suzanne Disheroon Green 13

The Fall and Rise of Kate Chopin and Her Works
  David J. Caudle 31

Annotated Bibliographical Entries
  A. Primary Texts 51
  B. Biographies 55
  C. Bibliographies 57
  D. Critical Books and Journal Articles, 1976-1999 61
  E. Essays in Edited Volumes 185
  F. Dissertations 215

Author Index 247
Title Index 253
Subject Index 267

Preface

The intent of this volume is to give scholars, students, and others interested in the study of Kate Chopin and her works an overview of the critical work that has appeared during the past two decades. The coverage of this volume begins in 1976, where the first survey of Chopin criticism, Marlene Springer's volume *Edith Wharton and Kate Chopin: A Reference Guide* leaves off.

As the title indicates, the bulk of the volume consists of enumerated and annotated entries for each of Chopin's works that appeared between 1976 and 1998, and also includes annotations of major books and essays which are scheduled to appear in 1999 as this volume goes to press. In addition, this volume contains two biblio-critical essays, a selective primary bibliography and a critical introduction by Pulitzer Prize nominated biographer Emily Toth. Toth's essay, "Kate Chopin's Life and Literary Career" provides a discussion of Chopin's life and focuses specifically on new biographical data that she has discovered since the publication of her comprehensive Chopin biography in 1990. "Where Are We Going? Where Have We Been? Twenty Years of Chopin Criticism," by Suzanne Disheroon Green, offers a survey of the critical studies of Chopin's works and suggests an organizational structure for the large body of scholarly study. "The Fall and Rise of Kate Chopin and Her Works," by David J. Caudle, examines the early critical reception of Kate Chopin's fiction, focusing particularly on *The Awakening* and its later rise to prominence in American letters.

The enumerative entries in this volume are prepared in accordance with the second edition of the *MLA Style Manual*. While we have attempted to include annotations for each study enumerated in this volume, for a variety of reasons, we were unable to obtain six items. These few items are enumerated but not annotated.

Methodology

The body of *Kate Chopin* is organized into five sections, with each section cataloging a major group of publications concerning Chopin's work. These sections are described below:

Primary Texts: This section offers an enumerative list of Chopin's works, most of which are currently in print. Two texts that appeared before the 1976-present time frame are included, as they are important texts for those new to Chopin studies.

Biographies: Biographical studies and sketches constitute this section. Similar to the Primary Texts section, all book-length studies of Chopin's life undertaken to date are enumerated and briefly annotated, even if they do not fall within the stated time parameters of the bulk of the volume.

Bibliographies: Bibliographic essays, as well as enumerative and annotated bibliographies that appeared after Springer's 1976 volume, are included in this section.

Critical Books and Journal Articles: This section contains the majority of the entries. These entries are arranged chronologically, beginning with 1976 and ending with 1999. The chapters in this section fall into two categories: (1) book-length studies and/or articles from book length studies, and (2) journal articles. The information in each of these categories is arranged alphabetically by the last name of the author.

Titles of journals that frequently publish essays dealing with Chopin and her works are abbreviated. The list of abbreviations at the front of this volume provides a key to these titles.

Essays in Edited Volumes: Entries in this section come from volumes which are devoted exclusively to the study of some aspect of Chopin and her work. Many of the essays in this section are reprints of works previously published, and accordingly, cross-references point the reader to the original sources of these reprinted articles. The annotations for articles that have been reprinted one or more times appear with the *most recent reprinting of the essay*. Annotations for the volumes as a whole may be found in the Critical Books and Journal Articles section.

Dissertations: Brief annotations of dissertations that offer substantial studies of Chopin and her work appear in this section. These annotations are drawn in large part from the information provided to *Dissertation Abstracts International*. Like the Critical Books section, the dissertation section is arranged in chronological chapters, with entries in these chapters appearing in alphabetical order.

Indexes: The volume also includes three extensive indexes that categorize the critical studies by author, title, and subject, so that work by specific scholars or dealing with particular topics might be located efficiently.

Acknowledgments

As is the case with any project of this magnitude, the list of individuals who helped to make this book a reality is lengthy. We owe a great debt of gratitude to our families for their support, both emotional and financial: Charles L. Green, Jay and Jolene Caudle, Fred Disheroon and Diane Donley, Richard and Elaine Green, Kathryn A. Green and J. Alexander Green.

Alexander Pettit of the University of North Texas was instrumental in helping us plan this volume, and in making initial contact with Greenwood Press. James T. F. Tanner, Haj Ross and Barbara Rodman have not only taught each of us an enormous amount about American literature and literary research, but have been tremendously supportive mentors toward our research efforts and wonderful friends in the bargain. The efforts of Lisa Abney of Northwestern State University in helping us to edit and revise the final version of the manuscript were invaluable as well. Emily Toth of Louisiana State University was also an indispensable resource, both for her contribution of the introduction to this volume, as well as for her advice and suggestions for revision. Able assistance with translations of materials in French and German was provided by Marie Françoise Conin-Jones, Derek Foster, and Jerry Erath.

Barbara Ewell of Loyola University, New Orleans not only helped us locate a copy of her essay, but gave us advance copies of the special section of *Southern Quarterly* devoted to Chopin. We are grateful for her kindness in helping us make this volume as up-to-date as possible. Susan Bonifer and Gisela Brinker-Gabbler also assisted us in locating hard-to-find items.

We also owe a debt of gratitude to Fleming Thomas, the Interlibrary Loan Librarian at Northwestern State University, who diligently and repeatedly attempted to help us locate the last few hard-to-locate items. Laura Stuart of Louisiana State University, Shreveport, David Weeks of Xavier University, Nancy Brown of the Center for Southwestern Studies at the University of New Mexico, and Robert Skinner at Xavier University were also indispensable in this regard. The reference librarians at the Library of Congress, as well as the reading room staffs of that institution, were very helpful as the LOC served as our base of operations while we completed the bulk of our research. Substantial research was also undertaken at the University of North Texas Libraries, University of Maryland at College Park McKeldin Library, Georgetown University Library, and Texas Woman's University Blagg-Huey Library. We are also grateful to the reference staff at the Missouri Historical Society for their willingness to provide information over the phone and through the U.S. mail. The databases of *Dissertation Abstracts International* were an invaluable aid in annotating doctoral dissertations.

James Harner has said that part of the frustration involved in compiling a study such as this one is that you don't really know how to write such a book until you've written one. Without a doubt, his monograph, *On Compiling an Annotated Bibliography*, helped us avoid many of the pitfalls. Without the benefit of Harner's sage and timely advice, we might still be wandering the halls of the Library of Congress like a couple of lost tourists.

Abbreviations

The following abbreviations appear throughout the enumerative entries:

ALR   American Literary Realism
AmLit   American Literature
ArQ   Arizona Quarterly

KCN   Kate Chopin Newsletter

LaLit   Louisiana Literature
Legacy   Legacy: A Journal of American Women Writers

MissQ   Mississippi Quarterly

RegF   Regionalism and the Female Imagination

SLJ   Southern Literary Journal
SoQ   Southern Quarterly
SoSt   Southern Studies
SSF   Studies in Short Fiction

Kate Chopin's Life and Literary Career

Emily Toth

In 1967, Professor George Arms of the University of New Mexico wrote what may be the first essay summarizing Kate Chopin's achievements as an author. His "Kate Chopin's *The Awakening* in the Perspective of Her Literary Career" appeared in a *Festschrift* at a time when such collections honoring retiring scholars were common. (Now, with declining university press subsidies, they're extremely rare.) Arms wrote at a time when literature seemed to matter more than it does today.

Arms's essay was a pioneering work, for he attempted to delineate the shape of Chopin's career before Per Seyersted's biography (1969) and *Complete Works* (1969) even existed. Arms's essay on a woman writer also appeared before the second wave of the women's movement transformed American life and swept over the literary canon — opening it up, at last, to authors like Kate Chopin.

At the time that Arms was crafting his essay, I was a lowly instructor with a Master's degree, at Morgan State College in Baltimore. I had never heard of Kate Chopin. Nor had I been assigned to read any women writers at all in college and graduate school, except the big five British novelists (Jane Austen, the Brontës, George Eliot, and Virginia Woolf). Through omission and silence, I had been taught that no American women writers, and no writers of color, had ever been great enough for us to study them in school.

I had never heard of George Arms, either. Three years later, I would enter a Ph.D. program and eventually write a dissertation on Kate Chopin. Mine would also be the first Johns Hopkins dissertation to grapple with what feminist criticism —

a union of the personal and the political, applied to literature — might be. But rereading Arms's essay now, three decades later, brings back the ways that critics during the era of New Criticism approached authors: private life was essentially denied. One was supposed to concentrate on "the work itself," and biographical speculation was mostly taboo. (If we dug out juicy stuff, we kept it to ourselves.)

In any case, there was very little biographical information available to Arms. Although he mentions Daniel Rankin's 1932 biography, Arms does not quote from it nor comment at all about the author's life outside her achievements as an author. He speculates about whether she identified with Edna, but gives no evidence outside the text of *The Awakening*. In fact, he disagrees with other critics' claims that "The Story of an Hour" expresses Chopin's "attitude toward husbands" (225). But neither he, nor the critics he quotes, give any evidence to support their interpretation.

In short, Arms's definition of "career" means "publications." That is not, today, what we mean by a woman's career. Now, we mean her work and her life, in both the public and private spheres. We also do not hesitate to do research, and to speculate, about how the private woman came to produce the public writings that so many critics have analyzed. Our gazes have moved; our paradigms have shifted.

Daniel Rankin's *Kate Chopin and Her Creole Stories*, published in 1932, is a warmly-written picture of the author's life, but it makes her seem thoroughly conventional. Kate O'Flaherty, as described by Rankin, was born in St. Louis and educated at the Sacred Heart Academy, where she was popular and noted for her storytelling. In 1870, she married Oscar Chopin of Louisiana, and after a three-month European honeymoon, they settled in New Orleans, and later in rural Cloutierville, Natchitoches Parish, northwest Louisiana. (Rankin does not give pronunciations: "Shów-pan"; "Cloochyville"; "Nák-I-tush.")

The Chopins had six children in nine years, and Oscar died suddenly. Kate returned to St. Louis where, after a few years, she began writing stories critical of marriage. Yet, says Rankin, her own marriage had been extremely happy. As a widow, she dedicated herself loyally to her husband's memory — although many (unnamed) men did admire her, and she did leave the Catholic Church. (Rankin, it should be noted, was a priest.)

According to Rankin, Chopin's 1899 novel, *The Awakening*, had been removed from library circulation. She died a few years later, in 1904.

Thirty-seven years after Rankin, Per Seyersted's *Kate Chopin: A Critical Biography* (1969), painted a similar picture of her life. Seyersted's main purpose was to resurrect and promote her writings, and he did discover "The Storm," the shocking, delightful sexual fantasy Chopin wrote in 1898 but never published.

"The Storm" appeared in print for the first time in Seyersted's *Complete Works* in 1969. (It is now reprinted everywhere, often with no acknowledgment that it could not be published in the 1890s, or for that matter, in some venues in the 1960s: Seyersted was told he could not publish it in the Missouri Historical Society's *Bulletin* in the early 1960s).

But Seyersted, in 1969, also did not question Rankin's conventional narrative of Chopin's life, which fell neatly into three parts: a Girl in St. Louis; a Wife and Mother in Louisiana; and an Author and Chaste Widow in St. Louis. Seyersted found a few more sources who remembered her, but no one seems to have speculated, at least in print, about why a happy wife and devoted widow would write stories like "The Storm," *The Awakening*, and other tales of forbidden desires, including "A Respectable Woman," "La Belle Zoraïde," "A Lady of Bayou St. John," and many more.

Seyersted further added to the legend that *The Awakening* had been banned — a legend circulating freely after Rankin's book. Seyersted found a former library clerk who blamed the banning on a committee, and Kate Chopin herself made some ironic statements that could be interpreted as references to a banning. That legend — that *The Awakening* was a dirty book, and that the public was kept from reading it — was what resurrected the book in the early 1970s. One had to read it, and I did. And I wondered about its author and her marriage.

(I also wondered, much later, about whether *The Awakening* had actually ever been banned. Library records show it never was banned at all. But the legend retains a marvelous life of its own, which I describe in "The Alleged Banning of *The Awakening*.")

I first read *The Awakening* in the early 1970s, and then studied Rankin's and Seyersted's biographies. By the mid-1970s, I had finished a dissertation on Chopin's use of literary conventions for depicting women and people of color, and then I put her aside — only to return when I had learned more about women's lives. When scholars like Carolyn Heilbrun, Linda Wagner-Martin, and others began looking more closely at women's lives, they began suggesting that we needed to ask different questions. We needed to stop defining women primarily in relation to others, especially husbands and children: we needed new narratives of the quest as well as the nest.

Eventually, I set out to write a new narrative of Kate Chopin's life because I felt — to put it most succinctly — that Rankin and Seyersted had mostly not looked at Kate Chopin through women's eyes (Snitzer; Toth, "Shadow").

Rankin, I think, could not have done so; Seyersted, whose mother was a Norwegian feminist leader, asked some of the right questions, but could not find the women with the right answers. But I, an American woman benefitting from the ferment of the feminist movement, could discover information and insights that were not available to my predecessors. I was able to talk candidly with female descendants of those who'd known Kate Chopin in Cloutierville, for instance, and I discovered that there had indeed been another man.

His name was Albert Sampite, and he inspired the characters named Alcée in her fiction. (Alcée Laballière in "At the 'Cadian Ball" and "The Storm," as well as Alcée Arobin in *The Awakening*.) In my 1990 Chopin biography, I saw him as the key to much of what Kate Chopin wrote about men.

In 1999, I am not so sure. And so, after this long introduction, let me present a life of Kate Chopin that may illuminate her career, both public and private, for readers of this volume.

Kate O'Flaherty was born in 1850. (Many sources still say 1851, but her baptismal certificate and the U. S. Census show 1850 as the undoubted date.) At the age of five, she was sent to boarding school — highly unusual for a child from an intact family. There was a new baby, and Kate was a bit of a handful. But it is also possible that her father was involved with his family's female slaves (who produced several children designated in the census as "mulatto"). Kate may have been sent away to keep her from asking impertinent questions.

In any case, her father died that year in a train crash (Chopin readers will recognize that event from her "Story of an Hour"). Her mother, like generations of women in her family before and after her, was widowed young and never remarried. Eliza O'Flaherty took her place in a line, and in a household, of independent, smart widows who controlled their own money and their own lives. They were also the ones who educated young Kate O'Flaherty.

The effect of a female household on young Kate's development cannot be overemphasized. Wealthy homes without husbands were extremely rare, but the only male voices in Kate's household were her brother and half-brother, a couple of cousins, and male slaves. There was no patriarch in charge, and women ruled — as they also did at the Sacred Heart Academy.

At home and at school, Katie O'Flaherty saw intelligent women who could do everything. Her later stories suggest that she knew self-sufficiency was not for every woman, but she creates memorably self-sufficient characters in, among others, "The Maid of St. Phillippe," "Lilacs," "Regret," and *The Awakening*. That a woman might live alone and enjoy it was not an impossible thought.

She also had a best friend, Kitty Garesché, but only women know how important a best friend is (Apter). The Civil War, which both Rankin and Seyersted pass over quickly, was in fact a watershed for Kate O'Flaherty's girlhood. During those years she, following her family, was a Confederate sympathizer and came close to being arrested for tearing down a Union flag. She also grieved for the deaths of two close family members: her half-brother, who was a soldier, and her great-grandmother, her first teacher.

But my research into those years turned up two other events that may have been even more traumatizing. One was the loss of her best friend — for Kitty, with her Confederate family, was banished from St. Louis. The second was an "outrage" committed at the O'Flaherty household, according to a neighbor's letter. It included an invasion by Union soldiers, bayonets pointed at Eliza O'Flaherty — and whatever else it included, for young Kate, can only be imagined.

What we do know is that after the War, she suffered what modern psychologists call a "loss of voice." She went into a deep depression, a silence that was healed only by a warm and gifted nun, Madam Mary O'Meara of the Sacred Heart sisters. Kate O'Flaherty's young life had been devastated by war and by her encounters with patriarchal power. What restored her were the strengths, the voices, and the intelligence of women.

When she came to marry Oscar Chopin, at the age of twenty in 1870, Kate O'Flaherty had chosen an unusual man (and there is no evidence that the marriage was in any way arranged for her). Oscar, six years older, had been born in rural Louisiana but spent the Civil War years in France. He had a cosmopolitan background, was as comfortable in French as in English, and he had something else that would have attracted young Kate O'Flaherty: he had a sympathy for women.

We know that Oscar's father, Dr. Victor Jean-Baptiste Chopin, was a brutal man who mistreated both his wife and his slaves (Armand, when he is brutal in "Désirée's Baby," certainly has traces of Dr. Chopin). But when Oscar was fourteen, he ran away from home and went to live with relatives — as did his mother. It seems that Oscar, in fact, defended his mother against his battering father.

By the time Kate married into the family, Oscar's mother was dead; his father would follow just a month after the newlyweds settled in New Orleans, in the fall of 1870. But the family stories continued, and Oscar's appreciation of Kate's individuality was remarked upon by everyone. He did not try to coerce her into her "duty." Rather, he enjoyed her humor, her music, and even her imitations of animals, birds, priests, and his own relatives.

Oscar was a cotton factor, the gentlemanly middle man between the cotton traders and the growers. In that profession he met, among others, the relatives of Edgar

Degas, the French painter who spent several months in New Orleans in 1873. Degas painted an office like the one in which Oscar worked (*Bureau de Coton*), but the not-yet-famous painter also, obviously, met Kate Chopin at that time.

Degas, in France, had been close friends with the painter Berthe Morisot, whose painter-sister had married, given up her art, and been unhappy for the rest of her life. The sister's name was Edma Pontillon — too close to Edna Pontellier to be accidental. (Other correspondences and connections also appear in my *Unveiling Kate Chopin*.)

Beyond the fact that she took long walks and listened to others' stories and came of age as a wife and mother, we know little about Kate Chopin's New Orleans years. She was immersed in bearing and raising children and often spent months at a time with her mother in St. Louis (a form of birth control). There were also some summers at Grand Isle, just becoming a Creole resort, but we do not know which summers, or how many, the Chopins actually spent there. In 1874 Oscar took part in the Battle of Liberty Place, a White League attack against the police — but whether Kate shared his racial politics is unknown. (At the time of the battle, she was in St. Louis, awaiting the birth of their third son.)

By the time Oscar's business failed, in 1879, the couple had five sons. Kate was pregnant with their last child and only daughter when they moved to Oscar's family lands in Cloutierville, toward the end of the year. There, Kate was freer to indulge her curiosity — and the locals, likewise, scrutinized her freely.

They did not like what they saw. She was a sophisticated city woman who wore flamboyant clothes, smoked cigarettes, and flirted with other women's husbands. She was also, inevitably, seen as an outsider — an experience which helped her to create the outsider character Edna Pontellier, a Kentucky Presbyterian often bewildered by the Creoles' ways in *The Awakening*. (Melicent, the heartless St. Louis flirt in Chopin's first novel, *At Fault*, also reflects in some ways Chopin's experiences in Cloutierville.)

And then, suddenly, Oscar Chopin died of malaria, just before Christmas in 1882. Kate had six children, the youngest not yet three years old, and was $12,000 in debt. As Rankin and Seyersted both note, she took over Oscar's business, collected the debts, sold off some properties, and put it all on a solid footing. In that, she reflected the practicality of the women who raised her in her female-run household in St. Louis.

But there was also a serpent during her widowhood: her neighbor Albert Sampite ("Sám-pi-tay"), a married man who had a habit of consoling widows. He was handsome and tempting, and according to village gossip, they definitely had a romance (years later, his estranged wife said that Kate Chopin had broken up her marriage). We know that they mingled their money, or perhaps he attempted to take hers over.

But Albert Sampite was also a dangerously violent man. Charming when sober, he turned vicious when he drank, and beat his wife with a leather strap. He followed what we now recognize as the pattern of the classic batterer — isolating her from her friends and family, preventing her from finding help, destroying her confidence, and terrifying their children (Koppelman).

But Kate Chopin was different. She had not grown up in a patriarchal household where violence was the norm — and she was not his wife. Abruptly, in 1884, she left Cloutierville and moved back to St. Louis. She would live with her mother; her children would attend the finest public schools in the country; and she would escape an impossibly painful situation in Cloutierville.

That move back to St. Louis — leaving her lover for a mother-woman, just as Edna does toward the end of *The Awakening* — was what enabled Kate Chopin to become an author.

Chopin's mother, who was also her best friend, died within a year. A few years later, Chopin had essentially stopped being a Catholic and had become a published writer. Her first publication was a polka and her second a poem, but then she turned to the short stories that would make her name. She tried Missouri local color, but there was little interest. What sold was Louisiana — and so she mined her memories.

She used the quaint language and customs that fed the vogue for local color but shaped her stories to make universal comments about women and men and human relationships. Her two novels (*At Fault* - 1890 and *The Awakening* - 1899) and nearly a hundred short stories, essays, poems, reviews, and a play are a mature woman's reflections on romance, death, generosity, greed, violence, family loyalty, and much, much more.

What she has to say is never truly confined to Louisiana, and neither was she. While she used her memories — including her thoughts about Albert Sampite — I think now that her memories and attachments to women, and perhaps to Oscar, were far more central to her life.

By the early and mid-1890s, Kate Chopin had created the first literary and artistic salon in St. Louis, with herself at the center. Essentially, she invented networking, as her friends — journalists, in particular — were the ones who promoted her career, as well as abetting her more avant garde forays. She was famous as a smoker and an advanced literary lady, and she had great ambitions.

She carefully crafted a certain public image as a nonchalant writer, a tosser-off of stories who refused to work very hard at being an Author. She would write, she said in one essay, unless housework distracted her, and she claimed that she did not have a writing room, preferring to have her children "swarming" around her. In fact, she had a room of her own, pictured in a newspaper drawing by one of her sons. And her children, in their teens and twenties when she was writing in the 1890s, were far too large to swarm.

Yet in the 1890s, as in the 1990s, women with public fame routinely claim to put their families first and to be un-serious about their careers. Rankin, in his book, promoted that portrait of Kate Chopin and contributed to that image in a particularly sinister way that was revealed only sixty years later.

In the late 1920s and early 1930s, Rankin borrowed some of Chopin's manuscripts from her descendants, promising to return them. Some he did give to the University of Pennsylvania library, where he did his dissertation, although the family wanted them to be housed at the Missouri Historical Society in St. Louis. But other, handwritten manuscripts he squirreled away in a warehouse in Worcester, Massachusetts in 1932 — and they stayed there, untouched, until new owners began cleaning out the building in 1992 (Toth).

They found a cache of handwritten story manuscripts by Kate Chopin. Fragile, written in pencil on newsprint, the manuscripts are mostly drafts for stories she later revised for print: there are scribbled-over parts of "A Little Country Girl," "Charlie," "A Vocation and a Voice," and others. There are also a few fragments of stories that Chopin began but never finished.

What the Rankin-Marhefka Fragments (as they are now called) demonstrate is that Kate Chopin was a committed, ambitious author. Along with her manuscript account notebooks (called the Bonnell and Wondra Books in *Kate Chopin's Private Papers*), they show how dedicated she was to her career. Like the women in her family, she knew how to control her job and her money. She strove to improve her writing and especially to improve her marketing. She wanted to appear in the top magazines, and within five years after beginning her career, she had succeeded: she was in the *Atlantic* and the *Century* magazines.

The narrative of Kate Chopin's life, in the last part, is not primarily the tale of a chaste widow. Rather, it is the story of an ambitious author. Like many women whose lives are famous enough to be written about, she stopped following the traditional path of a woman — and became an individual.

Individuality in women is not always easy to see. Often, without even knowing what we are doing, we look for the typical, for the familiar wife-and-mother behind the dynamic career. We look for the demure belle or the suffering widow — and see women primarily as appendages to men or as seeking the approval of men.

Except professionally, Kate Chopin seemed not to be all that interested in men's approval as she grew older.

Her pictures show that she did not particularly dress to suit men's notions of fashionability. She was a woman of substance, with a figure more like the grandiose Lillian Russell than the lithe Gibson Girl, and after her teen years, none of her pictures look flirtatious. Her gaze is much more like Edna Pontellier's: quick, bright, and direct.

Nor were her stories always attuned to the tastes of literary men. She broke into the *Atlantic* with "Athénaïse," the tale of an immature young woman who runs away from her husband but returns once she discovers she is pregnant — an ending that rather celebrates a conventional female condition. It was one of very few Chopin stories ever accepted by the *Atlantic*. Mostly, she could not write the traditionally pleasing story.

The stories for which she is best known today include "Désirée's Baby" and "The Story of an Hour," as well as "A Lady of Bayou St. John" and "La Belle Zoraïde" and "A Respectable Woman." All those stories first appeared in the first issues of a fashion magazine edited by a woman: *Vogue*, edited by the eccentric, independent Josephine Redding. By herself, with her own tastes, Josephine Redding created the Kate Chopin whose discovery was such a shock and a delight for Per Seyersted in the 1950s and the rest of us in the 1970s.

(In this instance, George Arms's piece shows his lack of knowledge about women's forms of resistance. He writes disparagingly that some of Chopin's work is "in a juvenile vein or from the conventional angle of a woman's magazine" (221)).

Chopin, in any case, could not confine herself to the well-made, easy-selling story built on local color. She kept stretching the subject matter, and two of her most radical stories are mostly forgotten. Both were hard to place, since they do not concern romance; they are not upbeat, and they fit no comfortable late nineteenth-century story paradigm. One, "Odalie Misses Mass," is probably the only story of its era showing a female friendship between a young white girl and an old African American woman: they cross the races and the generations. The other, "In Sabine," seems to be the only story of its era in which a battered wife escapes from her violent husband (Koppelman).

"Odalie Misses Mass" appeared in the *Shreveport Times*, the only newspaper that would take it. "In Sabine" was slipped into Chopin's first story collection, *Bayou Folk* (1894), for which a publisher was guaranteed.

In the latter part of the 1890s, Chopin's stories no longer conformed to what editors wanted. They were confused by her stories that seemed to ramble, lyrically, rather than end in a way that tied up loose ends. Her earlier tale, "A Matter of Prejudice," for instance, ends in the conversion of a curmudgeonly woman who hates everything "American." But "An Egyptian Cigarette" — a late, *Vogue* story — is about a woman who smokes an hallucinogenic cigarette, has some bad visions, and is unhappy.

Kate Chopin, though, had not stopped writing when she published *A Night in Acadie* (1897), her second story collection, and then *The Awakening*, two years later. The first had fewer than a dozen reviews (*Bayou Folk* had over 200), and Chopin was getting less national attention.

The Awakening, while it was not banned, did get many negative reviews. Men found it "morbid," as well as distasteful, unpleasant, and unclean. They objected not only to Edna's adultery, but also to her not being a "mother-woman." She was, of course, a rebel against the patriarchal order — although no one actually said so, in print, until the 1970s.

Chopin's contemporary women, though, generally liked *The Awakening*. A young Pittsburgh reviewer, Willa Cather, disliked the story but praised the author's storytelling ability. Other women in St. Louis felt that Chopin was being truthful about women's lives. They wrote her fan letters, some of which are still in the Missouri Historical Society in St. Louis, and they invited her to give readings. A women's club day honoring St. Louis writers — at a time when Kate Chopin was supposedly ostracized and banned everywhere — in fact drew the largest crowd in its history, with Chopin as the central attraction.

The Awakening appeared in April, 1899, and within a year, Chopin's publisher had canceled her next short story collection, *A Vocation and a Voice* (which did not appear until ninety years later). It appears that the negative reviews (and poor sales) of *The Awakening* may have been a factor.

Chopin herself was ailing by the turn of the century. She may have had emphysema and diabetes, but she was definitely saddened by family illnesses. Her son's wife died in childbirth, sending him into a nervous breakdown from which he never fully recovered. Chopin herself wrote a few more short stories in the 1900s, but after a strenuous and exciting day at the St. Louis World's Fair in 1904, she had a cerebral hemorrhage and died on August 22. She is buried in St. Louis's Calvary Cemetery.

Kate Chopin was buried with the expectation that she might very well be forgotten. There was no reason to expect that an American priest and a Norwegian scholar would keep her memory and her life alive — or that I, an American feminist, would develop an obsession with Chopin that has lasted through my own career. As I grow older, I redefine what I think is most important about the lives and choices of the women before me — and Kate Chopin, who managed to be that rare writer who had both a family and a writing career, is a model for wresting control of our own lives, and our own narratives.

All this would not have been gibberish to George Arms some thirty years ago. When I first read *The Awakening*, I was Edna's age, and identified with her; now I'm much closer to Kate Chopin's age when she created Edna; and I agree with Arms's assessment: "instead of identifying herself with Edna's actions, Mrs. Chopin tends to regard them as romantically motivated rather than as realistically considered" (218). He did not know that Kate Chopin herself moved away from being a romantic, scandalous widow toward being a hardheaded, realistic novelist — but he clearly recognized and appreciated the result.

I also think George Arms, based on his practice, would have a certain sympathy for literary critics who reject jargon and abstract theorizing and prefer clear-spoken statements. Kate Chopin's critics have, for the most part, followed her lead and tried to communicate, as Arms did, with a literate audience, not merely a lit crit one.

The best Chopin criticism, as summarized in this excellent volume by Suzanne Green and David Caudle, is written with simplicity and grace. Those who study Chopin's prose style, like those who study Edith Wharton's, often imitate, or absorb, the clarity of her writing. Like all of us, she had mixed motives, and can be differently interpreted according to the age, style, and interests of the interpreters. Which is all by way of saying that, like all interesting women, she was ultimately unknowable.

And that is the unending fascination.

Works Cited

Apter, Terri and Ruthellen Josselson. *Best Friends: The Pleasures and Perils of Girls' and Women's Friendships*. New York: Crown, 1998.

Arms, George. "Kate Chopin's The Awakening in the Perspective of Her Literary Career." *Essays on American Literature in Honor of Jay B. Hubbell*. Ed. Clarence Gohdes. Durham: Duke, 1967, 215-228.

Chopin, Kate. *A Vocation and a Voice*. Ed. Emily Toth. New York: Penguin Classics, 1991.

Heilbrun, Carolyn. *Writing a Woman's Life*. New York: Norton, 1988.

Koppelman, Susan, ed. and comp. *Women in the Trees: U. S. Women's Short Stories about Battering & Resistance, 1839-1994*. Boston: Beacon, 1996.

Rankin, Daniel S. *Kate Chopin and Her Creole Stories*. Philadelphia: U of Pennsylvania P, 1932.

Seyersted, Per, ed. *The Complete Works of Kate Chopin*. Baton Rouge: Louisiana State UP, 1969.

Seyersted, Per. *Kate Chopin: A Critical Biography*. Baton Rouge: Louisiana State University and Oslo: Universitetsforlaget, 1969.

Snitzer, Maria Fernandez. "Telling the Lives of Kate Chopin, Edith Wharton, and Willa Cather: The Effects of Social Change and Ideology Upon Literary Biography." Diss. St. Louis University, 1992.

Toth, Emily. "The Alleged Banning of *The Awakening*.'" *Kate Chopin: A Life of the Author of The Awakening*. New York: Morrow, 1990. 422-425.

—. *Kate Chopin: A Life of the Author of The Awakening*. New York: Morrow, 1990; Austin: U of Texas P, 1993.

—. "That Outward Existence Which Conforms: Kate Chopin and Literary Convention." Diss. Johns Hopkins University, 1975.

—. "The Shadow of the First Biographer: The Case of Kate Chopin." *Southern Review* 26 (1990): 285-292.

—. *Unveiling Kate Chopin*. Jackson, MS: UP of Mississippi, 1999.

—. "*A Vocation and a Voice*: Why Was It Killed?" *Kate Chopin: a Study of the Short Fiction*. Ed. Bernard Koloski. New York: Twayne, 1997. 135-140.

Toth, Emily and Per Seyersted, with Cheyenne Bonnell, eds. *Kate Chopin's Private Papers*. Bloomington: Indiana UP, 1998.

Wagner-Martin, Linda. Telling Women's Lives. New Brunswick, NJ: Rutgers UP, 1994.

Where Are We Going? Where Have We Been? Twenty Years of Chopin Criticism

Suzanne Disheroon Green

The recovery of Kate Chopin's writings in the late twentieth century marks the beginning of a success story to which many of her contemporaries, whose works have been relegated to lonely archives, might aspire. Chopin's status was long reduced to that of marginalized female local colorist, with only two or three of her stories occasionally appearing in anthologies. She now holds a secure position in the canon that is arguably equivalent to nineteenth century writers of the stature of Herman Melville, Nathaniel Hawthorne, and Emily Dickinson. The result of this rekindled attention to Chopin's work is that a great deal of scholarly interest has focused on this remarkable writer. The magnitude of this interest has created the need for a volume such as the one you presently hold in your hands.

Before delving into the wealth of critical study detailed in this book, it is useful to consider the scope of these studies. What are the recent critical conversations that surround Chopin's work? How do these conversations inform our reading of Chopin's texts? What work remains to be done? This volume addresses critical studies undertaken between 1976 and 1998 – as well as forthcoming publications for 1999 that were available as we went to press in late 1998 – as studies prior to this time period are covered by Marlene Springer's 1976 volume *Edith Wharton and Kate Chopin: A Reference Guide.* Since the appearance of Springer's bibliography, the critical study of Chopin's work has largely evolved into four categories. These categories include: (1) biographical studies; (2) "ism" studies – scholarly endeavors which argue for the placement of Chopin's work within literary movements such as Naturalism, Realism, or Modernism; (3) studies drawing on feminist scholarship and thought, and (4) ethnographic studies. Not surprisingly, scholarly conversation has most often focused on *The Awakening* — Chopin's masterpiece — along with commonly anthologized pieces of her short fiction such as "Desiree's Baby," "The Story of an Hour," "At the 'Cadian Ball," and "The Storm." Over the past decade, *At Fault* has begun to elicit more extensive critical attention, as have the lesser-known pieces of short fiction.

In surveying the landscape of Chopin scholarship, readers will encounter an important early essay which contextualizes Chopin not only as a local colorist of interest only to those who study the literature of the Southern region, but as a woman writer. Marie Fletcher's "The Southern Woman in the Fiction of Kate Chopin" in many ways opens the conversation about Chopin as a writer with universal appeal because she writes of women's needs and desires in an era where women were told what they needed. Fletcher first addresses Chopin's status as a local colorist, attributing a good deal of her initial success to the "almost insatiable demand for Southern local color" in the decades leading up to the end of the nineteenth century (Fletcher 118). Local color pieces, especially those drawing on the Southern tradition, assumed that

> the woman's place . . . is still in the home rather than in politics or the professions; marital fidelity and strong maternal feelings, which keep home and family intact, are just as axiomatically demonstrated. Impetuous heroines may be somewhat more rebellious and unconventional than in the past; however, such unconventionality usually brings trouble rather than happiness. (Fletcher 118-19)

Fletcher points out, however, that although Chopin makes use of "the most colorful subdivision of Louisiana's culture" in her fiction, a "realistic presentation begins to replace the earlier romantic concept of Southern womanhood" (119). She goes on to conclude that Chopin "upholds the Creole belief in the purity of womanhood and those other aspects of the feminine mystique and Southern cult of family which follow from it" and presents a "'modern' honesty in her treatment of human situations, such as . . . [the] need for fulfillment" (132).

Fletcher's essay opens a Pandora's box containing issues with which critics continue to grapple, leading to much discussion of Chopin's works. Many early studies of Chopin's work concerned themselves largely with elements of local color and studies of biographical elements in her fiction. The second wave of criticism — more prolific than the first — has expanded the range of topics, and has tended to evolve into the categories mentioned above. Biographical studies and other research based in primary text materials, including typescripts, first editions, biographical source material and personal papers, constitute the first major category of Chopin study. The authoritative text for the majority of Chopin's works is Per Seyersted's 1969 *Complete Works*, although primary source materials, including previously unpublished stories, letters, diaries, and other personal documents appear in collections such as Per Seyerested and Emily Toth's two volumes, *A Kate Chopin Miscellany* (1979) and *Kate Chopin's Private Papers* (1998). Chopin's translations of Guy de Maupassant's fiction appear in Thomas Bonner's *Kate Chopin Companion*. *A Vocation and a Voice*, a volume which would have constituted Chopin's third collection of short fiction, was edited and introduced by Toth and appeared in 1991. This publication of *Vocation* marked the first time that these stories appeared together, as the author appears to have intended them. An exhaustive primary bibliography, complied by Heather Kirk Thomas, appeared in 1994 and catalogs the publication of all of Chopin's known works.

Per Seyersted's critical biography, although predating the scope of this volume, still provides useful information – of particular use are Seyersted's analyses of Chopin's works. The authoritative Chopin biography was written by Emily Toth, and remains unrivaled in both scope and quality of research. Toth also published numerous shorter essays on aspects of Chopin's life and works during the time that she was researching and writing the biography, including but not limited to "Kate Chopin's *The Awakening* as Feminist Criticism" which argues that Edna is the "embodiment of 19th century feminist criticism" and that *The Awakening* is indicative of the growing feminist consciousness during that era. One of the more intriguing of Toth's essays is "The Shadow of the First Biographer" in which she speaks at length of the difficulties of rewriting biography, especially when the first biography is riddled with errors, as is the case with Daniel Rankin's *Kate Chopin and Her Creole Stories*. Toth's book, *Unveiling Kate Chopin*, which is forthcoming from University Press of Mississippi in 1999, will reveal newly-discovered secrets and reinterpret some important aspects of Chopin's life.

Another substantial category of criticism may be dubbed the "ism debate." Studies in this category argue for the placement of Chopin's fiction in the context of various literary movements, ranging from local color, romanticism, and naturalism to impressionism, realism, and modernism. Several major studies, including Ottavio Casale's "Beyond Sex: The Dark Romanticism of Kate Chopin's *The Awakening*" compare Edna Pontellier's experience to those of protagonists in other important American romantic texts such as *The Scarlet Letter* and *Moby Dick*. Her awakening and search for a sense of self is equated with similar experiences described in *Walden* and the works of Emerson. In "Wagnerian Romanticism in Kate Chopin's *The Awakening*," Kelley Griffith argues that during Chopin's era, evoking the Wagnerian variety of Romanticism was common at the beginning of romances, and therefore, using compositions such as *Tristan und Isolde* as tools to aid in the interpretation of the romantic aspects of the novel provides insight into the motivations of the characters. W. Kenneth Holditch, in "The Broken World: Romanticism, Realism, Naturalism in *A Streetcar Named Desire*" points out the elements of each of these literary movements in *The*

Awakening, as well as in *Streetcar* and Faulkner's *The Wild Palms*. Jerome Klinkowitz counters these scholars in "Kate Chopin's Awakening to Naturalism," arguing that Chopin's work illustrates a series of movements, from Romanticism to local color to Realism to Naturalism. Carol Merrill points out in "Impressionism in Kate Chopin's *The Awakening*" that most chapters of *The Awakening* could be represented as impressionistic scenes on canvas and that Chopin's use of the sea as a unifying symbol illustrates an impressionistic influence. Michael Gilmore attempts to place Chopin in the modernist camp in his essay titled "Revolt Against Nature: The Problematic Modernism of *The Awakening*." Gilmore argues that *The Awakening* marks a turn toward the anti-naturalist, self-referential agenda of Modernism. Virginia Kouidis also places Chopin in the Modernist school, supporting her argument with the idea that Chopin uses Emerson to represent the system from which Edna struggles to escape. The common trait of each of these studies is the attempt to firmly establish Chopin within a specific movement.

In recent years, an evolving topic in Chopin criticism has centered on the debate over her status as a canonical writer, in contrast to her traditional categorization as a local colorist. Although early critics treated her work as if it amounted to little more than charming stories about life on the Louisiana bayou that provided glimpses into Southern life, more recent scholars have refuted this argument. Contemporary critics point to her prose style, her use of universal themes, and the humanity of her characters, arguing that readers generally relate to Chopin's characters because they can identify with their experiences. Elmo Howell's essay "Kate Chopin and the Creole Country" argues that Chopin was not a local colorist at all. Although she devoted much of her fiction to describing life in Creole Louisiana and locale is important in understanding her meanings, her subject matter is human nature, not Creole nature. Thomas Bonner, in his essay "Kate Chopin: Tradition and the Moment," compares Chopin with her literary contemporaries, pointing out that Grace King and Ruth McEnery Stuart were "guardians of the French civilizations—Creole and Acadian" (Bonner 141). Chopin, on the other hand "perceived that a decisive change already had occurred and that more changes were to come" (Bonner 141). While Chopin places her fiction in the "social milieu of post-Civil War French Louisiana," she illustrates that the "bonds of caste had been broken and that a freer society was in the process of formation" (Bonner 141). Like Howell, Bonner acknowledges Chopin's deep attachment to Louisiana life and culture, but argues that her work should not be judged solely as a product of that culture. Dorys Grover cites Chopin as one of four major Louisiana writers of her time, along with George Washington Cable, Lafcadio Hearn, and Grace King. These four writers each took advantage of the public taste for exotic stories about the South, and especially Creole society. Grover concludes that Chopin never overcomes this public perception of literary regionalism, even though her themes are universal in the Southern setting, addressing issues such as the need for freedom and the false base upon which Southern culture was built.

Closely related to the "ism" debate are questions regarding the religious aspects of Chopin's work, such as those raised in Thomas Bonner's 1982 essay "Christianity and Catholicism in the Fiction of Kate Chopin." Bonner argues that religious elements give structure to Chopin's fiction, and that she often satirizes excessive religious piety and fervor. Paul Giles points out, in *American Catholic Arts and Fictions: Culture, Ideology, Aesthetics* that Chopin was a Catholic apostate who, as a Modernist, was torn between two opposing forces: the papal order to adhere to the standards of the church and the pressure from the literary establishment and the reading public to escape the restrictions of those standards. In two essays, Bert Bender departs radically from Bonner's view, describing Chopin as a follower of Darwin, arguing that she thought of Darwin as something of a mentor. However, while she accepted the major theses of *On the Origin of Species*, she rejected his argument on the role of sexuality in selection. According to Bender, Chopin vehemently disagreed with Darwin's argument that women were by nature passive in sexual encounters and inferior to men in that arena. He argues that *The Awakening* is a study of Darwin's theory of sexual selection which attempts to disprove Darwin's views on female sexuality. He further suggests that Chopin's fiction grows into a "darkening meditation" on Darwinian thought.

By far the largest body of scholarship that has developed around Chopin's writing is that produced by feminist writers. In the earliest stages of Chopin's revival, which marks its beginning with the reissuing of *The Awakening* in 1969, feminist readings of her texts have been in the forefront of Chopin studies. In *The Second Sex*, Simone de Beauvoir argues that "in song and story, woman's role is to wait: her life is static; ahistorical, the course it enacts is the antithesis of *Bildung*" (de Beauvoir 271). However, de Beauvoir's description of the plight of women provides a progression in which "sleep and quiescence in female narratives represent a progressive withdrawal into the symbolic landscapes of the innermost self. As such, they make possible a form of development, albeit one-dimensional" (Hirsch 23). Scholars have often addressed the idea of the *bildungsroman*, or the novel of development or formation, arguing that

> development is a relative concept colored by many interrelated factors, including class, history, and gender . . . Literature, especially the novel, offers the complexity of form necessary to represent the interrelationships shaping individual growth. The desire to translate these interrelationships into a coherent narrative has produced a distinctive genre, the *Bildungsroman*, or novel of formation. (Abel 4)

Although the *Bildungsroman* originally focused on male protagonists (Abel 5), it has proved a useful tool for understanding texts with female protagonists. The experience of a successful *Bildung*, however, "requires the existence of a social context that will facilitate the unfolding of inner capacities, leading the young person from ignorance and innocence to wisdom and maturity" (Abel 6). The unfortunate plight of many female protagonists, including those created by Kate Chopin, is that they do not exist in a social context that allows the unfolding that Abel describes.

Susan Rosowski looks at the female "novel of awakening," contrasting it with the male *Bildungsroman*. She defines the "awakening" novel in terms of numerous 19th-and-20th century novels from both sides of the Atlantic, including *The Awakening* in her analysis. Rosowski argues that prior to her study, the "definitions and examples that follow the [examination of the *Bildungsroman*] are notably masculine, omitting developments of this theme in literature by and about women" (Rosowski 49). She suggests that the *Bildungsroman* has been used in literature in two distinctly different ways: the "novel of apprenticeship" which largely applies to male protagonists, and the "novel of awakening" which is more relevant to female characters. She argues that these two types of *Bildungsroman* share common traits: they recount the "attempts of a sensitive protagonist to learn the nature of the world, discover its meaning and pattern and acquire a philosophy of life" (Rosowski 49). The end result of awakening for female protagonists is that they have in fact awakened "to limitations" (Rosowski 49). Edna Pontellier experiences this "reality of limitation" and finds it unacceptable. She then "completes the process of awakening by placing her romantic dreams for escape in the context of time and change" and she makes a "final attempt to escape" (Rosowski 54). In a similar, though more recent, essay, Thomas Matchie argues that the *bildungsroman* was especially important to nineteenth century literature because of the severe testing of social mores with which these authors engaged. He suggests that Edna awakens to the possibility of equality between people of opposite genders, and revolts against a society that sanctions sex but allows people to be treated as property. In this sense Edna is "courageous," as her suicide acts as an affirmation of the importance of being oneself and as evidence that one isn't alive if one is not free. Marianne Hirsch examines the conventions of the androcentric *bildungsroman* in *The Awakening* as an alternative to the tradition of "female bildung." She explains that childhood and death are closely interrelated because the beginning and ending of life are nearly identical. The female experience follows the pattern of *künstlerroman* up to the point of withdrawal into an inner life. To find satisfaction, women must find unconventional, individual fulfillment because of their fragmented and discontinuous development. The "solution" that male heroes find that "saves them from the heroine's death, the solution of art . . . is virtually unavailable to the young woman in the nineteenth-century novel" (Hirsch 28). Accordingly, for Edna Pontellier, "death becomes an escape from female plot and the only possible culmination of woman's spiritual development" (Hirsch 44). Linda Huf discusses the *künstlerroman* as well, saying that Chopin's novel is "a tale of a young woman who struggles to realize herself—and her artistic ability. Of course, as a *künstlerroman*, it reveals something of the author's own struggle and, what is more important, something of the struggle of all women artists" (69).

Additional influential feminist studies of Chopin's fiction include essays by Cynthia Griffin Wolff, Joyce Coyne Dyer, and Kathleen Lant. Wolff's essay, "Kate Chopin and the Fiction of Limits: Désirée's Baby" examines the story in terms of its somewhat "scattered" critical responses, calling the piece one of Chopin's most "vivid and direct" (42). Dyer analyzes the nature of female awakenings in Chopin's short fiction and in *The Awakening*, but since she sees Chopin as sensitive to male perspectives, she argues that Chopin's true subject is not limited to an examination of female nature, but encompasses human nature. Lant's essay "The Siren of Grande Isle" takes exception to Dyer's point of view, saying that measuring Edna's development based on her relationships with Léonce, Alcée, and Robert is "male centered" and represents a "failure to read the novel as Chopin has written it" (Lant 168). She argues instead that Edna's awakenings are centered around the female characters in the novel—Adele's femininity, Mademoiselle Reisz's sensuality as illustrated through her music, and Edna's ultimate awakening to a sense of herself. The female characters of the novel represent "various possible selves to Edna" (Lant 173). Ultimately, Adele sends Edna to her death, for Edna realizes that she will never be able to reconcile the "inner life which questions" with the "outward existence which conforms." Adèle is identified with the classical Sirens, as she both lures and imperils Edna, a human counterpart to the seductive sea that beckons Edna's soul. She first awakens Edna near the sea, enticing her to speak of her childhood, and to recognize the missing elements in her life. Adele's lying-in seals Edna's fate, reminding her that while she may be able to escape from societal expectations, she can not escape the fact that she has two children, with all of the accompanying responsibilities. Her remaining choice is to reject her biological ties by renouncing her physical self, thus leading to her final swim into the Gulf.

Scholars have discussed the role of *eros* and female sexuality in Chopin's fiction. For example, Wendy Martin, in her introduction to *New Essays on The Awakening*, describes Chopin's tendency to "explore the tension between emotional and erotic inclination and traditional social mores" and her "unabashed explorations of eros and its consequences" (4). Karen Day has argued that Chopin's stories of female sexuality "can be read as fictionally exemplifying the French feminist theory of female sexuality as the Other in patriarchal discourse" and argues for the need for a "space for female sexuality and desire" (108) which Chopin's fiction begins to create.

The ground-breaking study on erotic desire in Chopin's fiction is Sandra Gilbert's essay "The Second Coming of Aphrodite: Kate Chopin's Fantasy of Desire." Originally printed in the *Kenyon Review*, this essay has been reprinted in a number of other volumes, including Harold Bloom's *Kate Chopin: Modern Critical Views*. Most recently, this essay appears in volume 2 of Gilbert and Gubar's *No Man's Land* series, which examines the development of the female tradition in literature. Gilbert bases her argument on the premise that the major women writers of the late nineteenth century, whose works chronicled the emergence of "New Women," either "suffer from or repudiate the erotic, the relationship between late nineteenth-century feminism and female desire" (Gilbert 84). While in reality, suffragists were hesitant to embrace as sisters women such as Victoria Woodhull, who argued for and actively pursued free love, women writers of this era began "not only to excuse or justify but to celebrate the transgressive sexuality of the 'fallen woman'" (Gilbert 84). Gilbert argues that Kate Chopin extended this thinking, making "such a woman paradoxically . . . [a] resonant symbol of the same need for drastic social change. Ultimately, Aphrodite, the goddess of love . . . became Chopin's ideal" (Gilbert 84). The forbidden passion that Aphrodite comes to represent in Chopin's fiction was a major theme in her work and led to the shocked reviews of *The Awakening* when it first appeared. Gilbert argues that Chopin's work was "excoriated or deprecated" because "unlike many of her female contemporaries, Chopin was aligned with a particularly sensational, largely male-dominated *fin-de-siècle* rhetoric, a rhetoric which explored, and often defended, what society defined as 'damnation'" (Gilbert 86).

Joyce Dyer further explicates Chopin's use of classical mythology in *The Awakening: A Novel of Beginnings*, exploring the archetypal function of Greek goddesses in the novel. Arguing that Edna Pontellier is "Diana/Artemis, Eve, Venus/Aphrodite, and Ariadne," she shows that this character is "surrounded by symbols and settings" taken from the classical tradition, and that "no scene remains untouched by the emblems and significances" of this tradition (Dyer 56). Each of these archetypes represents a different aspect of Edna's "sexual rebirth"(Dyer 72). Although Edna grows as a result of this rebirth, it does not provide the solution to her dissatisfaction with her life. Allusions to Diana and her traditional association with fertility and childbirth, as well as Aphrodite and her association with passion, "hint that Edna will eventually have to admit that female biology can liberate, but that its reproductive aspect can enslave" (Dyer 72). She further argues that in the nineteenth century, women sought "maternal dignity" rather than "human dignity." Edna's search for an identity extends beyond that of the "mother-woman" role to which she is assigned and that ultimately "forces [her] into the sea. She sees no way for a mother to keep the freedom of her soul—no way, that is, except to dissolve her attachment to her children" (Dyer 101).

Andrew Delbanco's essay "The Half-Life of Edna Pontellier" discusses the function of the men in Chopin's novels, describing them as "a recognizable sort in turn-of-the-century American fiction" (92). He suggests that Chopin makes a major theme of "male attenuation," the fall of a "once haughty privileged class on the edge of extinction, nominally led by men who were in a condition too shriveled to lead" (93). Delbanco makes an interesting argument, especially given Léonce Pontellier's overall ineffectualness as a husband. Although Léonce offers the appearance of the perfect husband, in reality he is petty, peevish, and can exercise little real control over his wife. He fumes and complains that Edna casts off her "at home" days and takes steps to cover up her socially unacceptable move to the pigeon house, but ultimately he is powerless to stop Edna from taking such drastic steps. Delbanco postulates that Léonce's powerlessness is in part a result of "rebellions of his own. He is, quietly and without anything like his wife's risk of shame, disowning his own culture" (Delbanco 93). Delbanco further argues that Edna's sexuality is largely autoerotic: she meets her husband "at breakfast," rather than in the boudoir; she frightens Robert Lebrun when he glimpses her sexuality, and "even Arobin, though less hesitant to test her desire [than either Léonce or Robert], is more a voyeur than lover" (96).

Similarly, Phyllis Barrett focuses on Chopin's male characters and takes a seemingly anti-feminist approach, arguing that the female characters mirror the well-defined "Adamic" American male hero. However, in the end Barrett's argument reconfirms the empowerment of female characters, as these "Adamic" characters are not presented as wives and mothers but are characterized, much like their male counterparts, as self-centered, vital, and irresponsible. Barrett then compares Edna's experience with those of Hester Prynne and Isabel Archer, pointing out that the consequences are what differ among these characters. While Hester and Isabel triumph, Edna's only option is death. Elizabeth Ammons extends Barrett's argument, saying that one of Edna's major awakenings is the acknowledgment of the simple fact that she is not a mother-woman, but rather that she has artistic tendencies and needs erotic love. Elaine Apthorp, in her essay dealing with *The Awakening* and Willa Cather's *Lucy Gayheart*, suggests that the reason women's awakenings are not accepted is that the linguistic forms necessary to explain their dilemmas do not exist. The strength of both novels is their capacity to suggest what Cather termed "the presence of the thing not named." The result of this presence is that Edna struggles to express ideas that have no nomenclature and no models. Citing the work of Nancy Chodorow and Carol Gilligan, Apthorp concludes by calling for an alternative model of creativity between the mainstream and the Other which is both receptive and interactive—a model that will be difficult to achieve because of the patriarchal constructs that dominate the standard models of language and creativity.

Miriam Shillingsburg argues that women's writing from the end of the nineteenth century not only tells modern readers about the feelings of a large segment of the population, but also that a change in those feelings became apparent in the latter half of the century. She describes Edna Pontellier, as well as the characters of Caroline Lee Hentz and Grace King, as bucking both convention and their places in society. While Hentz and King write more traditional romances, in which marriage is the reward for demonstrating acceptable values, Chopin questions the basic assumptions which underlie marital relationships. Martha Cutter's essay continues in this vein, arguing that in Chopin's early fiction, women who attempt to overtly voice desires and experience are dismissed as meaningless or insane, and citing as her examples stories such as "Mrs. Mobry's Reason" or "Wiser than a God." In her later fiction, however, Chopin's female characters develop covert voices which allow them to undermine patriarchal structures from within their own paradigms. Each of these critics argues that women needed a space in which to find and define themselves. That space might be linguistic, emotional, or paradigmatic, but it has to exist.

Even before her Chopin biography appeared, Emily Toth had contributed several essays dealing with women's issues in Chopin's fiction. She also founded the *Kate Chopin Newsletter* (*KCN*) in 1976, which published numerous short pieces of textual analysis, biographical data, and miscellany. Notable articles include Jacqueline Berke's "Kate Chopin's Call to a Larger 'Awakening,'" which contextualizes *The Awakening* as a feminist manifesto and "The Literature of Birth and Abortion," by Irene Dash, which points out that the birth of Adèle's baby at the end of the novel makes Edna's suicide inevitable. The *KCN* also includes interesting marginalia about Chopin's life and times. The *KCN* was later renamed *Regionalism and the Female Imagination*, and while it no longer focused exclusively on studies related to Chopin, the journal continued to offer numerous pieces on the writer. Yet despite a common theoretical focus, feminist scholars often disagree over the interpretation of Chopin's texts. For example, Gina Burchard has argued that Chopin would not have considered herself a feminist because the bulk of her work deals with human relationships in a generalized way. She further argues that Chopin explores and subverts female nonconformity, concluding that Edna's suicide is unjustified. Whatever the particulars of the disagreement, however, feminist scholars have contributed a large and useful body of work to Chopin studies.

The final major category of secondary criticism deals with racial issues in Chopin's fiction. Two book-length studies have appeared in the last decade: *Gender, Race and Region in the Writings of George Washington Cable, Ruth McEnery Stuart, and Kate Chopin* by Helen Taylor and *Women on the Color Line* by Anna Shannon Elfenbein. Taylor and Elfenbein take opposing viewpoints on the subject of Chopin's view of racial issues. Taylor describes Chopin's significance as stemming from her "particular use of Local Color techniques, and of regional and historical themes and allusions that challenged European male and English and American female fictional definitions of femininity and female sexuality" (139). Taylor describes Chopin's attraction to Louisiana as the setting for her fiction as "derived from its function as an imaginary Other that did not require Kate Chopin to accept a version of the South different from that of her family and class" (143). She further attributes a "bitter suspicion of emancipation" to Chopin, because her brother died while serving in the Confederate army. In fact, Taylor considers both Chopin and her works as "unequivocally racist" (Lundie 126). This argument ignores the fact that Chopin troubles her contemporaries' idea that one's place is defined by one's race in stories such as "Beyond the Bayou" and "Désirée's Baby." Catherine Lundie examines Taylor's argument, and in finding that Chopin often offers a "complex exploration of race and ethnicity" (126), she concludes that Chopin "had enlightened views on the subject of race" (129).

Anna Shannon Elfenbein also describes Chopin's racial attitudes in a more flattering light, describing her, in essence, as a writer who was somewhat ahead of her time in even attempting to deal with racial issues. Elfenbein begins with a thorough discussion of the plight of the "tragic octoroon"—the woman of mixed racial ancestry—in society, and more specifically, in literary texts. While acknowledging that "dark women characters are frequently peripheral or ambiguously identified in [Chopin's] fiction," Elfenbein points out that a close study of Chopin's women of color heightens our "appreciation of Chopin's achievement as a sexual realist" (117). She argues that Chopin depicts

> the destructive symbiosis of power and powerlessness, measuring the distance between romantic views of marriage and motherhood and the reality of the sexual lives of women on both sides of the color line. Those attempting to solve the riddle posed by the white women Chopin portrays, however, have neglected to examine this symbiosis and with it the dark women characters through whom she first tested and transgressed the Victorian proprieties in her fiction. (Elfenbein 117)

Elfenbein's position is supported by Toth, who states that Chopin's "most skillful use of blacks in fiction" offers a "critique of Southern social mores through the conventional figure of the tragic octoroon" (Toth, *Outward* 120). Chopin's black characters are "usually carefully drawn and realistic" (Elfenbein 118), and in many cases the writer "clearly anticipates the dawning racial awareness of white women of her generation" (119).

In *The Myth of New Orleans in Literature*, Violet Harrington Bryan argues that an "*implied* and sometimes *explicit* dialogue" (44) existed among Kate Chopin, Grace King, and Alice Dunbar Nelson, a dialogue which at times extended to include Charles W. Chestnutt and George Washington Cable. According to Bryan, Chopin and her contemporaries re-created the New Orleans environment—Creoles, miscegenation, racial stereotypes, dialects, culture conflicts between races and immigrant ethnic groups. In many of their stories, King, Chopin and Dunbar-Nelson also used the city to confront women's social issues: the restrictions of gender roles, especially as these influenced marriage and divorce, career, social networking and motherhood. (44)

Bryan further argues that Chopin was aware of "the period's racial climate" (53). New Orleans becomes the "site of social change" in Chopin's fiction, both for her female characters and her characters of color.

In addition to these discussions in book-length studies, numerous essays have appeared that deal with Chopin's treatment of race. Elaine Showalter, for example, argues that although Edna awakens sexually and emotionally, she "never awakens . . . to the dimensions of her social world . . . never sees how the labor of the mulatto and black women around her makes her narcissistic existence possible" (145). In part because of the "servitude of others" (Delbanco 100), Edna enjoys freedom of movement, a release from responsibility for the day-to-day needs of her children. Elizabeth Ammons points out that the presence of women of color in the fiction of this era allows their white counterparts the luxury of actions such as suicide. Because the women of color are present, dissatisfied white women could feel assured that their children would be cared for even if they themselves were not present to assist in the process. Accordingly, Ammons argues that no awakening would have occurred had there been no women-of-color to take up the slack.

Ammons's argument is seconded by Ellen Cantarow, who essentially calls for rebellion against societal norms and stereotypes. She argues that *The Awakening* describes Edna's imprisonment by upper-middle-class values, which were the norm during Chopin's lifetime, and describes the possibilities of freedom, which, although available to a white woman, would not be available to a woman of color. One of the ways of achieving freedom is through productive, remunerative work; the other possibilities rely on a course of rebellion and isolation before ultimately leading to self-fulfillment. The limited options available to women of color, both in reality and in fiction, perpetuated this over-reliance on women of color as undervalued child care providers.

Janet Goodwyn stops short of calling Chopin a racist in her 1994 essay, yet argues that the writer privileges things European over their Creole counterparts. Chopin's culture, and thus her fiction, is informed and biased by its roots in European arts and thought processes. Chopin places greater value on "the higher things derived from Europe" (3), by definition making any individual or group which is not privy to the aesthetics of European cultures natural outsiders. She concludes that Chopin's Creole stories are "stilted," using "self-conscious language which is typical of Chopin when not quite at ease with her material" (8).

Critics have found the tools of psychology useful in analyzing Chopin's fiction as well. Marina Roscher takes a psychoanalytic approach to Edna's suicide, arguing that, despite the explanations offered by other critics, Edna takes her own life because she is immature. Citing Edna's early loss of her mother, her lack of close female companions, and her resulting solitary nature as major contributing factors to her demise, Roscher associates this tendency to solitude with the generally accepted truism that the solitary primate is an abnormal primate. She couples this information with R. D. Laing's argument that losing one's mother at the wrong stage of development often thwarts the adequate development of a sense of self. Roscher analyzes Edna as possessing an incompletely developed *animus*, which prevents the integration of her personality and blinds her to reasonable alternatives and mature relationships. Ultimately, her immaturity drives her into the sea. Roscher concludes with the argument that the ending of *The Awakening* is not ambiguous but merely complicated, in that it contains multiple and hidden meanings, meanings larger than the author's conscious purpose. Sam Girgus also applies Laing's research to Chopin's fiction, suggesting that the plight of the modern woman, as described by Chopin, is that she is forcibly estranged from those around her by the social roles imposed on her. He concludes that Edna suffers from a divided personality, which causes her to lead a dual life and ultimately withdraw from society and life itself. Elizabeth Fox-Genovese addresses this withdrawal in her essay "Kate Chopin's Awakening," arguing that Edna's suicide acts as the organizing principle for the novel. In this view, *The Awakening* contains two narrative voices—one that is institutional and another that is personal, with the two narrative voices representing Edna's internal experience and the Creole social structure, respectively. Edna's subjective experience is contrasted with social institutions, and the strengths and weaknesses of each is revealed. Fox-Genovese further argues that by fully accepting a feminist reading of Chopin's text, her readers would have to reject Creole society as patriarchal and oppressive, yet a psychoanalytic reading would necessitate viewing Edna as a failure. Combining these two schools of thought creates an approach which allows Chopin to illustrate the negative aspects of Creole society for women without rejecting the entire system.

In addition to the sea of individual critical works, several edited volumes of studies of Chopin's work have appeared in the past decade. These volumes, which include Harold Bloom's 1987 *Kate Chopin: Modern Critical Views* and Iqbal Kaur's 1995 volume *Kate Chopin's The Awakening: Critical Essays*, offer reprints of important essays. Bloom's volume is useful in that it assembles many of the most important early essays addressing Chopin's work, such as Sandra Gilbert and Susan Gubar's "Aphrodite" essay and Wolff's "Thanatos and Eros." Kaur's volume includes many new essays, as well as the fourth reprinting of Margit Stange's essay.

Bernard Koloski's *Kate Chopin: A Study of the Short Fiction* offers critical analysis of the short stories, including reprints and original articles, and this volume is the first book-length study devoted exclusively to Chopin's short fiction. Koloski also edited *Approaches to Teaching Kate Chopin*, which offers a substantial selection of pedagogical essays. This collection of essays, authored by noted scholars, offers down-to-earth, hands-on discussions of how to go about teaching Chopin's texts to students at levels ranging from high school to Ph.D. candidates. Alice Hall Petry's volume *Critical Essays on Kate Chopin* also includes both reprints of important articles and original studies of Chopin, with a heavy emphasis on the short fiction.

Despite the abundance of articles, books, and approaches dealing with Chopin and her work that have appeared over the last several decades, excellent scholarship continues to appear, and the volume of such work is increasing. For example, *Degas In New Orleans: Encounters in the Creole World of Kate Chopin and George Washington Cable*, by Christopher Benfey, presents a fascinating analysis of the cultural milieu and interlocking social and family relationships that greatly influenced these three artists. Janet Beer's *Kate Chopin, Edith Wharton and Charlotte Perkins Gilbert: Studies in Short Fiction* employs original methods of analysis while focusing her attention on some of Chopin's less frequently studied short fiction. She also draws valuable comparisons between Chopin and two of America's most important turn-of-the-century women writers. Other works too numerous to mention here, many by prominent scholars, are on the horizon; neither scholarly nor popular interest in Chopin's fiction appears to be waning as we approach the centennial of her masterpiece, *The Awakening*.

Thus, both those new to the field and seasoned scholars face a large and varied body of critical works dealing with Chopin's fiction. The task before the reader is presumably simple: to identify the scholarly works that are relevant to the research project under consideration. However, many of the works mentioned in this essay, and the many other fine studies that space forces us to slight, defy easy categorization. Therefore, the preceding discussion merely offers the most basic of road maps to those new to the study of Chopin's works.

Works Cited

Abel, Elizabeth. Introduction. *The Voyage In: Fictions of Female Development.*
    Ed. Elizabeth Abel, Marianne Hirsch and Elizabeth Langland. Hanover,
    NH: UP of New England for Dartmouth College, 1983.
Ammons, Elizabeth. *Conflicting Stories: American Women Writers at the Turn
    into the Twentieth Century.* Oxford: Oxford UP, 1991.
Apthorp, Elaine Sargent. "Re-Visioning Creativity: Cather, Chopin, Jewett."
    Legacy 9 (1992): 1-22.
Barrett, Phyllis W. "More American Adams: Women Heroes in American
    Fiction." *Markham Review* 10 (1981): 39-41.
de Beauvoir, Simone. *The Second Sex.* Trans. H. M. Parshley. New York:
    Vintage-Random House, 1952, 1989.
Beer, Janet. *Kate Chopin, Edith Wharton and Charlotte Perkins Gilman: Studies
    in Short Fiction.* London: Macmillian and New York: St. Martin's P,
    1997.
Bender, Bert. "Kate Chopin's Quarrel with Darwin before *The Awakening.*"
    Journal of American Studies 26 (1992): 185-204. Rpt in *Critical Essays
    on Kate Chopin.* Ed. Alice Hall Petry. New York: G. K. Hall - Simon
    and Schuster, 1996.
—. "The Teeth of Desire: *The Awakening* and *The Descent of Man.*"
    *American Literature: A Journal of Literary History, Criticism, and
    Bibliography* 63 (1991): 459-73.
Benfey, Christopher. *Degas in New Orleans: Encounters in the Creole World of
    Kate Chopin and George Washington Cable.* New York: Knopf, 1998.
Bonner, Jr., Thomas. "Christianity and Catholicism in the Fiction of Kate
    Chopin." *Southern Quarterly* 20 (1982): 118-25.
—. *The Kate Chopin Companion.* Westport, CT: Greenwood, 1988.
—. "Kate Chopin: Tradition and the Moment." *Southern Literature in Transition:
    Heritage and Promise.* Ed. Philip Castillo and William Osborne.
    Memphis: Memphis State UP, 1983.
Bryan, Violet Harrington. *The Myth of New Orleans in Literature: Dialogues of
    Race and Gender.* Knoxville: U of Tennessee P, 1993.
Burchard, Gina M. "Kate Chopin's Problematical Womanliness: The Frontier of
    American Feminism." *Journal of the American Studies Association of
    Texas* 15 (1984): 35-45.
Cantarow, Ellen. "Sex, Race and Criticism: Thoughts of a White Feminist on
    Kate Chopin and Zora Neale Hurston." *Radical Teacher* 9 (1978): 30-
    33.
Casale, Ottavio Mark. "Beyond Sex: The Dark Romanticism of Kate Chopin's
    The Awakening." *Ball State University Forum* 19.1 (1978): 76-80.
Cutter, Martha J. "Losing the Battle but Winning the War: Resistance to
    Patriarchal Discourse in Kate Chopin's Short Fiction." *Legacy* 11:1
    (1994): 17-36.

Day, Karen. "The 'Elsewhere' of Female Sexuality and Desire in Kate Chopin's *A Vocation and a Voice*." *Louisiana Literature* 2.1 (1994): 108-17.

Delbanco, Andrew. "The Half-Life of Edna Pontellier." *New Essays on The Awakening.* Ed. Wendy Martin. New York: Cambridge UP, 1988.

Dyer, Joyce. *The Awakening: A Novel of Beginnings.* New York: Twayne, 1993.

—. "Gouvernail, Kate Chopin's Sensitive Bachelor." *Southern Literary Journal* 14.1 (1981): 46-55.

—. "Kate Chopin's Sleeping Bruties." *Markham Review* 10 (1980-81): 10-15.

Elfenbein, Anna Shannon. *Women on the Color Line: Evolving Stereotypes and the Writings of George Washington Cable, Grace King, Kate Chopin.* Charlottesville: UP of Virginia, 1989.

Fletcher, Marie. "The Southern Woman in the Fiction of Kate Chopin." *Louisiana History* 7 (1966): 117-132.

Fox-Genovese, Elizabeth. "Kate Chopin's Awakening." *Southern Studies* 18 (1979): 261-90.

Gilbert, Sandra. "The Second Coming of Aphrodite: Kate Chopin's Fantasy of Desire." *No Man's Land: The Place of the Woman Writer in the Twentieth Century. Volume 2: Sexchanges.* New Haven: Yale UP, 1989.

Giles, Paul. *American Catholic Arts and Fictions: Culture, Ideology, Aesthetics.* New York: Cambridge UP, 1992.

Gilmore, Michael T. "Revolt Against Nature: The Problematic Modernism of *The Awakening.*" *New Essays on The Awakening.* Ed. Wendy Martin. Cambridge: Cambridge UP, 1988.

Girgus, Sam B. "R.D. Laing and Literature: Readings of Poe, Hawthorne and Kate Chopin." *Psychological Perspectives on Literature: Freudian Dissidents and Non-Freudians. A Casebook.* Ed. Joseph Natoli. Hamden, CT: Archon, 1984.

Goodwyn, Janet. "'Dah you is, settin' down, lookin' jis' like w'ite folks!': Ethnicity Enacted in Kate Chopin's Short Fiction." *Yearbook of English Studies* 24 (1994): 1-11.

Griffith, Kelley. "Wagnerian Romanticism in Kate Chopin's *The Awakening.*" *English Romanticism: Preludes and Postludes. Essays in Honor of Edwin Graves Wilson.* Ed. Donald Schoonmaker and John A. Alford. East Lansing: Colleagues P, 1993.

Grover, Dorys Crow. "Kate Chopin and the Bayou Country." *Journal of the American Studies Association of Texas* 15 (1984): 29-34.

Hirsch, Marianne. "Spiritual Bildung: The Beautiful Soul as Paradigm." *The Voyage In: Fictions of Female Development.* Ed. Elizabeth Abel, Marianne Hirsch and Elizabeth Langland. Hanover, NH: UP of New England for Dartmouth College, 1983.

Holditch, W. Kenneth. "The Broken World: Romanticism, Realism, Naturalism in *A Streetcar Named Desire.*" *Confronting Tennessee Williams's A Streetcar Named Desire: Essays in Cultural Pluralism.* Ed. Philip C. Kolin. Westport, CT: Greenwood, 1993.

Howell, Elmo. "Kate Chopin and the Creole Country." *Louisiana History* 20 (1979): 209-19.

Huf, Linda. *A Portrait of the Artist as a Young Woman: The Writer as Heroine in American Literature*. New York: Frederick Ungar, 1983.

Kaur, Iqbal, ed. *Kate Chopin: Critical Essays*. New Delhi: Deep & Deep, 1995.

Koloski, Bernard. *Approaches to Teaching Chopin's The Awakening*. New York: MLA, 1988.

—. *Kate Chopin: A Study of the Short Fiction*. New York: Twayne - Simon and Schuster, 1996.

Klinkowitz, Jerome. "Kate Chopin's Awakening to Naturalism." *The Practice of Fiction in America: Writers from Hawthorne to the Present*. Ames: Iowa State UP, 1980.

Kouidis, Virginia M. "Prison into Prism: Emerson's 'Many-Colored Lenses' and the Woman Writer of Early Modernism." *The Green American Tradition: Essays and Poems for Sherman Paul*. Ed. H. Daniel Peck. Baton Rouge: Louisiana State UP, 1989.

Lant, Kathleen Margaret. "The Siren of Grand Isle: Adèle's Role in *The Awakening*." *Southern Studies: An Interdisciplinary Journal of the South*. 23.2 (1984): 167-75.

Lundie, Catherine. "Doubly Dispossessed: Kate Chopin's Women of Color." *Louisiana Literature* 11 (1994): 126-44.

Martin, Wendy, ed. Introduction. *New Essays on The Awakening*. New York: Cambridge UP, 1988.

May, John. "Local Color in *The Awakening*." *Southern Review* 6 (1970): 1031-40.

Merrill, Carol. "Impressionism in Kate Chopin's *The Awakening*." *New America* 3.2 (1977): 50-52.

Rankin, Daniel S. *Kate Chopin and Her Creole Stories*. Philadelphia: U of Pennsylvania P, 1932.

Roscher, Marina L. "The Suicide of Edna Pontellier: An Ambiguous Ending?" *Southern Studies* 23.3 (1984): 289-98.

Rosowski, Susan J. "The Novel of Awakening." *Genre* 12 (1979): 313-32.

Seyersted, Per. *The Complete Works of Kate Chopin*. 2 vols. Baton Rouge: Louisiana State UP, 1969.

—. *Kate Chopin: A Critical Biography*. Baton Rouge: Louisiana State UP, 1969, 1980.

Seyersted, Per, and Emily Toth, eds. *A Kate Chopin Miscellany*. Natchitoches: Northwestern State UP, 1979.

Shillingsburg, Miriam J. "The Ascent of Woman, Southern Style: Hentz, King, Chopin." *Southern Literature in Transition: Heritage and Promise*. Ed. Philip Castille and William Osborne. Memphis: Memphis State UP, 1983.

Showalter, Elaine. *Sister's Choice: Tradition and Change in American Women's Writing*. Oxford: Clarendon, 1991.

Taylor, Helen. *Gender, Race and Region in the Writings of Grace King, Ruth McEnery Stuart and Kate Chopin.* Baton Rouge: Louisiana State UP, 1989.
Toth, Emily. "Kate Chopin's *The Awakening* as Feminist Criticism." *Louisiana Studies* 15 (1976): 241-51.
—. "Kate Chopin's New Orleans Years." *New Orleans Review* 15.1 (1988): 53-60.
—. "The Shadow of the First Biographer: The Case of Kate Chopin." *Southern Review* 26 (1990): 285-292.
—. "That Outward Existence Which Conforms: Kate Chopin and Literary Convention." Ph.D. Diss. Johns Hopkins U, 1975.
—. *Unveiling Kate Chopin.* Jackson, MS: UP of Mississippi, Forthcoming 1999.
—, ed. *A Vocation and a Voice* by Kate Chopin. New York: Penguin, 1991.
— and Per Seyersted, with Cheyenne Bonnell. *Kate Chopin's Private Papers.* Bloomington: Indiana UP, 1998.
Wolff, Cynthia Griffin. "Kate Chopin and the Fiction of Limits: Désirée's Baby." *Southern Literary Journal* 10 (1978): 123-33.

The Fall and Rise of Kate Chopin and Her Works

David J. Caudle

Since Per Seyersted published *The Complete Works of Kate Chopin* in 1969, the interest in this author — all but ignored for more than sixty years — has increased dramatically, causing her work to be elevated to the canon of American letters. Thirty years after Seyersted restored Chopin to the attention of academic critics and casual readers alike, the popularity of her writings and the number of scholarly essays dealing with her work continues to increase each year. In the last two decades, only three critical essays and one book review have taken exception to the quality and importance of Chopin's work — these from a body of scholarship that includes some five hundred studies, and none of them has exerted any noticeable influence on either critics or casual readers[1]. The critical community of the late twentieth century largely argues that Chopin's fiction was ahead of its time. A similar perception among Chopin's contemporaries, coupled with her frank portrayal of female sexuality, is often cited as an explanation for the disappearance of most of her work.

Most critics overlook the fact that within less than twenty years of Chopin's death her most controversial piece, *The Awakening*, would have been perceived by both casual readers and critics alike as almost discreet in its sexual content. Chopin's work thus faced more intransigent and profound obstacles to widespread acceptance than those presented by Victorian sexual mores. In addition, Chopin's work was, and remains, difficult to classify. The last decade of the nineteenth century was a time of transition in both American society and American literature. The Romantic indulgences of the Transcendentalists and their followers were out of fashion in the aftermath of the Civil War, yet no clear literary vision arose in the wake of the American Renaissance. Most of the literary establishment — both publishers and critics — were staunchly conservative, resisting the forces that would eventually lead to Realism and Naturalism even as the more conventional forms of Romanticism became increasingly exhausted. Thus, for some time, no literary movement or critical perspective even existed in which to place Chopin — a writer who subverted the conventional genre of local color to create her distinctive works — to lay claim to or which might in turn champion her art.

This lack of a critically sanctioned space in which to place Chopin's work, along with the problems that she faced as a woman seeking recognition in a male-dominated profession — a profession whose power structure mirrored other social institutions — are often used to explain the mixed critical reception of her masterpiece. This neatly-packaged analysis begs the larger question of why her work went largely unnoticed for over sixty years, despite the fact that, as Bernard Koloski reminds us, some of her short fiction never went out of print. The answer to this question is buried in the cultural milieu of turn-of-the-century America, a culture that has become quite foreign to many readers and critics at the close of the twentieth century.

In order to publish successfully in the late nineteenth century, Chopin had to work within a literary and cultural establishment that was not only dominated by males but one dominated by a very specific group of males. This group was composed almost exclusively of white Anglo-Saxon Protestants; it was also affluent, the product of elite educational institutions, and centered in Boston and New York. The group was, because of these factors, powerful and insular, as exemplified by such figures as Henry Adams and William Dean Howells. Such a group could be expected to possess its own political, economic, and literary agenda. As the *de facto* leader of the commercial side of the literary world, Howells, the editor of *Harpers*, defined what was the "best" of American literature for the last quarter of the century. He set the agenda for the small and like minded group who controlled the large publishing houses in Boston and New York, the ones that really mattered. These men decided which authors would have a national audience and which would have no audience at all, as well as whether or not a particular work was likely to be well received, since they either wrote or commissioned many of the most prominent reviews. On the academic side was Adams, a professor at Harvard, a prolific writer, and a respected opinion maker who was descended from two presidents and born to wealth , power, and connections with other wealthy and powerful individuals. He was the epitome of the nineteenth century American aristocracy, a group of men accustomed to defining culture and taste for an acquiescing public. This was the age of the robber barons — Rockefeller, Carnegie, Mellon — in other words, an age of concentrated power and insular power relationships, and the literary establishment was no exception. Such groups typically act in their own interests and are usually reluctant to recognize or accept outsiders and unconventional ideas.

An author such as Chopin thus faced a number of disadvantages in having her work accepted by such a literary and social establishment. In addition to the limitations imposed by her gender, a well-defined niche for "women's fiction" still existed and her work also bore the indelible mark of the provincial. Her residence in St. Louis and the fact that she set much of her work in Louisiana marked Chopin as a regionalist. In the eyes of literary opinion makers, her work would, by definition, have had marginal literary merit outside the realm of light entertainment. Women, and for that matter most men, were not considered to be capable of producing "serious" literature, leaving space for them to work only within the well-defined constraints of the local color or domestic fiction genres. To stray too far from these conventions could severely damage careers, if such adventurous authors could publish at all. Chopin experienced this problem first hand when, in the aftermath of the scandal surrounding the publication of *The Awakening*, her publisher revoked the contract for her third collection of short stories, *A Vocation and a Voice*. Despite the fact that her first two collections were well received and that her career up to that point seemed to be advancing, these works were not published in the form that she intended until 1991.

The fact that a number of Chopin's female characters, particularly Edna Pontellier in *The Awakening*, attempted to take control of their own sexual and economic destinies would also have been quite disturbing to the turn-of-the-century literary establishment. Aside from the offense to late Victorian prudery, Chopin's novel implied a profound threat to the economic and political *status quo*. It strongly suggested that established social institutions were inadequate and oppressive, and that American women, and by extension others excluded from the power structure, could and should attain equality and independence. The men who would determine the circumstances of Chopin's publication and who would be most influential in her works' critical reception were the group most threatened by some of the social changes implicitly suggested by her work.

Evidence of this dilemma, which was faced by both Chopin and other women writers of the time, can be seen in their fiction. Martha Cutter argues that much of Chopin's short fiction demonstrates the development of a covert voice that allowed her to undermine established power structures from within their own paradigms. Doreen Saar further argues that Chopin presented some of her most radical ideas while employing one of the nineteenth century's most conventional literary genres — local color. The very existence of such subversive tactics demonstrates the difficulty faced by writers who would challenge the established power structure. This dilemma was intensified by the fact that Chopin was forced to deal with a literary establishment that consisted of the group that was the greatest beneficiary of the type of society that *The Awakening* challenged.

The implicit challenge of Chopin's work to the position of the male elite might be expected to have received an enthusiastic reception among the middle and upper class women who composed much of her audience. After all, Edna was like them in many ways, though she offered a life completely different from the traditional one that most upper class women experienced. Yet if this was the case, the enthusiasm was evidently short-lived, since most of her work passed out of print shortly after her death. Perhaps female readers were as covert in their reading material as many female writers were subversive in the presentation of their themes, and her works were perhaps more widely read than conventional reporting methods indicate. Although, on the face of it, this seems highly speculative, it becomes much more likely when viewed in light of the fact that Chopin herself provides an example of such a possibility — the surreptitiously circulated novel that Edna finds so embarrassing in *The Awakening*. In describing the absence of prudery among the Creoles summering at Grand Isle, Chopin describes a book making the rounds that Edna felt compelled to read in "secret and solitude," hiding it "at the sound of approaching footsteps" (890). Further, Toth notes that the St. Louis Public Library and the Mercantile library — the ones that supposedly banned it — held seven copies of *The Awakening* and removed multiple copies from circulation in the early 1900's because they were worn out. Replacement copies were being purchased as late as 1906, seven years after it first saw press (Toth, *Biography* 367-368). Given the controversy surrounding Chopin's novel, *The Awakening* itself may have been such a secret and solitary book for many of its readers. Nevertheless, Chopin's female audience likely understood the dilemma of a character such as Edna Pontellier because of their similar circumstances. As Eleanor Flexner observes, changes in the status of American women were not the sole accomplishment of a relatively small group of activists. These changes were brought about by the consensus of the "woman on the street," who was not only the impetus of social change, but without whom the activists would have been far less influential (*xiii*).

Indicative of Chopin's early lack of impact is the fact that although her two short story collections were readily available while in print, sales had become rather modest by the time her second novel was published (Toth, *Biography* 367). Willa Cather's pointedly negative review of *The Awakening*, which she called "trite and sordid" in *The Pittsburgh Leader*, illustrates the fact that the male literary elite was not alone in rejecting Chopin's novel. A possible reason for these facts is that while Chopin clearly depicted the double-bind faced by women during this time, she was unable to publicly articulate any realistic solution. Joseph Candela argues that Edna Pontellier is a symbolic representation of this inability to directly address issues raised by the growing women's rights movement. Given the lack of clear alternatives available to turn-of-the-century women, many of Chopin's readers might have reasonably preferred the bliss of ignorance.

These facts influenced the world of American letters as well, and their influence is exemplified in the person of Howells, the preeminent editor and critic of late nineteenth-century America. As editor of *Harper's*, his pronouncements in the world of American letters all but carried the weight of law. He stated his opinion that authors should focus on "the more smiling aspects of life, which are the more American," avoiding "certain facts of life which are not usually talked of before young people, and especially young ladies" (Toth 278). Howells was referring to more than just sexually oriented material; he also meant anything that disturbed the culturally sleeping nation and its "American dream." The literary establishment exemplified by Howells defined a particular space for women writers, specifying acceptable subject matter, tone, and style. Fiction in general was automatically suspect, and anything controversial or threatening to the established social order was condemned, if it ever saw the light of day at all. Against these odds, a number of female writers were able to convey subversive social critiques using sanctioned genres such as domestic fiction and local color. Other women writers in addition to Chopin — Sarah Orne Jewett and Mary E. Wilkins Freeman among the most prominent — were able to express biting social criticism by masking it in the conventions of such traditionally acceptable genres. However, the very fact that subversion was necessary illustrates the rigidity of the system and the difficulty of making new voices heard, much less accepted by literary opinion makers.

Opinions such as those expressed by Howells, along with a tendency toward misogyny in the world of publishing and society in general, certainly played a role in the mixed and often openly hostile reception to Chopin's novel. However, neither of these factors completely explain the level of hostility, or more importantly, the reasons that the novel disappeared from the attention of literary scholars for such an extended period of time. Although most novels disappear, usually forever, *The Awakening* is unusual because few such novels are recovered, (or deserve to be) and fewer still generate such sustained interest among both critics and casual readers. Given the virtually uncontested literary merit of both *The Awakening* and much of the rest of Chopin's work, other issues must have played a role, among them economic issues associated with the rise of industrial capitalism and class issues deriving from both industrialization and urbanization. Miriam Shillingsburg suggests that Chopin, more so than most writers, questioned some of the most basic assumptions of her time, and perhaps this fact explains some of the animosity seen in the more negative reviews of her work.

As anyone who has taught *The Awakening* in a classroom knows, questions such as "If Edna was so unhappy with her life, why didn't she just leave Léonce?" are commonly asked by both male and female students. Despite the obvious shortcomings of late twentieth century society in terms of gender equity, we often underestimate the plight of women at a time when they were denied even the most basic rights of citizenship. The alternatives to the carefully circumscribed social roles available to women such as Chopin's female readers ranged from appallingly bad to completely unavailable. While the late nineteenth century was a time of growing social change and many social reformers in the women's rights movement effectively challenged the *status quo*, Flexner notes that full political citizenship was the long awaited culmination of the first wave of the women's movement. The advent of suffrage finally allowed the long struggle to bear its most significant fruit (Flexner *ix*). It is no coincidence that the revival of Chopin's work began at the same time that the second wave of the women's movement began to effectively assert itself in the social order. Greater, if not complete, equality for women allowed a novel such as *The Awakening* to inspire and resonate with modern readers in a way that would have yielded only frustration for Chopin's contemporaries. Fundamental changes in society at large were necessary before individual women could realistically contemplate acceptable solutions to the dilemma portrayed in *The Awakening*.

At the end of the nineteenth century, the U.S., especially the Southern U.S. where Chopin lived and in which she set most of her fiction, had still not quite overcome the trauma of the Civil War and the turmoil of Reconstruction. The generation that held power at the time *The Awakening* was published in 1899 still had strong personal memories of this tragic period of American history. The excesses of the Gilded Age were in many ways a reaction to the turmoil of the Civil War and its immediate aftermath. The social elite of the nation became focused on accumulating material comforts and enhancing their economic power through the growth of industry and technology. Many people became almost instinctively suspicious of any suggestion of social change, especially if it might be construed as a "movement." The struggle for the abolition of slavery, as noble and necessary an effort as it was, had torn the nation apart and cost the blood and fortunes of hundreds of thousands of its citizens — a cost still unprecedented in any of America's other conflicts. Even after such an heroic struggle, who could honestly say that the conditions faced by most African-Americans were even close to acceptable — or likely to improve much in the near future? The former slaves were "free" in name, but seldom in any other sense — the ideals espoused by the power structure had changed without the social relations of caste, race, or gender improving in practice. At least from the standpoint of the affluent white male American, had it all been worth it, and would anything else ever be worth such an effort? As it was, the power elite of American society became viscerally reluctant to entertain other potentially divisive or disruptive movements, regardless of their merit.

This post Civil War reaction combined with what Elaine Showalter, in her study *Sexual Anarchy*, terms the "end of the century disease." Showalter uses this term to describe the angst and uncertainty of upper class males regarding social change, especially those changes involving gender roles, that pervaded Anglo-American culture in the last half of the nineteenth century. The threat of the "new woman" was met by a brief flurry of male "revenge" literature in which uppity suffragists were put back in their place — for their own good, of course. This response seems to be perhaps a more virulent expression of Nathaniel Hawthorne's railings against "that damned mob of scribbling women," by which he meant that female writers should leave the literary marketplace to "serious" writers such as himself and his friend, Herman Melville[2]. At least he was no hypocrite in this regard, and therefore Hawthorne put his wife's not insignificant literary talent to work editing his own manuscripts, without attribution. Not only were established gender roles being questioned, but the late nineteenth century was also a period of unprecedented urbanization and industrialization, with all the social upheaval that these changes imply. It was a time of fundamental challenge to some of the basic cultural underpinnings of society as well. The publication of Charles Darwin's *The Origin of the Species* in 1859 presented a direct assault on many closely held religious doctrines. The theory of evolution accompanied the discovery of geologic time and the uncovering of the fossil remains of extinct exotic species. These discoveries combined with the realization that many pagan religious traditions that predate the Judeo-Christian tradition contained remarkably Biblical parallels, especially in their creation stories.

These events led to a pointed questioning of both the truth and the merit of *any* religious belief. Chopin was aware of Darwin's work, and a number of critics, such as Stephen Heath argue that Chopin was not only influenced by him but also by other biological determinists such as Thomas Huxley and Herbert Spencer. Bert Bender takes an even stronger position on the question of such influences on Chopin and her works[3]. Nevertheless, America's intellectual and social elite were becoming disillusioned with their long held belief in the inevitability of providential progress. The response of many of them, at least at first, was to become more reactionary and intransigent in the face of any perceived threat to the established social order. Thus, change was in the air in turn-of-the-century America. The Seneca Falls convention of 1848, marking the inception of the American women's rights movement and the passage of the fourteenth amendment to the constitution, which gave citizenship to the former slaves, both promised better days ahead. The sad fact is that most of a century would pass before the civil rights movement of the 1960's would begin to fulfill the promises.

Nevertheless, the waning of religious faith and the willful, sometimes enforced, ignorance with regard to troubling social issues did not leave a vacuum in the collective American consciousness. Chopin herself was well read, and the salon that she founded in St. Louis provided further opportunities to keep abreast of intellectual and social trends. Even if she was not greatly influenced by the intellectual currents of her time — and most writers find it impossible not to be influenced to some degree — many of those who would determine whether or not to publish her work, and the reviewers who would influence its popularity and longevity, no doubt were. Social Darwinism, a perverse rendering of Darwin's own thought based largely on the determinism of Herbert Spencer and other, even less scientifically credible theories such as eugenics, was one of the more influential ideas of the time. This theory provided a popularized, pseudo-scientific lens through which to view society that the established elite, feeling somewhat threatened by progressive ideas, used to its great advantage. Social Darwinism not only justified the status quo, it adapted nicely to the rise of full-blown, *laissez faire* capitalism, especially from the perspective of its beneficiaries and promoters. It had the added advantage of being perfectly consistent with the Calvinist doctrine that it was beginning to replace in popular folk theories of economics and sociology, as Science became a new, if poorly understood, religion. Unrestrained industrial capitalism was embraced by the economic elite and promoted to the rest of society with an almost religious fervor — the invisible hand of the marketplace posited by Adam Smith, and worshiped by industrial capitalists, became the hand of God.

Such an astute observer of turn-of-the-century American society as Henry Adams noted, with some dismay but with little doubt, the inevitability of this transition. In "The Dynamo and the Virgin," from *The Education of Henry Adams*, he laments the ascension of force and technology at the expense of art and community. Adams might be expected to have an instinctive resistance to industrial and urban expansion, but nevertheless, he accurately perceived this change in society as it was happening. Most of the social establishment, of which Adams himself was a member, embraced and worshiped the change with the blind faith of the zealot, calling it progress and pressing it on the rest of society. Chopin's first novel, *At Fault*, shows that even the isolated Cane River region of Louisiana was not immune to the effects of a changing economy. The two central characters of the novel, Thérèse Lafirme and David Hosmer, come together for the first time because Hosmer needs the raw timber from Lafirme's land to feed his new lumber mill, demonstrating that even the old plantations were having to adapt to a more industrial economy.

The rise of science, and the advent of pseudo-sciences such as social Darwinism were important, providing the often unstated underpinnings of the social establishment. In addition to the thread of biological determinism weaving its way through society, Thorstein Veblen examined late nineteenth century America and formulated a theory, based on a form of sociological determinism, that should ring true to readers of Chopin. Veblen's *The Theory of The Leisure Class*, published in the same year as *The Awakening*, describes the role of the upper class wife as primarily a means of conspicuous consumption for her husband. Thus, she is obligated to perform ritualized duties around the home to assure that "she does not occupy herself with anything that is gainful or that is of substantial use" (68). This clearly describes a large part of Edna's dilemma in *The Awakening* and also explains her conflict with Léonce and his distress when she begins to neglect her household obligations and begins to pursue her own, sometimes "gainful," interests. Late Victorian society sanctioned only the role of the "mother-woman" for a woman of Edna's social class, and Veblen notes the inherent conservatism of such societies and "the revulsion felt by good people at any proposed departure from the accepted methods of life" (139).

Since, as Veblen notes, a woman such as Edna would have been viewed by many of her contemporaries as little more than an accessory to her husband's well appointed home, perhaps one effective way of understanding the early reception of Chopin's controversial novel is to attempt to view both the novel and its female hero in a late nineteenth century context. Her male critics and reviewers, and even many of her female readers, could be expected to view Edna Pontellier in the way that society viewed most women — through the men in her life. Social Darwinism, as well as the sociological determinism described by Veblen, provided a hunter-gatherer metaphor in which the male entered the strange urban jungle, complete with its exotic population of recent immigrants, to do battle in a zero sum game with others of his kind. This arrangement required the support of a female counterpart to provide domestic support for these forays, and perhaps most important of all, to see that his superior genetic material was passed on to the next generation. Energetic competition and accumulation of material goods was a virtue, second only to dominating one's foes. This way of viewing life at least provided a rationalization for the elite of society to pursue their own ends.

Edna's husband, Léonce, in the context of mainstream American society of the time, is a paragon — a living example of the American dream in its most benevolent form. For a male audience, which would have included virtually every critic, reviewer, editor, and literary scholar, Léonce was, if not a role model, at least a man to admire. He has all the traditional trappings of success. In addition to a very successful business, he has an attractive wife and numerous servants to attend to domestic chores and provide for his comfort. He also has two sons who "usually prevailed" (887) over their companions—chips right off the old Darwinian block. He reigns imperiously over his cottage at Grand Isle, as illustrated in the novel's first scene, and he has mastered the manly arts of gambling and playing pool. At Grand Isle, where his idle and pampered family serves as a living status symbol, he is a man's man in a woman's place, and he can hardly wait to return to the rough and tumble world of business back in New Orleans. Yet he is a generous and benevolent dictator, as much regarded by the community for generosity and tolerance as for his business acumen and wealth. The women and children of Grand Isle adore him, or at least his gifts, and even Edna "was forced to admit" that when it came to husbands, "she knew of none better" (887).

Given the gender roles of turn of the century America, Léonce's attitudes and behavior would have been viewed by most of Chopin's readers as progressive and tolerant, if not enlightened. His conversation with Dr. Mandelet would have been seen as a sincere attempt to understand Edna and help her with whatever was troubling her. One can easily imagine many of Chopin's male readers wondering why Léonce did not simply put his foot down and order Edna to snap out of it and behave, much as they would have, and probably sometimes did, in their own homes. At the same time, many of Chopin's female readers may have found themselves wondering why Edna was so dissatisfied with her life, especially when they could never hope to have it so good, either in terms of material comforts or the free time to explore their own thoughts.

In this regard, other literary husbands of the time prove instructive. For example, Frank Norris' "Fantaisie Printaniere," presents the examples of McTeague, generously described as a "brute," and Ryer, described as a "sadist," with equal generosity. Both reside in an urban tenement, have failed at business or professional life because of lack of credentials or ethics, drink heavily, and regularly abuse their wives. Sadly, both are closer to the late nineteenth century norm than is Léonce. The irony of this darkly humorous and disturbing story is that not only do the female characters tolerate their own systematic abuse, but they actually take pride in it. This illustration is by no means meant to suggest that nineteenth century women tolerated physical abuse, but unfortunately, as David Reynolds observes in *Beneath the American Renaissance*, such behavior was common enough to have been one of the motivating forces behind the temperance movement and one of the reasons that so many of its members — and its most effective leaders — were women.

Toth points out in her essay for this volume that Chopin herself was involved for a time with a man who, if not abusive to her, was abusive toward his wife. Her pointed response was to end the relationship and return to St. Louis. She also found such abusive behavior objectionable in literature, attacking the "Chicago School," of which Norris is a prime example, in her essay "Development of the Literary West." In the case of Léonce, by comparison, one can easily imagine many of Chopin's readers scratching their heads, and asking themselves alternatively, "What more could the poor man do?" and "What does that silly woman want, anyway?" Edna's affluence and relative freedom, at least in terms of economic advantage and physical comfort, would make her plight difficult for many readers — especially the males — to understand. Much of Chopin's female audience would likely have been happy to trade places with Edna and at least be able to face their other problems from relative financial comfort. Though many women undoubtedly understood Edna's situation, *The Awakening* would have had relatively little impact on their daily lives. As Toth observes, it is a novel of empathy and consciousness raising, not an advice manual. To male readers, most of whom would have been beneficiaries of the status quo, Edna's privileged social position would make Chopin's themes all the more threatening to those who grasped their implications, and a hostile reaction should come as no surprise.

One could compare the critical reception of Norris' *McTeague,* published in the same year as *The Awakening. McTeague* deals, in a frank and melodramatic fashion with both male and female sexuality, as well as with a large number of other "unwholesome" and "immoral" themes. In contrast to *The Awakening*, Norris' work was enthusiastically received and has remained in the critical eye ever since. Unlike the affluent Creole society in which Chopin's novel is set, the characters in Norris' novel are uneducated, often either stupid or scheming, and unvariably from the lower socioeconomic classes of recent immigrants and unskilled workers. Their behavior, shocking as it might be to conventional society, should come as no surprise — both Calvinism and Social Darwinism tell us so. In this analysis, gender roles take a secondary position to class expectations, even to the extent that the Victorian sense of literary *noblesse oblige* dictates a range of acceptable behavior for the upper classes, thus setting a good example for the "great unwashed" in fiction as in life. Behavior that was expected, if not acceptable, in the lower class — even to the extent that it could be played for dark comedy — was both profoundly disturbing and threatening to society when seen in the upper class, even if in a far less pronounced form.

A convention of Chopin criticism is that *The Awakening* was rejected by many of her contemporaries because of its frank portrayal of female sexuality. This observation, while at least superficially true, is belied by the themes presented in Chopin's rather well received short fiction, as well as by a novel often compared to *The Awakening* — Theodore Dreiser's *Sister Carrie*. Dreiser's book is every bit as frank as Chopin's in terms of its portrayal of female sexuality and presents a far harsher vision of American society as well. One would expect *Sister Carrie* to have been far less acceptable to a contemporary audience than *The Awakening*, and in fact, Dreiser seems to have had greater difficulties publishing his novel than Chopin did. While no evidence exists one way or the other regarding editorial interference with *The Awakening, Sister Carrie* was clearly subjected to severe editing for content prior to publication. In addition, Dreiser's publisher attempted to void his contract upon reading even the highly expurgated version of the novel, and when he finally accepted the fact that he was obligated to publish it, he did everything in his power to cause its failure. Despite being far more frank in its treatment of sexuality and far harsher in its critique of society, *Sister Carrie* never disappeared from the landscape of American fiction. Of course, Dreiser had advantages that Chopin lacked, such as friends in the publishing industry, however, the usual reasons cited for the rejection of *The Awakening* — its sensuality and its dark, ambiguous ending — are difficult to accept in light of the success of far darker and more explicit works. Chopin challenged the social establishment at a far more fundamental level than is commonly recognized. The theme of her novel implies social changes — and subtly indicts established institutions — that go far beyond sexual frankness. It challenges the very founding principles upon which upper class hegemony is built and by which it justifies its existence.

The most critical difference between Carrie and Edna, and hence the reason for Carrie's success and Edna's failure in the literary marketplace, is that of their social class. Dreiser, ever the master of the redundant prepositional phrase, describes Carrie leaving her rural birthplace for Chicago with "four dollars in money" (Dreiser 3) in her purse, speaking both to her economic situation and to his skill as a writer. The contrast with Chopin's skill and Edna's situation could not be more dramatic. Chopin's acknowledged craftsmanship as a writer and Edna's obvious economic and social advantages serve to make the themes of *The Awakening* far more threatening to the political and literary establishment, and they might be expected to elicit a commensurately more shrill response. Nancy Walker argues that this threatening exploration of cultural relations is what makes *The Awakening* such an important and powerful novel. The implicit threat that such a work presented could also be expected to lead the social establishment, including those in the publishing community and the academy, to happily ignore such a novel after the initial, obligatory, negative review.

Thus, the work of a Dreiser or a Norris can be viewed by the elite as informative and instructive, while Chopin's work would have been seen as a menace to be ignored, if not suppressed. This tendency would have been especially pronounced in the case of *The Awakening*. While much of her short fiction dealt with themes every bit as controversial as those of her second novel, the short stories' most controversial characters were either Creole, African-American, or of mixed race. Most readers found them and their cultures to be somewhat exotic, and regardless of their economic status, they each "knew their place" and, ultimately, behaved accordingly. Similar themes portrayed in the life of Edna, a privileged woman who is described in the novel as from "good Kentucky Presbyterian stock," a background specifically mentioned in one of *The Awakening*'s most critical reviews (Culley 170), proved far more difficult and threatening for much of Chopin's audience to accept. Pearl Brown argues that rebellion on the part of a member of the privileged classes suggested the possibility of social disorder of such a magnitude that a hostile reception was inevitable. Antony Harrison argues in his essay "Swinburne and the Critique of Ideology in *The Awakening*" that Chopin's novel attacked not just certain social mores but the very social and religious institutions upon which the power structure was based. Thus, the implications of female autonomy, for the male establishment, would have been far more pervasive and troubling than issues related only to the sexual content of the novel.

Another crucial difference between Chopin and either Norris or Dreiser is that Chopin died suddenly, just as she was reaching the pinnacle of her artistic powers. Had Dreiser died within a few years of the publication of the expurgated version of *Sister Carrie*, prior to producing his other major works and without giving social and literary conventions time to catch up to his vision, he likely would have been lost for a time as well. Norris experimented with a number of literary forms and genres before the space of Naturalism opened in the critical community that allowed him to make the transition from experimentalist to leader of a literary movement. Unlike either Norris or Dreiser, Chopin's work is especially difficult to pigeonhole, and this too helps explain her disappearance from the critical scene. Even a brief survey of recent Chopin criticism will find her work described, accurately, as being representative of or influenced by virtually every "-ism" recognized by literary scholars, a subject addressed by Suzanne Disheroon Green's essay in this volume. This very complexity is a large reason that Chopin's work has attracted such interest and shown such popular longevity, however, it also serves to fragment and obscure critical discourse. Such a situation presented a particularly serious problem during Chopin's lifetime, since no artistic or critical school of the time could truly claim her as its own.

As Richard Ruland and Malcolm Bradbury note in *From Puritanism to Postmodernism,* prior to the twentieth century, American literature was seen as a branch of English literature, and a "genteel," New England branch at that. The rising respectability of American literature in the early - to mid-twentieth century was accompanied by the co-opting of the critical establishment by the university. As criticism became a purely academic discipline, the evolution of an American canon was at least partly driven by the demands of pedagogy and the rigidity demanded by course syllabi. Even had Chopin been included with local colorists — a sub-genre that Chopin herself viewed critically, as illustrated in her essays "The Western Association of Writers" and "'Crumbling Idols' by Hamlin Garland" — the fit would have been uneasy because of her themes and perhaps led to the exclusion of some of her best work. Until feminist scholars in the 1970's made the study of women writers acceptable in, and then a necessary part of literature, there was no well defined space in the American canon in which to place Chopin's work. Such is often the effect of rigid institutional definitions, and we owe an enormous debt to those early Chopin scholars who brought her work back to the attention of casual readers and students of literature alike.

Thus, the reasons for the early critical rejection and subsequent disappearance of Chopin's work, especially *The Awakening*, are more complex than have generally been recognized. Certainly Chopin's depictions of female sensuality and the resistance of the male-dominated establishment to themes of female freedom were a factor. However, the attitudes of the late nineteenth century social establishment related to economic and social status played an even larger role in the negative reception of Chopin's work. If women claim the rights and benefits of full citizenship, what then of people-of-color? What of the poor? The very existence of the literary and social elite who stood in judgment of Chopin's work was predicated on a rigid hierarchy, and any suggestion of leveling it could not be taken lightly. *The Awakening* not only threatened the accepted norms of affluent society — more importantly, it threatened the very dream of Gilded Age capitalism, materialism, and the entire economic and social order being built by the elite. The threat to the validity of existing institutions and the establishment's dream of continued dominance was far more problematic than any of the particular issues raised in the novel. Absent this "American dream," all of the troubling issues and uncertainties of the *fin de siècle* would have burst forth into the shared consciousness of the age. In other words, many of Chopin's contemporaries would have been willfully resistant to her message — they did not want to ponder its implications for their privileged position.

Chopin's work fell from critical attention because of the organization of the academic literary community and its single-minded determination to classify works and develop an officially sanctioned canon. This trend was compounded by Chopin's death, at the height of her artistic power, which prevented any of the self promotion necessary to a developing career. Given the fact that Chopin remained productive until her health began to decline, shortly before her untimely death, we could have expected her body of work to grow in both quality and quantity, had she lived. This fact, along with her self confidence and business acumen, would have undoubtedly made her a strong contender to take advantage of the changes in American society and letters that occurred in the next twenty years. Unfortunately, at the turn of the century no mainstream categories, either social or literary, existed in which to place work such as Chopin's. Thus, after a brief spark of controversy, it was doomed to fall from sight until society began to catch up with Chopin's vision. This temporary obscurity is the real tragedy of Chopin's career — that an entire generation of readers had almost no access to her best work.

Notes

¹ Jane P. Tompkins in "*The Awakening*: An Evaluation," finds Chopin's novel to be melodramatic, ambiguous, and emotionally unmoving, while Yves Clemmens' "Photographic Politics" describes it as unfocused and illusive. Perhaps the most scathing critic is Hugh J. Dawson, who in "Kate Chopin's *The Awakening*," states that the novel should be removed from the canon. He calls it pretentious, inflated and juvenile, criticizing its "over-cute" language, its shallowness, and its lack of plot and character development. Developed or not, he does not care for most of the characters either, calling Robert a "foppish parasite," Mlle. Reisz intentionally cruel, and Edna confused, selfish, and self-destructive. James W. Tuttleton, in *Vital Signs*, reserves most of his critical remarks for certain Chopin scholars, rather than the author and the works themselves. In a generally favorable review of Toth's biography, he argues that *The Awakening* has been "ransacked" by feminist critics, and that Chopin was never in fact a "lost author."

² Emily Toth has observed that *The Awakening* is in the process of replacing Herman Melville's *Moby Dick* in the canon, an opinion that rings true to anybody who has recently taught or taken classes in nineteenth century American literature.

³ Bert Bender in "The Teeth of Desire" and "Kate Chopin's Quarrel with Darwin before *The Awakening*" argues that the influence of Darwinism is pervasive in Chopin's work. However, Bender's analysis implies that Chopin herself was much more of a determinist than many of her themes indicate. In my forthcoming article, "Kate Chopin and Nineteenth Century Determinisms," I argue that such an analysis is incompatible with Chopin's clear rejection of traditional women's roles and upper-class social mores.

Works Cited

Adams, Henry. *The Education of Henry Adams.* in *Henry Adams.* Ed. Ernest Samuels and Jayne N. Samuels. New York: Library of America, 1983.

Bender, Bert. "'The Teeth of Desire': *The Awakening* and *The Descent of Man.*" *AmLit* 63 (1991): 459-73.

—. "Kate Chopin's Quarrel with Darwin before *The Awakening.*" *Journal of American Studies* 26 (1992): 185-204.

Bonner, Thomas Jr. "Christianity and Catholicism in the Fiction of Kate Chopin." *In Old New Orleans.* Ed. W. Kenneth Holditch. Jackson, MS: UP of Mississippi, 1983.

"Book Reviews." *The Awakening: An Authoritative Text, Biographical and Historical Contexts, Criticism* by Kate Chopin. Ed Margo Culley. New York: W. W. Norton, 1994.

Brown, Pearl L. "Kate Chopin's Fiction: Order and Disorder in a Stratified Society." *University of Mississippi Studies in English* 9 (1991): 119-34.

Candela, Joseph L. Jr. "Domestic Orientation of American Novels, 1893-1913." *ALR* 13 (1980): 1-18.

Cather, Willa. "A Creole Bovary." *The Awakening: An Authoritative Text, Biographical and Historical Contexts, Criticism* by Kate Chopin. 1st ed. Ed. Margo Culley. New York: Norton, 1983.

Chopin, Kate. *The Awakening.* in *The Complete Works of Kate Chopin.* Ed. Per Seyersted. Baton Rouge: Louisiana State UP, 1969.

—. *At Fault. The Complete Works of Kate Chopin.* Ed. Per Seyersted. Baton Rouge: Louisiana State UP, 1969.

—. "The Western Association of Writers." *The Complete Works of Kate Chopin.* Ed. Per Seyersted. Baton Rouge: Louisiana State UP, 1969.

—. "'Crumbling Idols' by Hamlin Garland." *The Complete Works of Kate Chopin.* Ed. Per Seyersted. Baton Rouge: Louisiana State UP, 1969.

Clemmen, Yves. "Photographic Politics: The Text and Its Readings in Kate Chopin's *The Awakening.*" *SoQ* 32.4 (1994): 75-79.

Cutter, Martha J. "Losing the Battle but Winning the War: Resistance to Patriarchal Discourse in Kate Chopin's Short Fiction." *Legacy* 11 (1994): 17-36.

Daigrepont, Lloyd M. "Edna Pontellier and the Myth of Passion." *New Orleans Review* 18.3 (1991): 5-13.

Dawson, Hugh J. "Kate Chopin's *The Awakening*: A Dissenting Opinion." *ALR* 26.2 (1994)1-18.

Flexner, Eleanor. *Century of Struggle: The Women's Rights Movement in the United States.* Cambridge: Harvard UP, 1968.

Harrison, Anthony H. "Swinburne and the Critique of Ideology in *The Awakening.*" *Gender and Discourse in Victorian Literature and Art.* Ed. Anthony H. Harrison and Beverly Taylor. Dekalb: Northern Illinois UP, 1992.

Heath, Stephen. "Chopin's Parrot." *Textual Practice* 8 (1994): 11-32.

Koloski, Bernard. "The Anthologized Chopin: Kate Chopin's Short Stories in Yesterday's and Today's Anthologies." *LaLit.* 2.1 (1994):18-30.

Mitchell, Angelyn. "Feminine Double Consciousness in Kate Chopin's 'The Story of an Hour.'" *CEA Magazine* 5.1 (1992): 59-64.

Norris, Frank. *McTeague: A Story of San Francisco.* Ed. Donald Pizer. New York: Norton,1977.

—. "Fantaisie Printaniere." *Heath Anthology of American Literature.* 3rd ed. Ed. Paul Lauter. 2 vols. Boston: Houghton Mifflin: 1998.

Reynolds, David. *Beneath the American Renaissance: the Subversive Imagination in the Age of Emerson and Melville.* Cambridge: Harvard UP, 1988.

Ruland, Richard and Malcolm Bradbury. *From Puritanism To Postmodernism: A History of American Literature.* New York: Penguin, 1991.

Saar, Doreen Alvarez. "The Failure and Triumph of 'The Maid of Saint Phillipe': Chopin Rewrites American Literature for American Women." *LaLit* 2.1 (1994): 59-73.

Shillingsburg, Miriam J. "The Ascent of Woman, Southern Style: Hentz, King, Chopin." *Southern Literature in Transition: Heritage and Promise.* Ed. Philip Castille and William Osborne. Memphis: Memphis State UP, 1983.

Showalter, Elaine. *Sexual Anarchy: Gender and Culture at the Fin de Siècle.* New York: Penguin, 1990.

Toth, Emily. "Timely and Timeless: The Treatment of Time in *The Awakening* and *Sister Carrie.*" *SoSt* 16(1977): 271-76.

—. Kate Chopin: *The Life of the Author of The Awakening.* New York: Morrow, 1990.

—. "Feminist or Naturalist: The Social Context of Kate Chopin's *The Awakening.*" *SoQ* 17.2 (1997): 95-103.

Tompkins, Jane P. "*The Awakening*: An Evaluation." *Feminist Studies* 3.3-4 (1976):22-29.

Tuttleton, James W. *Vital Signs: Essays on American Literature and Criticism.* Chicago: Ivan R. Dee, 1996.

Veblen, Thorstein. *The Theory of the Leisure Class: An Economic Study of Institutions.* New York: Mentor Books, 1953.

Walker, Nancy. *The Disobedient Writer: Women and Narrative Tradition.* Austin: U of Texas P, 1995:

ANNOTATED BIBLIOGRAPHICAL
ENTRIES

Primary Texts

The following list includes references to primary texts which have been published as of 1998. Penguin Classics plans to reissue Chopin's short story collections *Bayou Folk* and *A Night in Acadie* as one volume in March, 1999. We do not attempt to comprehensively list all editions of *The Awakening* that are currently in print, as such a listing is beyond the scope of this volume. The references below refer to the authoritative versions of Chopin's texts. Two editions of *The Awakening* are included in this list in addition to Seyersted's *Complete Works* because they also include a substantial selection of secondary criticism.

A.1 Bonner, Thomas, Jr. *The Kate Chopin Companion*. Westport, CT: Greenwood, 1988.
   LOC: PS1294.C63 B6 1988
   Bonner's volume includes Chopin's translations of Guy de Maupassant's stories and a comprehensive dictionary of Chopin's characters.

A.2 Culley, Margo, ed. *The Awakening* by Kate Chopin. 2nd ed. New York: Norton, 1994.
   LOC: PS1294.C63 A6 1994
   This reprint of *The Awakening* also includes a facsimile of the manuscript's title page, a biographical sketch by Emily Toth, selections from women's advice and etiquette manuals of Chopin's era, selections from contemporary reviews, letters to Chopin from

readers of *The Awakening*, as well as Chopin's "retraction," selections of excerpts from more recent critical essays, a chronology of Chopin's life and literary career, and a selected bibliography of primary works, biographies, bibliographies, criticism, and numerous editorial notes.

A.3   Seyersted, Per. *The Complete Works of Kate Chopin*. 2 vols. Baton Rouge: Louisiana State UP, 1969.
      LOC: PS1294.C63 1970
      Seyersted's volume is the *de facto* standard edition of all of Chopin's extant texts as of 1969. The volume includes an apparatus, a publishing history, and a biographical sketch of Chopin. Seyersted uses the last published versions of Chopin's works as his base texts.

A.4   Seyersted, Per and Emily Toth, eds. *A Kate Chopin Miscellany*. Natchitoches: Northwestern State UP, 1979.
      LOC: PS1294 C63A6 1979
      This volume includes several previously unpublished stories and poems by Chopin.
      See also: D.44

A.5   Toth, Emily, ed. *A Vocation and a Voice*, by Kate Chopin. New York: Penguin, 1991.
      LOC: PS1294.C63 A78 1991
      Toth's volume includes the stories that Chopin intended to publish as *A Vocation and a Voice* before the contract for the volume was canceled. Toth presents the stories in the order in which Chopin intended to arrange them. The volume also includes a critical introduction.

A.6   Toth, Emily and Per Seyerested, eds. *Kate Chopin's Private Papers*. Bloomington, IN: Indiana UP, 1998.
      LOC: PS1294.C63A6 1998
      Along with a chronology of Chopin's life, the volume details her surviving private papers, which include her: (1) adolescent autograph book, (2) commonplace book, (3) manuscript account books, (4) 1894 diary, (5) letters and inscriptions, (6) newspaper pieces, (7) translations, (8) musical composition the "Lilia" Polka, (9) transcriptions of re-discovered short stories, including the Rankin-Marhefka fragments, (10) poems, (11) statements on *The Awakening*, (12) reminiscences about her friend Kitty Garesché, and (12) Chopin's last will and testament. The volume also includes a listing of her complete works and a core bibliography for Chopin scholars. All of the material is placed in its historical and scholarly context.
      See also: D.307

A.7   Walker, Nancy, ed. *The Awakening* by Kate Chopin. Boston and New
       York: Bedford Books – St. Martin's P, 1993.
          Walker's volume includes a text of *The Awakening* drawn from
          Seyersted's *Complete Works*. It also includes critical essays by Elaine
          Showalter, Margit Stange, Cynthia Griffin Wolff, Patricia Yaeger, and
          Paula Treichler. These essays represent a variety of theoretical
          approaches and are preceded by essays introducing the approaches
          presented. The volume also includes an essay analyzing the
          biographical and historical contexts of the novel.

          For annotations of the individual essays in this volume, please refer to
          section E.9.1-5.
          See also: E.9

Biographies

B.1 Rankin, Daniel. *Kate Chopin and Her Creole Stories*. Philadelphia: U of
Pennsylvania P, 1932.
LOC: PS1294.C63 R3 1932
    Based on his doctoral dissertation, Rankin's biography is the first
study of Chopin's fiction. The study places her firmly in the local color
tradition. His study has been superceded by the biographical studies of
Seyersted and Toth, as noted below.

B.2 Seyersted, Per. *Kate Chopin: A Critical Biography*. Baton Rouge:
Louisiana State UP, 1969, 1980.
LOC: PS1294.C63 S4
    First published in 1969, and reprinted in 1980, the volume provides a
somewhat dated but still useful analysis of Chopin's life and her major
works. Seyersted also provides a selected bibliography of archival
sources, a bibliography of primary texts and their original place of
publication, as well as selected early secondary criticism.

B.3 Toth, Emily. *Kate Chopin: A Life of the Author of The Awakening*. New
York: Morrow, 1990.
LOC: PS1294.C63 T68 1990
    Toth's biography offers a comprehensive study of Chopin's life and
works. The volume is thoroughly researched, highly detailed, and
imminently readable. A partial publication history and extensive
bibliography are included in the volume.

B.4   Toth, Emily. *Unveiling Kate Chopin.* Jackson, MS: UP of Mississippi, forthcoming 1999.

Toth's forthcoming volume tells how a 19th century schoolgirl from St. Louis learned to be an independent woman in the French mold of the women who raised her. Kate O'Flaherty Chopin was a clever daughter, a wife with a wicked sense of humor, a much-loved mother, a scandalous widow, and then the brilliant, ambitious author of the most radial, notorious novel of the late 19th century: *The Awakening,* which will be 100 years old on April 22, 1999.
See also: D.305

Annotated by Emily Toth, Louisiana State University.

Bibliographies

1976

C1. Springer, Marlene. *Edith Wharton and Kate Chopin: A Reference Guide*. Boston: G. K. Hall, 1976.
    LOC: Z8969.2.S66
    Springer's volume catalogs writings by and about Chopin from the time Chopin began writing until 1976. The volume includes an exhaustive enumerative bibliography, as well as brief annotations of many works. Of particular use are the annotations of contemporary reviews of Chopin's writing.

C.2 "Kate Chopin Bibliography." *KCN* 1.2 (1975-76): 32-37.
    LOC: PS1294 C63 Z7
    A selected, annotated bibliography, this article includes dissertations, conference papers, journal articles, bibliographies and books dealing with Kate Chopin and her works which appeared during 1975 and early 1976. The selections also include references to works about Chopin that were in press at the time that the *Newsletter* was printed.

C.3 "Kate Chopin Bibliography." *KCN* 2.1 (1976): 28-34.
    LOC: PS1294 C63 Z7
    A selected, annotated bibliography, this article includes dissertations, conference papers, journal articles, bibliographies and books dealing with Kate Chopin and her works which appeared during the spring and summer of 1976. The selections also include references to works about Chopin that were in press at the time that the *Newsletter* was printed.

C.4 "Kate Chopin Bibliography." *KCN* 2.2 (1976): 47-48.
   LOC: PS1294 C63 Z7
   A selected, annotated bibliography, this article includes dissertations, conference papers, journal articles, bibliographies and books dealing with Kate Chopin and her works which appeared during the fall of 1976. The selections also include references to works about Chopin that were in press at the time that the *Newsletter* was printed.

1977

C.5 "Kate Chopin Bibliography." *RegF* 3.1 (1977): 45-48.
   LOC: PS1294 C63 Z71
   A selected, annotated bibliography, this article includes dissertations, conference papers, journal articles, bibliographies and books dealing with Kate Chopin and her works which appeared during the early part of 1977. The selections also include references to works about Chopin that were in press at the time that the *Newsletter* was printed.

1981

C.6 Springer, Marlene. "Kate Chopin: A Reference Guide Updated." *Resources for American Literary Study* 11 (1981): 280-81.
   LOC: Z1225 R46
   Springer's update of her 1976 volume begins in 1973 but does not duplicate entries from the 1976 volume. She annotates items that she was able to obtain, omitting reviews of secondary sources, general works with minor discussions of Chopin, and MA theses. The update contains entries through 1980 and categorizes the entries as book-length studies or shorter critical pieces.

1983

C.7 Inge, Tonette Bond. "Kate Chopin." *American Women Writers: Bibliographical Essays*. Ed. Maurice Duke, Jackson R. Bryer, and M. Thomas Inge. Westport, CT: Greenwood, 1983.
   LOC: Z1229.W8 A44 1983 or PS147.W8 A44 1983
   Inge provides a brief biography of Chopin, followed by enumerative entries for bibliographic aids, editions of primary texts, manuscripts, letters, biographical data, and selected criticism through 1980. She also makes suggestions for further research.

1984

C.8 Gannon, Barbara C. "Kate Chopin: A Secondary Bibliography." *ALR* 17
(1984): 124-129.
LOC: PS1 A65
Gannon updates bibliographies appearing in the *Missouri Historical
Society Bulletin*, *Bulletin of Bibliography*, *Kate Chopin Newsletter*
and *Regionalism and the Female Imagination*, including editions from
1975-77, and then extends them through 1981. She offers an
enumerative bibliography of secondary sources, arranged
chronologically.

1996

C.9 Thomas, Heather Kirk. "Kate Chopin: A Primary Bibliography,
Alphabetically Arranged." *ALR* 28.2 (1996): 71-88.
LOC: PS1 A65
Thomas provides an alphabetical arrangement with variant titles from
Chopin's log books, including the titles of unlocated works. The essay
enumerates all known writings, except personal correspondence,
including commonplace books, diaries, stories, sketches, story
collections, novels, essays, reviews, published letters to editors, poems,
a musical composition, and a one-act play.

Critical Books and Journal Articles, 1976–1999

1976

Books and Book Chapters

D.1   Berke, Jacqueline and Lola Silver. "The 'Awakened' Woman in Literature and Real Life." *Proceedings of the Sixth Annual National Convention of the Popular Culture Association, Chicago, April 22-24, 1976.* Bowling Green, OH: Popular Press, 1165-79.
     Berke and Silver's analysis briefly mentions *The Awakening* in the context of works by Henrik Ibsen, along with a number of modern women writers. She addresses the futility of individual female awakenings absent a larger social awakening that would empower their newfound knowledge. Family therapist Silver uses Edna's situation as a paradigm for contemporary social problems that affect all members of society and propagate themselves across generations.

D.2   Fryer, Judith. *The Faces of Eve: Women in the Nineteenth Century American Novel.* New York: Oxford UP, 1976.
     LOC: PS374.W6F7
     Fryer notes that Chopin succeeded in creating a woman who was a complete person, whereas male writers of her era failed. She contrasts Edna with a wide variety of female protagonists, including Daisy Miller, Isabel Archer, Emma Bovary, and Anna Karenina. Edna shares characteristics of self-awareness and frank acceptance of her sexuality with these characters, however, Edna is different from all of the above, in that she is not after romance and is not

guilt-ridden. Fryer also compares female and male perceptions of women's death, drawing specific examples from Hawthorne's Zenobia and Plath's "Ariel."

D.3   Moers, Ellen. *Literary Women*. Garden City, NY: Doubleday, 1976.
       LOC: PN471 M63
       Moers discusses the influence of de Stael's *Corinne* on Chopin's personal life and demonstrates the similarity of Mademoiselle Reisz to the Klemser character in George Eliot's *Daniel Deronda*. She argues that the bird imagery in *The Awakening* sets Edna apart from the Creole mother-women and also points out the abundance of Freudian water imagery derived from Whitman. The essay concludes with a discussion of Edna's celebration of her transformed self, which Moers argues is reminiscent of Emily Dickinson's poetry. The essay contains a selected enumerative bibliography of primary works and an index of comments by critics.

Journal Articles

D.4   "The Bayou Folk Museum." *KCN* 2.1 (1976): 27.
       LOC: PS1294 C63 Z7
       This essay briefly describes the Bayou Folk museum in Cloutierville, Louisiana, which is housed in Kate Chopin's former home. It also provides a brief inventory of the museum's contents and driving directions to the house itself.

D.5   Berke, Jacqueline. "Kate Chopin's Call to a Larger 'Awakening.'"
       KCN 1.3 (1975-76): 1-5.
       LOC: PS1294 C63 Z7
       Berke argues that *The Awakening* serves as a contemporary manifesto for feminism, due to the changes in social and gender roles that became necessary during the 19th century. These changes, which affected both men and women, were beginning to take place during Chopin's lifetime.

D.6   Borish, Elaine. "*The Awakening* Awakens England." *KCN* 2.1 (1976): 1-5.
       LOC: PS1294 C63 Z7
       Borish recounts her experience teaching *The Awakening* as an instructor at London's Morley College at a time when the novel was unavailable in England. She notes that despite greater levels of sexism and conservatism in England at that time, students responded favorably to the text.

D.7   Davidson, Cathy N. "Chopin and Atwood: Woman Drowning, Woman Surfacing." *KCN* 1.3 (1975-76): 6-10.
LOC: PS1294 C63 Z7
Davidson argues that Margaret Atwood's *Surfacing* serves as a modern revision of Chopin's *The Awakening*. She also argues that the major characters of both novels are in similar situations in relation to their societies, and that their different responses reflect differences in their respective societies.

D.8   "Frédéric Pronounced It the Same Way." *KCN* 2.1 (1976): 27.
LOC: PS1294 C63 Z7
This essay notes that, according to her relatives, Kate Chopin's name is pronounced 'SHOW-pan,' not 'Choppin,' though the latter is favored by some New Orleans natives. The article also notes that the famous composer, Frédéric was not related to Chopin's husband Oscar.

D.9   Gartner, Carol B. "Three Ednas." *KCN* 1.3 (1975-76): 11-20.
LOC: PS1294 C63 Z7
Gartner compares Edna of *The Awakening* to Edward L. Wheeler's Edna in "The American Wild Edna" of *Old Avalanche* and *The Great Annihilator: Or, Wild Edna, the Girl Brigand*. She also compares Chopin's Edna to Edna Kenderdine of Miss Mulock's *The Woman's Kingdom: A Love Story*. Gartner uses these comparisons to place *The Awakening* in the context of its time. She describes contemporary readers' widely-held expectations in order to illustrate how Chopin shattered them. She also examines specific parallels and divergences between *The Awakening* and the other works mentioned.

D.10 Gilbert, Jan. "Kate Chopin Up Against the Wall." *KCN* 2.2 (1976): 46.
LOC: PS1294 C63 Z7
Gilbert briefly transcribes a piece of graffiti referring to Chopin, touting the writer as a "teacher of women's liberation."

D.11 Hardmeyer, Steven G. "A Student's Response to *The Awakening*." *KCN* 2.1 (1976): 6.
LOC: PS1294 C63 Z7
Hardmeyer offers a brief response from the perspective of a first time reader to the conclusion of *The Awakening*.

D.12 Jasenas, Eliane. "The French Influence in Kate Chopin's *The Awakening*." *Nineteenth Century French Studies* 4 (1976): 312-22.

LOC: PQ1.N55

Jasenas suggests that although both French and Creole culture were foreign to Chopin, *The Awakening* shows the direct influence of French writers. She notes the influence of the French Symbolists on Chopin. She further argues that Maupassant, Flaubert, and Baudelaire influenced different parts of *The Awakening* and constitute "*influence critique*," defined by Jasenas as "the narrative turning against them or commenting upon them." She argues that Chopin ultimately rejects both the French and Creole influences, which represent bourgeois values and pessimism. Thus, Chopin had her own awakening as a writer as she learned from, but did not follow, the examples of these French writers.

D.13   Ladenson, Joyce Ruddel. "The Return of St. Louis' Prodigal Daughter: Kate Chopin After Seventy Years." *Midamerica* 2 (1976): 24-34.

Ladenson argues that contemporary male critics have overemphasized the sexuality and existential angst in Chopin's work at the expense of its themes of female rebellion. She examines the female characters in a variety of Chopin's short stories, *The Awakening* and *At Fault*, arguing that the majority of them experiences conflict with male authority that illustrates a gender phenomenon across economic, cultural, and racial lines. She argues that Chopin's work raises important questions about the role of women as wives, mothers, unmarried women, adolescents, and revolutionary pioneers.

D.14   Mills, Elizabeth S. "Colorful Characters from Kate's Past." *KCN* 2.1 (1976): 7-12.
LOC: PS1294 C63 Z7

Mills argues that not just local history, but family history, as related to Kate Chopin by her great-grandmother, influenced the characters, themes, and attitudes seen in her fiction.

D.15   "The Practical Side of Oscar Chopin's Death." *KCN* 3.1 (1975-76): 29.
LOC: PS1294 C63 Z7

This brief note reports that Oscar Chopin's coffin was apparently ordered seven days before his death, illustrating Kate Chopin's practicality and lack of sentimentality.

D.16   Tompkins, Jane P. "*The Awakening*: An Evaluation." *Feminist Studies* 3.3-4 (1976): 22-29.
LOC: HQ1101 .F46

Tompkins argues that despite its strengths, *The Awakening* does not
constitute a great work of art, citing as an example the abundance of
sensuous imagery, which she finds emotionally unmoving. Chapter
12 offers the most clear examples of these faults. The imagery
surrounding Edna's suicide is contradictory and raises unanswered
questions. Chopin's view of suicide vacillates between the Realistic
and the Romantic, without examining the consequences of suicide as
did Hawthorne and Melville. The novel does not involve the reader
in Edna's dilemma, and Chopin chooses a melodramatic ending
rather than revealing her stance on the conflicting values treated in
the novel. Tompkins finds this unsatisfying strategy reminiscent of
Chopin's short fiction.

D.17 Toth, Emily. "Comment on Barbara Bellow Watson's 'On Power and
the Literary Text.'" *Signs* 1 (1976): 1005.
LOC: HQ1101 .S5
Toth agrees with Watson's assertion that female critics and students
tend to view Edna's suicide as positive, while men see it as a failure.
She further agrees that women have a particular insight into power
relations and a greater willingness to look at literature in new ways.

D.18 Toth, Emily. "Kate Chopin Remembered." *KCN* 1.3 (1975-76): 21-
27.
LOC: PS1294 C63 Z7
Toth offers a short collection of anecdotes from the only two (likely)
people to have known Kate Chopin personally, as well as from
descendants of both Oscar and Kate and the descendants of those
who knew them. The essay also includes an abridged genealogy of
the Chopin family.

D.19 Toth, Emily. "Kate Chopin's *The Awakening* as Feminist Criticism."
Louisiana Studies 15 (1976): 241-51.
LOC: F366.L935
Toth takes exception to earlier critics who argued that *The
Awakening* is not a feminist novel. She points out that feminist ideas
were part of the late 19th century cultural milieu, in that the theme
of woman's escape from confinement derives directly from the
feminist works of Charlotte Perkins Gilman, John Stuart Mills, and
August Bebel. Toth argues that Edna is the "embodiment of 19th
century feminist criticism" and that *The Awakening* is a successful
representation of the growing feminist consciousness at the turn of
the century. *The Awakening* functions as social criticism, and this
fact allows insight into the 19th century itself, as well as into the
impact of the novel on its original audience.

D.20   Toth, Emily and Dennis Fitzgibbons. "Kate Chopin Meets *The Harvard Lampoon*." *KCN* 3.1 (1975-76): 28.
         LOC: PS1294 C63 Z7
         Toth and Fitzgibbons refer to a 1973 *Harvard Lampoon* article in which *The Awakening* is the topic of an example of an undergraduate paper, using the recommended academic "stretching" techniques.

D.21   Webb, Bernice Larson. "The Circular Structure of Kate Chopin's Life and Writing." *New Laurel Review* 6.1 (1976): 5-14.
         LOC: PN2 N3
         Webb draws on "Charlie," "Athénaïse," and "Nég Créol" to demonstrate that both Chopin's life and her best fiction followed a circular path. This path places the protagonist at the story's geographic point of origin and causes them to pass through New Orleans in the middle. A reversal of the protagonist's circumstances during the story causes the protagonist to return to the story's point of origin.

D.22   Wilson, Mary Helen. "Kate Chopin's Family: Fallacies and Facts, Including Kate's True Birthdate." *KCN* 2.3 (1976-77): 25-31.
         LOC: PS1294 C63 Z7
         A distant relative of Kate Chopin by marriage, Wilson provides detailed genealogical data and accounts of Chopin and her ancestors. She corrects a number of errors in early biographies, most notably, Chopin's birthdate.

1977

Books and Book Chapters

D.23   Allen, Priscilla. "Old Critics and New: The Treatment of Chopin's
        The Awakening." *The Authority of Experience: Essays in Feminist
        Criticism.* Ed. Arlyn Diamond and Lee R. Edwards. Amherst: U of
        Massachusetts P, 1977.
        LOC: PR151.W6 A9 1977

   Allen argues that modern critics, regardless of their positions,
   overstate and overemphasize Edna's sexual activity. They therefore
   misread the text. Accordingly, she takes several critics to task for
   their errors. Her argument is similar to those of early critics, in that
   she criticizes Edna's "failure" as wife and mother along with her
   struggle with herself and society. Allen suggests that critics
   dehumanize Edna by failing to see her struggle for freedom as
   universal and by failing to take her seriously because she is a
   woman. She finds most critics to be too sympathetic to Léonce and
   argues that because Mademoiselle Reisz is ugly, she is not taken
   seriously either by society or critics. Allen further argues that critics
   overplay Edna's neglect of her children, saying that to call *The
   Awakening* a sexual book is like calling *Moby Dick* a book about the
   whaling industry. The novel is more revolutionary than critics have
   realized because the true theme presents a portrait of a woman
   determined to have either full integrity and personhood or nothing at
   all.

Journal Articles

D.24   Berggren, Paula S. "'A Lost Soul': Work Without Hope in *The Awakening.*" *RegF* 3.1 (1977): 1-7.
LOC: PS1294 C63 Z71
Berggren argues that in Chopin's short fiction, the recurrent theme is reaching selfhood through self-sacrifice rather than a simple search for freedom. This theme is evident in "Ozème's Holiday" and "Cavanelle." Chopin rejects sexual stereotypes by expressing this search through male characters on the one hand, and woman's need for work outside the home on the other. She argues that Edna is caught between these two modes of self-expression, and that this leads to some of *The Awakening's* ambiguity. Berggren notes that "The Woodchoppers" and "Polly" illustrate Chopin's retreat from these adult themes following Edna's failure to reconcile them.

D.25   Bogarad, Carley Rees. "*The Awakening*: A Refusal to Compromise." *University of Michigan Papers in Women's Studies* 2.3 (1977): 15-31. Bogarad compares *The Awakening* to the 20th century *bildungsroman* as illustrated by the works of James Joyce and D. H. Lawrence. She notes that while male characters, such as Stephen Daedalus and Paul Morel persevere, prevail, and go on to lives as artists, the similar struggles of female characters end in either madness or suicide. *The Awakening* is the clearest statement of this female dilemma. The author compares *The Awakening* to works by female writers such as Gilman, Rhys, Walker, Plath, Parker, and Woolf. She further notes Edna's age, family, and social obligations, comparing them to similar male characters. These constraints combine with Robert's inability to escape the Victorian Madonna/whore dichotomy – represented by Adèle and Mariequita – that seals Edna's dilemma. She argues that Edna has two awakenings: the first is the desire for autonomy and freedom, and the second is her realization that the first is impossible, leading to overwhelming existential despair.

D.26   Bonner, Thomas, Jr. "Kate Chopin's *Bayou Folk* Revisited." *New Laurel Review* 7.2 (1977): 5-14.
LOC: PN2 N3
Bonner argues that critical interest in the *Bayou Folk* collection has focused excessively on characterization while leaving other aspects of these stories unexplored. He critically, but briefly, examines issues such as ethnicity, point of view and dialect, narrative structure, and themes. Bonner concludes that this early collection, though somewhat flawed, shows the promise that was realized in Chopin's later work.

D.27   Bonner, Thomas, Jr. "Kate Chopin's *At Fault* and *The Awakening*: A
        Study in Structure." *Markham Review* 7 (1977): 10-14.
        LOC: PS2363.M37
        This essay examines the growth of Chopin as a writer by looking at
        the structure of *At Fault* and *The Awakening*. Bonner notes that *At
        Fault* is episodic, subconscious, and awkward, while *The Awakening*
        effectively uses settings and patterns of images to draw characters
        and express themes. Bonner provides a careful examination of both
        texts and presents some of the major critical perspectives on
        Chopin's work.

D.28   Chopin, Kate. "Lilia Polka for Piano." *RegF* 3.1 (1977): 30-53.
        LOC: PS1294 C63 Z71
        This reproduction shows Chopin's only published musical
        composition, which was copyrighted in 1888.

D.29   Chopin, Kate. "The Joy of Spring." *RegF* 3.1 (1977): 34-39.
        LOC: PS1294 C63 Z71
        This reproduction shows the lyrics of Chopin's musical composition,
        which was copyrighted in 1913.

D.30   Dash, Irene. "The Literature of Birth and Abortion." *RegFI* 3.1
        (1977): 8-13.
        LOC: PS1294 C63 Z71
        Dash suggests that Adèle's birthing scene stimulates Edna's ultimate
        awakening to the irreconcilable struggle between the claims of
        motherhood and her desire for self-fulfillment. This event makes
        Edna's suicide inevitable, rather than her affairs or other possible
        reasons that critics have postulated.

D.31   Dickey, Imogene. "Kate Chopin: Her Serious Literary Ambition."
        Journal of the American Studies Association of Texas 8 (1977): 18-22.
        LOC: E169.1.A493
        Dickey argues that Chopin belongs to the Naturalist school. She
        notes the influence of Maupassant on Chopin's writing style as well
        as her well-documented, high literary ambitions after her husband's
        death.

D.32   Merrill, Carol. "Impressionism in Kate Chopin's *The Awakening*."
        New America 3.2 (1977): 50-2.
        Merrill argues that with the possible exception of two chapters, each
        chapter of *The Awakening* could be represented as an impressionistic
        scene on canvas. She notes that a person such as Chopin would have
        been aware of this artistic movement and that her use of light and

her presentation of nature conformed to its tenets. She also argues that Chopin's use of the sea as a unifying symbol illustrates an impressionistic influence and notes that her attention to color and her tendency to blur scenes is especially important to the lack of resolution in the final scene of *The Awakening*.

D.33   O'Brien, Sharon. "Sentiment, Local Color, and the New Woman Writer: Kate Chopin and Willa Cather." *KCN* 2.3 (1976-77): 16-24.
LOC: PS1294 C63 Z7
O'Brien notes Chopin's departure from the conventions of 19th century sentimentalism in *The Awakening* and especially in "Two Portraits." She argues that Chopin especially disdained moral didacticism and that she consciously, as opposed to Freeman and Jewett, distanced herself from the local color school. This can be seen in Chopin's review of Hamlin Garland's *Crumbling Idols*. Rather than dealing with local issues, Chopin's fiction dealt with universal human conditions.

D.34   Toth, Emily. "*Kate Chopin Newsletter*: History, Future, Apologies and Grovels." *KCN* 2.3 (1976-77): 32-34.
LOC: PS1294 C63 Z7
Toth offers a brief history of the *Kate Chopin Newsletter* and presents a number of changes that would occur as it becomes *Regionalism and the Female Imagination*.

D.35   Toth, Emily. "Kate Chopin's Music." *RegFI* 3.1 (1977): 28-9.
LOC: PS1294 C63 Z71
Toth discusses Chopin's love of music and includes passages from her childhood diaries written in the 1860s, noting the influence of music in her later life and in her literary works.

D.36   Toth, Emily. "Timely and Timeless: The Treatment of Time in *The Awakening* and *Sister Carrie*." *SoSt* 16 (1977): 271-76.
LOC: F366.I935
Toth notes the many superficial similarities between Chopin's *The Awakening* and Dreiser's *Sister Carrie*, but she argues that the two novels differ dramatically in their treatment of time. She argues that these differences illustrate the two modern trends in novelistic time. *Sister Carrie's* rhythm is purposeful, causal, and linear, corresponding to Dreiser's materialism. *The Awakening* is lyrical, epiphanic, and concerned with moments of consciousness rather than with upward striving. She argues that *Sister Carrie* follows a more masculine model and *The Awakening* a more feminine one.

1978

Books and Book Chapters

No critical books or book chapters were published this year.

Journal Articles

D.37   Candela, Gregory L. "Walt Whitman and Kate Chopin: A Further
        Connection." *Walt Whitman Review* 24 (1978): 163-65.
        LOC: PS3229.W39
   Candela demonstrates a biographical connection between the work of
   Chopin and Whitman. He argues that both the sea and bird images
   are drawn from Whitman. He argues that bird imagery, focusing
   especially on the mockingbird and Edna's eyes — which are
   "strikingly birdlike" — is tied to "Out of the Cradle Endlessly
   Rocking." Candela concludes by pointing out that the rhythm of
   repeated words and images in *The Awakening* is similar to the
   sounds of a mockingbird and Whitman's poem.

D.38   Cantarow, Ellen. "Sex, Race and Criticism: Thoughts of a White
        Feminist on Kate Chopin and Zora Neale Hurston." *Radical Teacher*
        9 (1978): 30-33.
        LOC: L11.R24
   Cantarow's paper is a version of one that was presented at a session
   of the 1977 MLA convention which was structured as a dialogue
   between Black and White feminists. She argues that *The Awakening*
   describes Edna's imprisonment by the upper-middle-class values that
   were the societal norm during Chopin's lifetime and also describes

the possibilities of freedom. Cantarow identifies two methods of achieving freedom: through the possibilities for productive, remunerative work or by following a course of rebellion, isolation, and ultimately self-fulfillment.

D.39   Casale, Ottavio Mark. "Beyond Sex: The Dark Romanticism of Kate Chopin's *The Awakening*." *Ball State University Forum* 19.1 (1978): 76-80.
        LOC: LH1.B18F6
        Casale argues that *The Awakening* is an example of the difference between American and European Realism. Unlike the characters of Flaubert, Edna is presented ironically, or as a victim of false Romanticism. He links her portrayal to the Transcendentalist ideal of "awakening to self" as shown in *Walden* and the works of Emerson and Whitman. The language and imagery of *The Awakening* especially support his view. He compares Edna to Hawthorne's Hester Prynne and Melville's Ahab, Bulkington, and Ishmael in terms of their mutually exclusive worlds. These characters yearn for harmony but find only ambiguity. He notes that these are romances of alienation and disorder, and that they are tragic because of the innocence of the characters. Casale notes the use of similar symbols and the technique of places reflecting states of "being in." He offers chapter 23 of *Moby Dick* as an example, with the sea representing both spiritual life and physical death.

D.40   Horton, Susan R. "Desire and Depression in Women's Fiction: The Problematics and the Economics of Desire." *Modern Fiction Studies* 24 (1978):181-195.
        LOC: PS379.M55
        Horton examines Edith Wharton's *House of Mirth*, Ellen Glasgow's *Barren Ground*, Willa Cather's *O Pioneers*, and Kate Chopin's *The Awakening*, looking at the differences between characters' instincts and impulses as well as the conflict that occurs when choosing between inclination and intention. The four works illustrate a melancholy "that comes not from a sense of powerlessness, but from an unexamined set of assumptions never explicitly expressed." Horton goes on to describe six themes of women's psyches: (1) instinct is bad and to be weeded out; (2) impulse is highly suspect and probably should be eliminated; (3) inclination is to be followed only if it leads to following intention; (4) intentionality is to be aspired to, but its fruition is bittersweet since its polar opposite, instinct, represents the loving attributes of a woman; (5) instinct and interaction can not be integrated; and (6) the battle is "endless, tiring" and can only lead to the death of one or the other aspect of

the self, whichever triumphs. Horton notes that this air of melancholy appears in all of female fiction. She views Edna as a "drifter" because she is willing to make a choice. Edna's dilemma is that she does not have the economic or physical strength to resist her impulses.

D.41   Justus, James H. "The Unawakening of Edna Pontellier." *SLJ* 10 (1978): 107-22.
        LOC: PS261.S527
        Justus views Edna *not* primarily as a woman victimized by a male society but as a romantic figure, contrary to the "critical fashion" of feminist critics. Unlike the characters in Chopin's short fiction, Edna awakens out of conventional society, but awakens into a child-like state where self-indulgence has no consequences. However, Edna has only limited insight and becomes regressive, passive, and self-destructive. Justus compares Edna to other contemporary characters caught between the roles of mother and artist, roles which were mutually exclusive. Since Edna requires freedom, this dilemma is so untenable that she can choose neither role.

D.42   Lattin, Patricia Hopkins. "Childbirth and Motherhood in Kate Chopin's Fiction." *Regionalism and the Female Imagination* 4.1 (1978): 8-12.
        LOC: PS1294 C63 Z71
        Lattin's study addresses "Athénaïse," "Ma'ame Pélagie," "The Godmother," "Désirée's Baby," "La Belle Zoraïde," "Mrs. Mobry's Reason," and *The Awakening*. Looking at both mothers and other female characters, she argues that Chopin's view of children and motherhood contrasts sharply with that seen in her own life. Lattin also argues that Chopin's views differ with regard to whether motherhood, much less conventional motherhood, exists as a central element in the short fiction. Only in *The Awakening* does the mother fully analyze her feelings toward her children, and this is also Chopin's only full portrait of the mother-woman. Chopin herself did not view 19th century motherhood as limiting, although the above works would indicate otherwise.

D.43   Wolff, Cynthia Griffin. "Kate Chopin and the Fiction of Limits: 'Désirée's Baby.'" *SLJ* 10.2 (1978): 123-33.
        LOC: PS261.S527
        See: E.2.9

1979

Books and Book Chapters

D.44   Seyersted, Per and Emily Toth, eds. *A Kate Chopin Miscellany*.
Natchitoches: Northwestern State UP and Oslo: Universitets-Forlaget,
1979.
LOC: PS1294 C63A6 1979
The one difficulty with Seyersted and Toth's volume is that it is out
of print and difficult to obtain. The volume contains three previously
unpublished stories, a fragment of a fourth story, numerous
unpublished poems, as well as portions of Chopin's diaries, letters,
photographs, and other personal papers. The volume also includes a
translation of Cyrille Arnavon's early, important discussion of
Chopin. A bibliography of primary and secondary works is also
included, and the volume covers the major critical studies through
1979. It concludes with the only piece of music that Chopin is
known to have composed.
See also: A.4

D.45   Showalter, Elaine. "Towards a Feminist Poetics." *Women Writing
and Writing About Women*. Ed. Mary Jacobus. Totowa, NJ: Barnes
and Noble, 1979.
LOC: PN481.W66 1979
Showalter's essay briefly mentions Edna in the context of other
female authors of the period. Edna exemplifies the agonizing
awakening from the drugged sleep of Victorian womanhood. In
fiction, women's awakening is much more likely to end in drowning
than discovery.

D.46   Ziff, Larzer. "An Abyss of Inequality." *The American 1890's: Life and Times of a Lost Generation*. New York: Viking, 1966. Rpt. Lincoln, NE: U of Nebraska P, 1979.
LOC: PS214.Z5 1979
See: E.2.10

Journal Articles

D.47   Fox-Genovese, Elizabeth. "Kate Chopin's Awakening." *SoSt* 18 (1979): 261-90.
LOC: F366.L935
Fox-Genovese suggests that feminist and psychoanalytic studies do not fully capture the contradictions of *The Awakening*. She argues that Edna's suicide is the organizing principle of the events leading up to it and must be understood at two levels: (1) "the accidental temporal sequence" and (2) the "necessary psychological permanence." *The Awakening* is structured similarly to Chopin's short fiction and contains two narrative voices — the institutional and the personal. She argues that Edna's personal experience contrasts with social institutions because social reality critiques Edna's subjectivity. This allows Chopin to deplore the subordination of women without challenging the underlying social foundations which she cherished.

D.48   House, Elizabeth Balkman. "*The Awakening*: Kate Chopin's 'Endlessly Rocking' Cycle." *Ball State University Forum* 20.2 (1979): 53-58.
LOC: LH1.B18F6
House emphasizes the critical dispute over the ending of *The Awakening* and compares the novel to Whitman's *Song of Myself* and "Out of the Cradle Endlessly Rocking," pointing to the two poems as the key to the novel's ending. She suggests that Chopin consciously adopted imagery and themes of death as one phase of a cycle of *eros*, birth, and death. Accordingly, throughout the novel the characters retrace their steps, even as Edna goes back to childhood as she is dying. In light of this retracing, Edna's suicide is an affirmation, which serves as both a beginning and an ending.

D.49   Howell, Elmo. "Kate Chopin and the Creole Country." *Louisiana History* 20 (1979): 209-19.
LOC: F366.L6238
Howell argues that Chopin was not a local colorist. Although locale is critical to her meanings, and she was devoted to Creole Louisiana, her true subject was human nature. For example, in *The Awakening*,

Edna, as an outsider, mirrors these influences because she is unfamiliar with local ways and more susceptible to the subtle influence of landscape. Howell states that although Seyersted captured local color, he missed the fact that Chopin was a creature of Creole culture and the South. Therefore, she was more like Adèle than Edna. Many newer critics yield readings entirely alien to Chopin's sympathies. He further argues that Chopin found happiness as a Southern wife and mother, where unhappiness only comes from what Marie Fletcher calls "women being unnaturally independent." He concludes that Chopin's work presents "an absolute accord of author and subject."

D.50   Howell, Elmo. "Kate Chopin and the Pull of Faith: A Note on 'Lilacs.'" *SoSt* 18.1 (1979): 103-09.
LOC: F366.L935
Howell examines the story "Lilacs" and equates Madame Farival with a Catholic Edna. He agrees with Seyersted's analysis that both author and character are modern counterparts of Emma Bovary. Like Emma Bovary, both of Chopin's characters are studies of romantic outlook and disillusionment. He contends that Chopin was a traditionalist, basing this argument on biographical data as well as evidence from her fiction, concluding that the purpose of her writing is to dramatize the conflict of body and soul.

D.51   Mayer, Charles W. "Isabel Archer, Edna Pontellier, and the Romantic Self." *Research Studies* 47 (1979): 89-97.
Mayer points out that *The Awakening* falls into an American tradition stretching from Cooper to Salinger. He notes expressions of belief in freedom and integrity of the self in the text, and states that Edna has more in common with Henry James' Isabel Archer than with Madame Bovary or Carrie Meeber, characters with whom she is commonly compared. Despite striking superficial differences, he argues that both characters illustrate an Emersonian idealism, and that their differences are those of early versus later Realists during the fifteen years that separate the works.

D.52   McIlvaine, Robert. "Two Awakenings: Edna Pontellier and Helena Richie." *RegF* 4.3 (1979): 44-48.
LOC: PS1294 C63 Z71
McIlvaine argues that Margaret Deland's "The Awakening of Helena Richie," written in 1906 — the same year *The Awakening* was reissued — shows Chopin's influence because it parallels *The Awakening's* plot. Its conclusion leads to the opposite view of women's relationships to society. He also compares the literary

careers and contemporary reviews of Chopin and Deland, noting that Deland's narrative criticism of Helena Richie is remarkably similar to critical reviews of *The Awakening*.

D.53   Paulsen, Anne-Lise Strømness. "The Masculine Dilemma in Kate Chopin's *The Awakening*." *SoSt* 18 (1979): 381-424.
LOC: F366.L935
Paulsen begins with a discussion of the meanings of masculine and feminine, drawing on the work of psychoanalysts such as Freud and Chasseguet-Smirgel, as well as sociological data from the Balinese culture. She also discusses the development of traditional Western sex roles. Her treatment of Chopin offers an analysis of sex role stereotyping, focusing on various types of male characters: the "successful businessman" as personified by Léonce Pontellier; the "strict military man" whom we see in Edna's father; the "sensitive young gentleman," portrayed by Robert Lebrun; the "man about town" in the form of Alcée Arobin; and the "symbol of non-modified masculinity," Victor Lebrun. Paulsen describes Dr. Mandelet, the "man of wisdom and insight," concluding with a discussion of Chopin's writing as a conversation between traditional and emancipated women.

D.54   Petry, Alice Hall. "Universal and Particular: The Local-Color Phenomenon Reconsidered." *ALR* 12 (1979): 111-26.
LOC: PS1 A65
Petry places Chopin's work in the context of the local color tradition, arguing that the literary merits of the movement should be re-evaluated in light of its influence on modern Realism. She discusses scenes from "At the 'Cadian Ball" and *The Awakening*, paying particular attention to the characteristics that these pieces draw from the local color genre. Although Chopin's works provide the basis for her discussion of local color, her major focus is on other authors and works.

D.55   Rosowski, Susan J. "The Novel of Awakening." *Genre* 12 (1979): 313-32.
LOC: PN80 G4
See: D.93, E.2.8

D.56   Skaggs, Peggy. "The Boy's Quest in Kate Chopin's 'A Vocation and a Voice.'" *AmLit* 51 (1979): 270-76.
LOC: PS1.A6
See: E.8.9

D.57   Walker, Nancy. "Feminist or Naturalist: The Social Context of Kate
         Chopin's *The Awakening.*" *SoQ* 17.2 (1979): 95 - 103.
         LOC: AS30.M58A2
         Walker argues that many critics have found "feminism where it
         doesn't exist" while downplaying the contemporary cultural and
         literary influences at work on Chopin. She points out that Chopin's
         portrait of Edna is based on Naturalistic conventions and the culture
         of Creole Louisiana. She also argues that Chopin's fiction examines
         the differences and points of conflict between Creole and Anglo
         society. *The Awakening* is an important novel because it examines
         cultural patterns and the collision between two dissimilar cultures.
         See also: E.5.5

D.58   Wolff, Cynthia Griffin. "Kate Chopin." *American Writers*,
         Supplement 1, Part 1. New York: Scribner's, 1979.
         Wolff offers a thorough summary of biographical data and the early
         critical reception of Chopin's work. She also discusses the major
         themes in Chopin's novels and short fiction and provides a selected
         bibliography of primary works, bibliographies, and biographies.

1980

Books and Book Chapters

D.59   Christ, Carol P. *Diving Deep and Surfacing: Women Writers on a Spiritual Quest.* Boston: Beacon P, 1980.
      LOC: BL458.C47 1980
      Christ examines whether Edna's suicide represents strength of character or failure to solve her problems. She discusses the differences between spiritual and social quests, arguing that Edna triumphs spiritually, but fails socially. A spiritual awakening that is not socially supported often leads to tragedy; thus, women must strive for both spiritual and social liberation.

D.60   Klinkowitz, Jerome. "Kate Chopin's Awakening to Naturalism." *The Practice of Fiction in America: Writers from Hawthorne to the Present.* Ames: Iowa State UP, 1980.
      LOC: PS371.K55
      Klinkowitz argues that the local color movement evolved from Romanticism and laid the groundwork for a sterner Realism by introducing more mundane themes that were simultaneously less sentimental and decorous. He views Chopin's development as microcosm of the movement from Romanticism to local color to Realism to Naturalism. He states that Chopin is no "American-girl Zola" nor is *The Awakening* an "American Bovary." Klinkowitz provides an analysis of Edna and *The Awakening* in terms of the Naturalistic novel.

D.61   Ridgley, Jo. *Nineteenth Century Southern Literature*. Lexington: UP
        of Kentucky, 1980.
        LOC: PS261 R44
        Ridgley makes reference to Chopin and *The Awakening*, arguing that
        the main point of the novel is the sexual desire of a woman. *At Fault*
        is criticized for its weakness, although *The Awakening* is praised for
        its uniqueness in a period when frankness and a "cool attitude
        toward extramarital gratification" were taboo. Ridgley further
        argues that Chopin "looked toward a newer South" in which women
        writers would not be bound by the "stultifying" stereotype of the
        Southern lady.

D.62   Stein, Allen F. "Kate Chopin's *The Awakening* and the Limits of
        Moral Judgement." *A Fair Day in the Affections: Literary Essays in
        Honor of Robert B. White, Jr.* Ed. Jack D. Durant and M. Thomas
        Hester. Raleigh: Winston P, 1980.
        LOC: PR14.F3
        Stein argues that Chopin's characters follow the demands of their
        "authentic" natures, pointing out that life is complicated enough to
        defy moral judgement. He states that Edna's suicide is inevitable
        because of her childhood experiences, and that the suicide is
        foreshadowed by *Zampa*. Though Edna asserts herself, her drive for
        authenticity and self-fulfillment is not freely chosen, but pre-
        determined behavior that may be justified or reviled, depending on
        the reader's moral stance. This lack of moral absolutes causes the
        ambiguity of the novel.

D.63   Treichler, Paula A. "The Construction of Ambiguity in *The
        Awakening*: A Linguistic Analysis." *Women and Language in
        Literature and Society*. Ed. Sally McConnell-Ginet, Ruth Borker and
        Nelly Furman. New York: Praeger, 1980.
        LOC: HQ1206.W872
        See: E.9.3

Journal Articles

D.64   Candela, Joseph L., Jr. "Domestic Orientation of American Novels,
        1893-1913." *ALR* 13 (1980): 1-18.
        LOC: PS1 A65
        Candela notes disturbing changes in late 19th century society,
        especially the effects of industrialization and urbanization on the
        traditional family. He analyzes *The Awakening* in terms of its use of
        understatement and symbolism to raise issues of, if not answer the
        questions raised by, the growing women's rights movement. He

argues that Edna's real rebellion is against nature, and "the cycle of sensuality, motherhood, and loss of self." Chopin connected feminist concerns to larger causes with the conflict between "freedom and responsibility, individuality and family" and argues that Edna was unable to strike a balance between them. He concludes that Chopin was more of a radical feminist than most of her contemporaries.

D.65   Lattin, Patricia Hopkins. "Kate Chopin's Repeating Characters."
        MissQ 33 (1980): 19-37.
        LOC: AS30.M58A2
        Lattin studies Chopin's repeating characters, especially the Santien, Laballière, and Duplan families. She argues that the Cane River characters foreshadow Faulkner's Yoknapatawpha County, basing her argument, in part, on the work of Donald Ringe. She follows these and other repeating characters through Chopin's fiction, arguing that knowledge from earlier stories provides insight in later stories that would otherwise be unavailable. Lattin also notes that few other repeating characters receive more than a passing mention. The repetition of characters provides continuity of setting and glimpses of human complexity that one story alone could not demonstrate.

D.66   Macpike, Loralee. "The Social Values of Childbirth in the Nineteenth-Century Novel." *International Journal of Women's Studies* 3 (1980): 117-30.
        LOC: HQ1101.I55
        Macpike argues that the childbirth metaphor was an important signal of social thought and change in the 19th century and examines childbirth metaphors in a number of 19th century novels. She argues that Adèle's birth scene illustrates Chopin's high opinion of both the mother and the artist.

D.67   Thornton, Lawrence. "*The Awakening*: A Political Romance." *AmLit* 52 (1980): 50-66.
        LOC: PS1.A6
        See: E.8.12

D.68   Wolstenholme, Susan. "Kate Chopin's Sources for 'Mrs. Mobry's Reason.'" *AmLit* 51 (1980): 540-43.
        LOC: PS1.A6
        Wolstenholme argues that Chopin's sources for the short story "Mrs. Mobry's Reason" come from Ibsen's *Ghosts* and Wagner's *Ring Cycle*. While conceding that it can not be proven categorically, she

argues that Chopin was certainly familiar with *Ghosts*, as it toured the U.S. in the late 1880's. A frequent theater-goer and opera enthusiast, Chopin was known to be especially fond of Wagner, whose *Ring Cycle* was commonly performed in the U.S. throughout the 1880's. The plot and theme of "Mrs. Mobry's Reason" are similar to those of its predecessors; however, Chopin reverses the male-female role of pursuer/pursued, placing the more aggressive qualities in Naomi, the female character, who eventually loses her reason. Naomi's loss of reason is especially reminiscent of Ibsen, whose protagonist goes insane as a result of syphilis, an allusion which adds some shock value to the ending of Chopin's story.

D.69   Wymard, Eleanor B. "Kate Chopin: Her Existential Imagination." *SoSt* 19 (1980): 373-84.
       LOC: F366.L935
       Wymard argues that Chopin's literary criticism provides clues to what she valued in literature and hoped to achieve in *The Awakening*. She refers to Chopin's statement that "a character should have the right to make choices, and the duty of the author is to remain objective." She states that Chopin is perhaps an existential psychologist writing ahead of her time, and that Edna provides a paradigm for Simone de Beauvoir's theory of the Other. The essay provides an existential analysis of *The Awakening*, with references to Sartre, Camus, and others.

1981

Books and Book Chapters

D.70   Jones, Anne Goodwyn. *Tomorrow is Another Day: The Woman Writer in the South, 1859-1936*. Baton Rouge: Louisiana State UP, 1981.
LOC: PS374.W6 J6

Jones examines Chopin's life and works in the context of the Southern tradition, concluding that she concerned herself with the South but did not personally identify with it. She rejected both the Old South and regionalism in general and found American society to be repressive, especially in its treatment of literature and art. This resulting divided self is expressed through the alienation of Edna in *The Awakening*. Jones provides a detailed explication of Chopin's novels and the major short fiction. She also addresses the work of Augusta Jane Evans, Grace King, Mary Johnston, Ellen Glasgow, Frances Newman, and Margaret Mitchell.

D.71   Lanser, Susan Sniader. *The Narrative Act: Point of View in Prose Fiction*. Princeton: Princeton UP, 1981.
LOC: PN3383.P64 L3

Lanser's study reprints "The Story of an Hour" in its entirety and then examines the narrator's clear, but not overtly dramatized ideology. Chopin's ideology is presented through the story's narrative structure and illustrates Chopin's situation as a female writer.

Journal Articles

D.72   Barrett, Phyllis W. "More American Adams: Women Heroes in
        American Fiction." *Markham Review* 10 (1981): 39-41.
        LOC: PS2363.M37
        Barrett argues that rather than establishing a separate female
        tradition, American women heroes mirror the well-defined Adamic
        American hero. The Adamic woman is never presented as primarily
        wife and mother, but instead is presented in terms of her male
        characteristics: innocence, self-centeredness, vitality and
        irresponsibility. Hawthorne's Hester Prynne, James' Isabel Archer,
        Chopin's Edna Pontellier, and Katherine Anne Porter's Miranda are
        offered as examples of a much larger class of Adamic women.
        Barrett states that Edna's impulses are similar to those of her male
        counterparts, but that it is the consequences which differ. She
        concludes by saying that Edna can only "light out" in death.

D.73   Dyer, Joyce Coyne. "Gouvernail, Kate Chopin's Sensitive Bachelor."
        SLJ 14.1 (1981): 46-55.
        LOC: PS261.S527
        See: E.2.1

D.74   Dyer, Joyce Coyne. "Kate Chopin's Sleeping Bruties." *Markham
        Review* 10 (1980-81): 10-15.
        LOC: PS2363.M37
        See: E.2.2

D.75   Dyer, Joyce Coyne. "Night Images in the Work of Kate Chopin."
        ALR 14 (1981): 216 - 230.
        LOC: PS1 A65
        Dyer examines Chopin's poetry and short fiction, tracing the
        recurrence of night symbolism from her early to her late works and
        notes its persistence and centrality in conveying theme. She uses the
        symbolism as an indicator of the variety and growth of Chopin's
        symbolic method. Chopin found that night images could do more
        than restate a theme, provide atmosphere, or even represent
        definable motions: "it could acquire an autonomous voice: it could
        utter truths that otherwise would never be heard."

D.76   Dyer, Joyce Coyne. "The Restive Brute: The Symbolic Presentation of
        Repression and Sublimation in Kate Chopin's 'Fedora.'" *SSF* 18
        (1981): 261-65.
        LOC: PN3311.S8
        See: E.8.6

D.77   Dyer, Joyce Coyne. "Symbolic Setting in Kate Chopin's 'A Shameful
        Affair.'" *SoSt* 20.4 (1981): 447-52.
        LOC: F366.L935
        Dyer compares "A Shameful Affair," published in 1891, to *The
        Awakening* in terms of both narrative technique and the theme of
        sexual awakening. The symbolism of landscape, natural growth, and
        fertility in "A Shameful Affair," though not as exotic or symbolically
        complex, foreshadows that of *The Awakening*. She suggests that
        Chopin developed this technique of using symbolic terrain to
        represent the unconscious mind in order to avoid alienating critics
        and readers, while still expressing her desired themes.

D.78   Klemans, Patricia A. "The Courageous Soul: Woman as Artist in
        American Literature." *CEA Critic: An Official Journal of the College
        English Association* 43.4 (1981): 39-43.
        LOC: PE1011.C22
        Klemans studies four portraits of early female artists, including
        Chopin's "Elizabeth Stock's One Story," Mary Wilkins Freeman's
        "The Poetess" and "A Village Stranger," and Dorothy Canfield
        Fisher's "The Bedquilt." Klemans notes that these stories share a
        common theme of oppression because of the low value placed on arts
        and because men, often ministers, are presented as the sole arbiters
        of success or failure. She argues that these attitudes limited options
        for gifted women. She then compares the four stories with Willa
        Cather's *Song of the Lark*, published in 1915, which she calls the
        first true success story. Cather's story is a success only because of a
        fortunate accident in which the hero's lover dies, leaving her the
        beneficiary of his insurance. She argues that these stories show
        women's art as unappreciated by society and easily dismissed by
        men. This dismissal leaves the women powerless and bitter. The
        exception to this devaluation is "The Bedquilt," in which art itself is
        diminished.

D.79   Portales, Marco A. "The Characterization of Edna Pontellier and the
        Conclusion of Kate Chopin's *The Awakening*." *SoSt* 20.4 (1981): 427-
        36.
        LOC: F366.L935
        Portales answers George Spangler's argument in *"The Awakening*: A
        Partial Dissent" which appeared in *Novel* 3 in 1970. Spangler argues
        that Edna's suicide is unsatisfactory to the reader because it is
        evasive. Portales points out Edna's increasingly impulsive actions
        after chapter 7, arguing that suicide is consistent with Edna's desire
        not to consider the consequences of her actions. He further argues
        that Chopin's representation of Edna is psychologically consistent

with suicidal individuals, such as the characters of Flaubert and
James.

D.80 Toth, Emily. "Kate Chopin and Literary Convention: 'Désirée's
Baby.'" *SoSt* 20.2 (1981): 201-8.
LOC: F366.L935
Toth notes Chopin's abhorrence of the conventional in both her
literature and her life, arguing that Chopin used accepted literary
conventions to attract her readers and then went beyond those
conventions to provide new insights. For example, in "Désirée's
Baby," she makes use of the convention of the tragic octoroon. The
feminine side is represented by Désirée's physical qualities, and the
male side is represented by Armand's psychological traits, thus
presenting a political and psychological analysis of a slave-owner's
character.

1982

Books and Book Chapters

No books or book chapters appeared during this year.

Journal Articles

D.81   Bonner, Thomas, Jr. "Christianity and Catholicism in the Fiction of Kate Chopin." *SoQ* 20 (1982): 118-125.
LOC: AS30.M58A2
   See: D.88

D.82   Fluck, Winfried. "Tentative Transgressions: Kate Chopin's Fiction as a Mode of Symbolic Action." *Studies in American Fiction* 10 (1982): 151-71.
LOC: PS370.S87
   Fluck's analysis focuses on Chopin's short fiction, arguing that critics give short shrift to local color and overemphasize the relative importance of *The Awakening*. Based on Chopin's diary entries, he argues that rather than presenting a firm point of view, her short fiction represents what Anne Scott called the "woman in the middle or in motion" who exists on a continuum between traditional and feminist values. The ambiguity in the short stories represents the tension of this unresolved conflict, both for Chopin herself and in society. The author may not be consciously aware of this tension. Fluck views literature as a testing ground upon which conflicting or contradictory impulses may collide and interact. He argues that Chopin's fiction is socially experimental, that it explores and

experiments rather resorting to didacticism. The ambivalent ending of *The Awakening* represents an evasive strategy and cuts off the dialogue between the conflicting demands of the self.

D.83   Gardiner, Elaine. "'Ripe Figs': Kate Chopin in Miniature." *Modern Fiction Studies* 28 (1982): 379-82.
        LOC: PS379.M55
        See: E.2.4

D.84   Lattin, Patricia Hopkins. "The Search for Self in Kate Chopin's Fiction: Simple Versus Complex Vision." *SoSt* 21.2 (1982): 222-235.
        LOC: F366.L935
        Lattin argues that Chopin's work departs from 19th century Realism and Transcendentalism by developing the theme of the search for the inner self. She argues that *The Awakening* serves as the climax of the themes in the short fiction. Lattin argues that Chopin attempts to view the world without illusion and implies that achieving selfhood is difficult, sometimes even impossible. She then traces the theme of rebirth through the complex and ambiguous final scene of *The Awakening*.

D.85   Levine, Robert S. "Circadian Rhythms and Rebellion in Kate Chopin's *The Awakening*." *Studies in American Fiction* 10 (1982): 71-81.
        LOC: PS370.S87
        Levine points out that critics have remarked on Edna's sleepiness, usually in a condemnatory manner, commenting that it is "the sleepiest novel in the American literary canon." Rather than indicating that Edna is sleepwalking passively through life, her irregular sleep habits and her habit of fighting sleep represent the ultimate rebellion — a rebellion against nature — as well as a rebellion against community standards. Her suicide indicates her strong desire to separate herself from the "Circadian rhythms of existence" and to resist compromising with the realistic world.

D.86   Miner, Madonne M. "Veiled Hints: An Affective Stylist's Reading of Kate Chopin's 'Story of an Hour.'" *Markham Review* 11 (1982): 29-32.
        LOC: PS2363.M37
        Miner analyzes "Story of an Hour" in light of the theory of phenomenology articulated by Stanley Fish and Wolfgang Iser. She argues that Chopin undermines the reader's confidence in the narrative by denying information and manipulating grammatical structures. She also argues that Chopin's manipulative strategies

create a vague sense of fear, apprehension, and scepticism in the reader. Thus, positive feelings about Léonce's self-assertion, as evidenced in chapter 3 and in his discussions with Dr. Mandelet, are subverted by the frustrated sense that something is wrong. This sense is confirmed by the ending of the novel.

D.87   Webb, Bernice Larson. "Four Points of Equilibrium in *The Awakening*." *South Central Bulletin* 42 (1982): 148-51.
LOC: PB1 S64
Webb describes a three or four point geographic circle in both Chopin's life and much of her short fiction. The circle originates in St. Louis, moves to New Orleans, then to Natchitoches Parish, Louisiana, and finally returns to St. Louis. In *The Awakening*, Webb views the cottage at Grand Isle, the Pontellier's home in New Orleans, the pigeon house, and Grand Isle as a circle. In Edna's first visit to Grand Isle, the sea represents an awakening into life. In the second visit, it offers an escape from life, and the search for innocence by drowning represents unthinking, unguided past acceptance. Edna thus becomes "irrevocably the victim of the circumstances of her existence." Webb also examines the symbolism of Edna's going-away dinner.

1983

Books and Book Chapters

D.88   Bonner, Thomas, Jr. "Christianity and Catholicism in the Fiction of
        Kate Chopin." *In Old New Orleans*. Ed. W. Kenneth Holditch.
        Jackson: UP of Mississippi, 1983.
        LOC: NX511.N39 I5 1983

   Bonner's study addresses *At Fault*, *The Awakening*, and selected
   short fiction. He demonstrates that themes of Christian love,
   criticism of ecclesiastical customs and practices, as well as feast
   days, icons, and rituals give structure to Chopin's work. He points
   out that Chopin satirizes legalism and excessive piety, noting that
   these factors are influenced by Chopin's education and the cultural
   influences of New Orleans and St. Louis.
   See also: D.81

D.89   Bonner, Thomas, Jr. "Kate Chopin: Tradition and the Moment."
        Southern Literature in Transition: Heritage and Promise. Ed Philip
        Castille and William Osborne. Memphis: Memphis State UP, 1983.
        LOC: PS261.S529 1983

   Bonner argues that Chopin, like Cable, but unlike King and Stuart,
   made no apologies for the Lost Cause of the Old South and
   forthrightly addressed the changes that had occurred and were to
   come in Southern society. Chopin's work provides a literary
   analysis of a French Louisiana in which the bonds of caste and
   gender had been broken to allow a focus on the individual and the
   search for selfhood. In contrast to the works of Emerson, Thoreau
   and Fuller, the genteel readers and critics of the Gilded Age could

not deal with these issues, resulting in Chopin's long-lasting critical obscurity. He examines *At Fault, The Awakening* and much of the short fiction to illustrate Chopin's bold yet ambiguous treatment of the volatile themes of race, caste and gender.

D.90   Hirsch, Marianne. "Spiritual Bildung: The Beautiful Soul as Paradigm." *The Voyage In: Fictions of Female Development.* Ed. Elizabeth Abel, Marianne Hirsch and Elizabeth Langland. Hanover, NH: UP of New England for Dartmouth College, 1983.
LOC: PR830.W6 V69 1983

Hirsch identifies the conventions of the androcentric *bildungsroman* in *The Awakening*, among other novels, as an alternative to the tradition of "female bildung." She explains that childhood and death are closely interrelated because the beginning and ending of life are nearly identical. The female experience follows the pattern of *künstlerroman*, or spiritual development, up to the point of withdrawal into an inner life. To find satisfaction, women must find unconventional, individual fulfillment — largely because of their fragmented and discontinuous development — rather than the universal solution that male heroes find that saves them from the female hero's fate, death. The solution of art is virtually unavailable to the young woman in the nineteenth-century novel. Accordingly, for Edna Pontellier, "death becomes an escape from female plot and the only possible culmination of woman's spiritual development."

D.91   Huf, Linda. *A Portrait of the Artist as a Young Woman: The Writer as Heroine in American Literature.* New York: Ungar, 1983.
LOC: PS374.W6 H78 1983

The chapter on *The Awakening* offers a bio-critical analysis and a close reading of the novel.

D.92   Lohafer, Susan. *Coming to Terms with the Short Story.* Baton Rouge: Louisiana State UP, 1983.
LOC: PN3373.L56 1983

One chapter contains a section on "Athènaïse," which is compared and contrasted with Hawthorne's "Roger Malvin's Burial." The essay provides a summary of the plots of the stories, followed by a summary of the pre-1970 secondary criticism. Lohafer then provides a structural analysis of "Athènaïse," based on the techniques outlined earlier in her book.

D.93   Rosowski, Susan J. "The Novel of Awakening." *The Voyage In: Fictions of Female Development.* Ed. Elizabeth Abel, Marianne Hirsch and Elizabeth Langland. Hanover, NH: UP of New England

for Dartmouth College, 1983.
LOC: PR830.W6V69 1983
  See: D.55, E.2.8

D.94   Shillingsburg, Miriam J. "The Ascent of Woman, Southern Style:
        Hentz, King, Chopin." *Southern Literature in Transition: Heritage
        and Promise.* Ed. Philip Castille and William Osborne. Memphis:
        Memphis State UP, 1983.
        LOC: PS261.S529 1983
        Shillingsburg argues that women's writing from the end of the 19th
        century not only tells modern readers about the "real feelings of half
        the population of the nineteenth century" but also about a change in
        those feelings which became apparent in the latter half of the
        century. She describes Chopin's Edna Pontellier, as well as the
        characters of Caroline Lee Hentz and Grace King, as individuals
        who challenge both convention and their "place" in society. While
        Hentz and King write more traditional romances, in which marriage
        is a reward for cultivating socially acceptable values, Chopin
        questions the basic assumptions which underlie marital
        relationships.

Journal Articles

D.95   Gilbert, Sandra. "The Second Coming of Aphrodite: Kate Chopin's
        Fantasy of Desire." *Kenyon Review* 5.3 (1983): 42-66.
        LOC: AP K426
          See: E.2.5, E.5.1

D.96   Leder, Priscilla. "An American Dilemma: Cultural Conflict in Kate
        Chopin's *The Awakening*." *SoSt* 22.1 (1983): 97-104.
        LOC: F366.L935
        Leder examines the cultural conflict between Creole society and
        Kentucky Presbyterian society, comparing Edna's situation with that
        of Tommo in Melville's *Typee*. She argues that Edna is
        simultaneously attracted to and repelled by a culture which seems
        more natural than her native one. Leder also argues that Edna can
        not live comfortably in either society. Tommo, in *Typee*, experiences
        a similar discomfort in an alien society. Edna's conflict is
        essentially the same as Tommo's but is complicated and intensified
        by the fact that she is a woman.

D.97   Rogers, Nancy E. "Echoes of George Sand in Kate Chopin." *Revue
        de Littérature Comparée* 57.1 (1983): 25-42.
        LOC: PN851.R4

Rogers' examination of the biographical data and literary works of George Sand and Kate Chopin concludes that Chopin read and was heavily influenced by Sand.

D.98   Walker, Nancy A. "Women Drifting: Drabble's *The Waterfall* and Chopin's *The Awakening*." *Denver Quarterly* 17.4 (1983): 88-96. LOC: AP2.U733

Walker draws on Margaret Drabble's *The Waterfall* and Chopin's *The Awakening* to examine women's passivity and sense of helplessness in the face of fate. She argues that this helplessness pervades literature about women by women. The two writers differ because of the time difference of the novels. They share themes of women being cast adrift into passivity and self-interest, and the characters of both Drabble and Chopin distance themselves from the mother-woman role. Their characters depend on other women for emotional well-being, and they make sacrifices for those commitments. Drabble's Jane is a character adrift, but Jane's narration is informed by the ironic 20th century insight that fate is truth and is bound by reality rather than by moral causation. Walker concludes by discussing the water imagery in both novels.

1984

Books and Book Chapters

D.99   Girgus, Sam B. "R.D. Laing and Literature: Readings of Poe, Hawthorne, and Kate Chopin." *Psychological Perspectives on Literature: Freudian Dissidents and Non-Freudians: A Casebook.* Ed. Joseph Natoli. Hamden, CT: Archon, 1984.
LOC: PN56.P93 P7 1984

      Girgus notes that in the 1960's, Laing was considered an extremist because he questioned the commonly accepted boundaries of reality and sanity. He extolled "the politics of anti-politics based on the psychology of anti-psychology," therefore yielding a highly personalized dissent without demanding any new systems of belief or social organizations. Girgus gives a long explication of Laing's ideas, his social rise and fall, and his influence on other writers and thinkers. Girgus' Laingian analysis of Adèle explores the plight of modern women forced into estrangement by socially imposed roles, and he draws heavily from Cynthia Griffin Wolff's work in making this argument. Girgus equates Laing's "schizoid personality" with Edna's dual life and ultimate withdrawal. Girgus also discusses Edgar Allan Poe, especially "The Fall of the House of Usher" from a Laingian perspective and touches lightly on works by Nathaniel Hawthorne.

D.100   Little, Judy. "Imagining Marriage." *Portraits of Marriage in Literature.* Ed. Anna C. Hargrove and Maurine Magliocco. Macomb, IL: Essays in Lit, 1984.
LOC: PN56 M27 P67 1984

Little examines the authors' imaginings of marriage in Virginia Woolf's *Between Acts*, Iris Murdoch's *A Severed Head*, Kate Chopin's *The Awakening*, Doris Lessing's "To Room Nineteen," and Margaret Drabble's *The Waterfall* and *The Garrick Year*. She argues that Drabble and Murdoch are reluctant to abandon romantic imaginings while Chopin, Woolf and Lessing attempt to avoid the hazards of romance. She argues that Edna consciously chooses a non-romantic match with Léonce after putting aside her early infatuations so as to avoid ever falling out of love. However, Edna's unexpected infatuation with Robert leads to a more far-reaching awakening to her incompatibility with middle-class social roles, leading to her suicide.

D.101   Stein, Allen F. *After the Vows Were Spoken: Marriage in American Literary Realism*. Columbus: Ohio State UP, 1984.
         LOC: PS374.M35 S74 1984
         Stein's discussion of Chopin focuses on the dichotomy between self-repression and self-assertion, a dichotomy that many of her marriage stories address. In most of Chopin's stories, successful marriages occur only when both partners are allowed the possibility for self-development. Marriages where the male partner seeks to control the female dissolve in one manner or another, either through separation, death, or emotional distance.

D.102   Toth, Emily. "A Laughter of Their Own: Women's Humor in the United States." *Critical Essays on American Humor*. Ed. William Bedford Clark and W. Craig Turner. Boston: G. K. Hall, 1984.
         LOC: PS430.C7 1984
         Toth argues that even as late as 1984, women humorists were not recognized and respected for their contributions. She discusses numerous American women writers, making passing reference to Chopin for the black humor of her fiction, which is at the same time social criticism.

Journal Articles

D.103   Burchard, Gina M. "Kate Chopin's Problematic Womanliness: The Frontier of American Feminism." *Journal of the American Studies Association of Texas* 15 (1984): 35-45.
         LOC: E169.1.A493
         Burchard states that Chopin would not have identified herself as a feminist because the bulk of her work treats human relationships in a generalized way. She points out that Chopin only presents female conflicts on rare occasions, and when she does, her ambivalence

undermines the argument that she harbored feminist sentiments. She further argues that only six of Chopin's stories even imply a feminist awakening. Citing the short fiction as evidence, Burchard argues that Chopin explores and then subverts female nonconformity. Therefore, Edna's suicide is unjustified and perhaps a result of Chopin's self-censorship. She concludes that Chopin was reluctant to portray female assertiveness and sexuality, showing her personal ambivalence to these subjects.

D.104   Collins, Robert. "The Dismantling of Edna Pontellier: Garment Imagery in Kate Chopin's *The Awakening*." *SoSt* 23.2 (1984): 176-90. LOC: F366.L935

Collins argues that garment imagery is symbolic of Edna's emotional development throughout *The Awakening*. He posits that Edna restlessly searches for a satisfying inner life at the start of the novel and develops a self-destructive urge because she yearns for the "infinite." Upon realizing that she can not achieve the infinite, and that she will always face limitations, she chooses to escape them through suicide. Each time she disrobes or loosens her clothing, she takes another step toward this realization of her limitations. Edna's disrobing further symbolizes her desire to "strip herself of all fictions, both realistic and romantic" and indicates that Chopin viewed Edna's suicide as a failure of imagination.

D.105   Dyer, Joyce Coyne. "Epiphanies through Nature in the Stories of Kate Chopin." *University of Dayton Review* 16.3 (1983-84): 75-81. LOC: AS30.U53

Dyer examines "Loka," "The Story of an Hour," "The Unexpected," "A Morning Walk" and *The Awakening* to illustrate Chopin's use of nature as a purveyor of epiphanies. She argues that Chopin's nature imagery is more than poetic, and it empowers nature to teach emotional lessons. The author cites biographical evidence to support this point. For example, Archibald and Dorothea live happier and more honest lives than other of Chopin's characters, while Loka holds back because of a sense of duty. Mrs. Mallard and Edna find ordinary life too dull because they expect more from nature's promises than it delivers. Chopin's characters learn or remember the critical role of instinct and the effect it has on their desire for freedom.

D.106   Dyer, Joyce Coyne. "Lafcadio Hearn's *Chita* and Kate Chopin's *The Awakening*: Two Naturalistic Tales of the Gulf Islands." *SoSt* 23.4 (1984): 412-26. LOC: F366.L935

Dyer's essay compares the Naturalism of Chopin and Hearn and argues that each author's version of Naturalism is different. Hearn most often links Louisiana's native creatures with explorations of death and the dead. Chopin associates Grande Terre, among other of the Louisiana chênières and islets, with sexual energy, and this is demonstrated through conversations between Robert and Edna. Images ranging from gold, slimy lizards wriggling in the sun to the muddy, slimy toes of Mariequita, with the Spanish-moss-covered shrimp in her basket, and even the vegetation on the islands — all of these images symbolize sexual force. Dyer concedes that Chopin's text is not devoid of allusions to death images but argues that this is not the predominant theme of Chopin's work. The sea is also invoked as a Naturalistic element, and in Chopin's work is "Whitmanesque." Dyer argues that Chopin portrays the sea as an alluring voice rather than a threatening presence, as it is portrayed in Hearn's writing. Chopin does not minimize the power of natural forces but instead uses them to underscore Edna's actions.

D.107   Dyer, Joyce Coyne. "A Note on Kate Chopin's 'The White Eagle.'" *AzQ* 40 (1984): 189-92.
LOC: AP2.A7265
Dyer argues that most of Chopin's fiction after the publication of *The Awakening* in 1899 is fraught with metaphors which merely "decorate a sentence" or "provide a convenient backdrop," rather than the expansive, meaningful metaphors and images which readers expect based on her earlier work. The essay gives an example of this decorative imagery in "The Wood Choppers." Dyer then argues that "The White Eagle," in which a statue of an eagle takes the place of a lover in the protagonist's life and ultimately comes to symbolize death, exhibits more of the ambiguous symbolism found in *The Awakening*. The essay concludes with a series of questions which invite further discussion about the story.

D.108   Franklin, Rosemary F. "*The Awakening* and the Failure of Psyche." *AmLit* 56.4 (1984): 510-26.
LOC: PS1.A6
Franklin argues that it is possible to find a reading of *The Awakening* other than the extremes of viewing Edna as either tragic or pathetic. She examines the novel in terms of the Eros and Psyche myth to show the struggle of the female hero to attain selfhood, and she argues that three male satellites are present in the novel, with each representing one of the personae of Eros. These three male satellites are Alcée, Victor and Robert. Edna plays the role of Psyche, the mortal outsider. Franklin views Edna as heroic, but argues that she

fails to finish her task because of the fear of a long and lonely
change. She also examines the strength of the Creole matriarchy as
it is portrayed in Chopin's novel.

D.109   Grover, Dorys Crow. "Kate Chopin and the Bayou Country." *Journal
of the American Studies Association of Texas* 15 (1984): 29-34.
LOC: E169.1.A493
Grover identifies Chopin as one of four major Louisiana writers of
her time, along with George Washington Cable, Lafcadio Hearn, and
Grace King. All four of these authors took advantage of a female
audience, which provided a natural readership for the local flavor of
the exotic Southern and Creole communities. She examines
Chopin's *At Fault* and some of her short fiction in this light, arguing
that Chopin did not transcend her regionalist roots, but that her
themes are universal in the South. Grover states that Chopin was
interested only in characters and ideas. Grover concludes by
pointing out that Chopin recognized the universal need for freedom,
and that she viewed the Southern class structure as being built on a
false base.

D.110   Lant, Kathleen Margaret. "The Siren of Grand Isle: Adèle's Role in
The Awakening." *SoSt* 23.2 (1984): 167-75.
LOC: F366.A935
See: E.2.6

D.111   Roscher, Marina L. "The Suicide of Edna Pontellier: An Ambiguous
Ending?" *SoSt* 23.3 (1984): 289-98.
LOC: F366.L935
Roscher presents a psychoanalytic approach to Edna's suicide,
arguing that despite the explanations offered by other critics, Edna
takes her life because she is immature. Citing Edna's early loss of
her mother, her lack of close female companions, and her resulting
solitary nature as major contributing factors to her demise, Roscher
associates this tendency to solitude with the psychological argument
that a "solitary primate is an abnormal primate." She couples this
information with R.D. Laing's argument that losing one's mother at
an early stage of development threatens the developing sense of self.
Roscher argues that Edna possesses an incompletely developed
animus, which prevents "the integration of her personality" and
prevents her from developing mature relationships. The stunted
development of her sense of self ultimately drives her into the sea.
Roscher concludes with the argument that the ending of *The*

Awakening is not ambiguous, but merely complicated because it contains multiple and hidden meanings that are larger than the author's conscious purpose.

D.112   White, Robert. "Inner and Outer Space in *The Awakening*." *Mosaic: A Journal for the Interdisciplinary Study of Literature* 17 (1984): 97-109.
LOC: PN2.M68

White analyzes "Emancipation: A Life Fable," which Chopin wrote at the age of nineteen, as a precursor to *The Awakening*. He compares the escape of the animal in the story to Edna's escape from the cult of motherhood and her proper place in society as a wife and mother. No cage can be gilded enough to make freedom unattractive, and accordingly, Edna's swim is a heroic response to her untenable situation.

1985

Books and Book Chapters

D.113 Aherne, John R. "Kate Chopin. An American de Maupassant."
Serendipity: Essays on Six Catholic Authors. nc: Merrimack College
P, 1985.
LOC: PR1110 .C3 A44 1985
   Aherne's essay poses two questions about Chopin's work: (1) based
   on a citation from Rankin, how could Chopin leave the Catholic
   church but "keep the faith" and (2) why, given her loving father and
   husband, her male characters are so negative. Aherne argues that
   although Chopin's female characters are masterfully portrayed, her
   male characters do not ring true. This assessment is based on an
   examination of the characters in the *Bayou Folk* collection. He
   further argues that the settings in these stories are not important, as
   many critics who view Chopin as a local colorist have argued, but
   that the dialogue is both important and well executed. He notes the
   influence of Maupassant and Flaubert and decries the lack of moral
   commentary, viewing Edna as selfish and destructive. He concludes
   that the novel represents abject surrender rather than a triumph of
   individuality.

D.114 Lupton, Mary Jane. "Women Writers and Death by Drowning." *Amid
   Visions and Revisions: Poetry and Criticism on Literature and the
   Arts.* Ed. Burney J. Hollis. Baltimore: Morgan State UP, 1985.
   LOC: PS221.A656 1985
   Lupton's essay discusses drowning in the works of George Eliot and
   Sylvia Plath, as well as in *The Awakening*. She argues that

drowning, for Edna, was equivalent to a promise of freedom from the societal restrictions under which she lived — those of her husband, her children, her father, her friends. Edna's self-destruction also serves as an act of defiance, a "going below the surface" to exercise her will in a society that preferred her to be powerless.

D.115   Rowe, Anne. "Kate Chopin." *The History of Southern Literature.* Ed. Louis D. Rubin, Jr., Blyden Jackson, Rayburn S. Moore, and Lewis P. Simpson. Baton Rouge: Louisiana State UP, 1985.
This brief bio-critical essay places Chopin's life and work in the context of the Southern literary tradition.

D.116   Skaggs, Peggy. *Kate Chopin.* Boston: Twayne, 1985.
LOC: PS1294.C63 S55 1985
Skaggs relates the characters in Chopin's short fiction to Edna Pontellier in *The Awakening.* The volume includes (1) a brief overview of Chopin's life, with attention to her literary career, (2) a brief survey of secondary criticism attempting to relate Chopin's work to main currents in the American intellectual and literary tradition, (3) an analysis of the stories collected in *Bayou Folk* and *A Night in Acadie*, (4) an examination of the stories collected for the posthumously published volume *A Vocation and a Voice*, (5) an analysis of the uncollected short stories, poems, and essays, (6) an analysis of *At Fault* and *The Awakening*, (7) conclusions based on the above analyses. She also includes a selected bibliography of primary and secondary sources with the latter being briefly annotated.

Journal Articles

D.117   Batten, Wayne. "Illusion and Archetype: The Curious Story of Edna Pontellier." *SLJ* 18.1 (1985): 73-88.
LOC: PS261.S527
Batten argues that in *The Awakening*, Edna and Dr. Mandelet speak at "cross purposes." Edna believes that motherhood has caused her to deny passion and to enter into and maintain a conventional relationship. Mandelet counters her belief, saying that it is a romantic nature that leads to motherhood. Edna tries to escape illusions, which "point to the suggestive power of illusion for both cause and cure." Edna's illusions may be broken into three categories: those suggested by other characters, those Edna creates for herself, and those which Chopin associates with Edna. The third category of illusions represents Edna's "real" experience.

D.118 Dyer, Joyce Coyne. "Techniques of Distancing in the Fiction of Kate Chopin." *SoSt* 24 (1985): 69-81.
LOC: F366.L935
Dyer discusses Chopin's use of distancing techniques. She plays on her audiences' prejudices by using characters who would traditionally have been marginalized, such as those suffering from mental illnesses. She offers as examples the distorted first person narration in companion stories such as "La Belle Zoraïde," and "The Night Came Slowly." The recurrence of minor characters often serves to veil sexual images and messages, in contrast to the more direct approach of *The Awakening*. The directness of Chopin's approach in *The Awakening* explains its hostile critical reception.

D.119 MacCurdy, Carol. "*The Awakening*: Chopin's Metaphorical Use of Clothes." *Publications of the Mississippi Philological Association* n.v. (1985): 58-66.
MacCurdy notes the well-documented use of natural symbols, such as the sun, sea, and birds to illustrate Edna's awakening to sensuality and freedom. The author contrasts these with the social constraints felt by Edna and argues that Chopin uses clothing to symbolize social conventions. She notes that Edna's changing forms of dress convey both the illusions that she wishes to establish for others as well as the ones she falls prey to herself. She compares *The Awakening* to Fitzgerald's *The Great Gatsby* in its metaphorical use of clothing.

D.120 McMahan, Elizabeth. "'Nature's Decoy': Kate Chopin's Presentation of Women and Marriage in Her Short Fiction." *Turn of the Century Women* 2.2 (1985): 32-35.
McMahan's essay argues that Chopin's presentation of marriage is remarkably modern, and that her work is a plea for changes which would allow women's self-direction. Within this framework, she examines women's reasons for marrying and the consequences of marriage in "Miss McEnders," "Athénaïse," "Charlie," "The Story of an Hour," "Désirée's Baby," and *The Awakening*. She argues that after a happy marriage of her own, Chopin experienced an awakening following Oscar's death. This awakening may have influenced the jaundiced view of marriage in her work.

D.121 Sacken, Jeanee P. "George Sand, Kate Chopin, Margaret Atwood and the Redefinition of Self." *Postscript* 2 (1985): 19-28.
Sacken compares George Sand's *Indiana*, Kate Chopin's *The Awakening*, and Margaret Atwood's *Surfacing* in terms of their protagonists' complex transformations. The novels share a sequence

of motifs that continue to influence women's fiction: (1) repressive domestic life, (2) flight from subjugation and dependence to a new social venue, (3) transformation through the discovery of latent strength and the true self, (4) the decision to either return to the male-oriented social structure or to remain separated from it and independent. The protagonists of these novels undergo more complex transformations than in the traditional male *bildungsroman* because having already mastered one set of social roles, they must deconstruct them and reconstruct themselves and perhaps those around them. This transformation precipitates their flights from domesticity.

D.122   Toth, Emily. "Crisis Alert: Kate Chopin House in St. Louis." *Legacy* 2.1 (1985): 13.
LOC: PS149 L43
Toth's note reports plans to raze the Kate Chopin House in St. Louis, and describes her remaining homes in New Orleans and Cloutierville, as well as in St. Louis.

1986

Books and Book Chapters

D.123 Bardot, Jean. "L'Influence Francaise dans la vie et l'oeuvre de Kate
Chopin." *Les Aspects Litteraires du Biculturalisme aux Etats-Unis:
Actes du Colloque du 1985.* Paris: Paris-Sorbonne, 1986.
LOC: PN843.A7 1986

  Bardot provides an extensive biographical sketch and a detailed
discussion of the influence of French writers on Chopin's work from
a French perspective. The authors addressed include de Stael, Sand,
Mirimie, Baudelaire, Goncourt, Daudet, Zola, Flaubert, and
Maupassant, noting that the latter two exerted the greatest influence
on Chopin. Bardot views Chopin's French literary influences in the
same way that she viewed the Creole society in her works: she loved
them but remained critical and transformed their influence into
something new and original.

  *Translated by Derek Foster, Northwestern State University;
Translated and annotated by Marie Françoise Conin-Jones,
University of North Texas.*

D.124 Ewell, Barbara C. *Kate Chopin.* New York: Ungar, 1986.
LOC: PS1294.C63 Z64 1986

  Ewell's critical biography includes a detailed chronology of
Chopin's life and literary career, with much of this data based on
documents owned by the Missouri Historical Society. Ewell includes
a selected bibliography of biographical, bibliographical, critical, and
primary works. She examines all of Chopin's works, with short

stories grouped by collection, as well as novels, poetry, and later short fiction. The volume is thoroughly indexed.

D.125   Foster, Shirley. "The Open Cage: Freedom, Marriage and the Heroine in Early Twentieth-Century American Women's Novels." *Women's Writing: A Challenge to Theory.* Ed. Moira Monteith. Sussex and New York: Harvester - St. Martin's P, 1986.
LOC: PN471.W58 1986

Foster's essay is a study of how female novelists incorporate protest and ambivalence into the novel, which she argues is a traditionally male form. The essay addresses *The Awakening, The House of Mirth* and *Song of the Lark.* Foster argues that Chopin was heavily influenced by Darwinism, and asserts the need for women to free themselves from societal conventions. She points out that successful heroes recognize these conventions and rebel against them. She argues that the novel is deliberately ambiguous, as opposed to presenting the notion of female separateness. She explores the symbolism and imagery of the novel and argues that the real image of womanhood presented is both pessimistic and hopeful.

D.126   Newman, Judie. "Kate Chopin: Short Fiction and the Arts of Subversion." *The Nineteenth Century Short Story.* Ed. A. Robert Lee. London: Vision, 1985. New York: Barnes and Noble, 1986.
LOC: PS374.S5 N5 1986

Newman argues that the short story is the product of marginalized individuals in isolated communities, and that the local color movement is a product of the same marginalization. Newman surveys the changes in critical responses to Chopin's work from the 1890's to the present. The author demonstrates how theme and technique interact, using "Charlie" as an example. She further argues that superficially, the story presents the feminization of and acculturation to patriarchal norms, yet the psychology of the story is carefully structured to subvert the roles constructed by and for the hero. Newman also examines the imagery of hands and rings in Chopin's writing and examines the hero's alternatives at the conclusion of the story. She also briefly examines other selected pieces of short fiction.

D.127   St. Andrews, Bonnie. *Forbidden Fruit: On the Relationship Between Women and Knowledge in Doris Lessing, Selma Lagerlof, Kate Chopin, Margaret Atwood.* Troy, NY: Whitson P, 1986.
LOC: PR888.W6 S74 1986

St. Andrews focuses on *The Awakening* and analyzes its early critical reception and historical contexts. She focuses on Edna's relationship with Léonce and her children and concludes that Chopin's literary technique is decidedly Impressionistic. Chopin blended Impressionism with the demands for detailed description brought about by the influence of Realism and local color. Ultimately, the novel presents a distinctly feminine quest for self-governance, despite the diverse critical approaches that have been applied to the text.

D.128   Tarpley, Philip. "Kate Chopin's Sawmill: Technology and Change in *At Fault.*" *Proceedings of the Red River Symposium.* Ed. Norman A. Dolch and Karen Douglas. Shreveport, LA: Red River Regional Studies Center, Louisiana State UP, 1986.
LOC: F377 R3 R47 1985
Tarpley examines *At Fault* in the historical context of the rise of the lumber industry in north-central Louisiana. He notes that *At Fault* is the earliest work of fiction set in the Cane River Country, and that it records and interprets the response to technology and change in this society in a very careful and authentic way. The essay provides a great deal of historical data related to the lumber industry and relates it to Chopin's novel.

Tarpley's name appears as "Tapley" both on the article and in the periodical databases.

Journal Articles

D.129   Gaudet, Marcia. "Kate Chopin and the Lore of Cane River's Creoles of Color." *Xavier Review* 6.1 (1986): 45-52.
Gaudet examines the history of Louisiana Creoles of Color, especially the Isle Brevelle community of Natchitoches Parish. She notes that Chopin accurately sets her Cajun stories outside of Natchitoches Parish, and that Chopin was the first writer to accurately depict the customs, traditions, and beliefs of the Cane River Region Creoles of Color. She argues that Chopin uses these elements of local color and folklore to present universal themes.

D.130   Mitsutani, Margaret. "Kate Chopin's *The Awakening*: The Narcissism of Edna Pontellier." *Studies in English Literature* n.v. (1986): 3-15.
LOC: PR1.S8
Mitsutani analyzes *The Awakening* in light of the Narcissus myth. She argues that the myth illuminates the desire to ignore society in favor of the world of the self and also illustrates the "horror of self-annihilation that complete fulfillment of that desire must inevitably bring." Mitsutani nonetheless sees the Narcissus myth as positive.

She argues that Edna poses a threat to the bastion of the 19th century home and was therefore met with ridicule and scorn. According to the author, Edna had three alternatives: (1) return to her marriage; (2) abandon herself to sensual pleasure; or (3) follow in the footsteps of Mademoiselle Reisz. Mitsutani takes issue with the analyses of Linda Huf and Elaine Showalter, stating that life itself becomes the unessential in terms of preserving Edna's awakened self. The awakening of self-love and the element of rebirth in the sea at the end of the novel demonstrate Chopin's view that marriage and motherhood do not and should not signal the end of a woman's growth. She suggests that Edna did not rebel against motherhood, *per se*, but against the role of the mother-woman that society foisted upon her. Edna saw the self as sacred and not to be sacrificed; therefore, she could not function in society in the same way as Adèle.

D.131   Mochizuki, Kaeko. "The Last Phase of Kate Chopin's Life - from 1900 to 1904." *Chu-Shikoku Studies in American Literature* 22 (1986): 68-78.

D.132   Moseley, Merritt. "Chopin and Mysticism." *SoSt* 25 (1986): 367-74.
        LOC: F366.L935
        Moseley explains the indeterminacy of the novel and the reticence of Edna and the narrator by arguing that Edna is a mystic. This argument is based on the time period during which Chopin wrote and on the influence of Transcendentalism on her work. The relationship of music to mysticism is explained in terms of William James' *The Varieties of Religious Experience*. Moseley compares Chopin's work to that of Melville, Whitman, and Freud.

D.133   Nye, Lorraine M. "Four Birth Dates For Kate Chopin." *SoSt* 25 (1986): 375-6.
        LOC: F366.L935
        Nye draws on census data and family genealogical records to conclude that Chopin's true birthday was 18 February 1849.

D.134   Simpson, Martin. "Chopin's 'A Shameful Affair.'" *Explicator* 45.1 (1986): 59-60.
        LOC: PR1.E9
        Simpson discusses "A Shameful Affair," arguing that Mildred Orme's exit from urban society represents a rejection of the civilized in favor of the natural, or sensuous, world. Mildred struggles with her sexuality, trying to escape from it by clinging to "symbols of civilization" but finds that she can not escape her sexuality in the

country with its symbolic fertility. She at first begins to abandon civilized social conventions by admitting her interest in Fred Evelyn, but she ultimately retreats to sexual repression. Simpson argues that this story is Kate Chopin's way of demonstrating that sexual repression is harmful because Mildred's retreat from sex causes her to be troubled and confused. She is incomplete because she does not come to terms with her sexuality.

D.135   Stone, Carole. "The Female Artist in Kate Chopin's *The Awakening*: Birth and Creativity." *Women's Studies* 13 (1986): 23-32.
         LOC: HQ1101.W77
         Stone views *The Awakening* as a *bildungsroman* of the female artist and views birth as a metaphor for Edna's rebirth as an artist. Edna's artistic birth is contrasted with Adèle, Mademoiselle Reisz, and Robert. Stone disagrees with the analyses of critics such as Cynthia Griffin Wolff and James Justus, who view Edna as regressive. She counters their arguments, saying that Edna's rebirth represents progress toward the conception of the self as an artist. She also views Edna's Romanticism as positive because it fuels her artistic imagination. Edna's final step toward autonomy is her realization that romantic love is a delusion and her witnessing of the horror of childbirth. The novel serves as a bridge in depicting conflicts of women wishing to become artists, a position which is supported by the fact that the name "Pontellier" means "bridge maker" in English.

1987

Books and Book Chapters

D.136   Bloom, Harold, ed. *Kate Chopin: Modern Critical Views.* New York:
         Chelsea, 1987.
         LOC: PS1294.C63 L38 1987
         Bloom's volume contains a chronology of Chopin's life and reprints
         of important scholarly articles. Bloom's introduction argues that
         Chopin's short fiction is inferior to *The Awakening* and takes
         exception to the arguments posed by feminist critics. He relates
         Chopin's work to that of Walt Whitman and calls Chopin "a belated
         American Transcendentalist." He further argues that a connection
         exists between Chopin's work and the auto-eroticism of *Song of
         Myself.* He concludes by noting the influence of Schopenhauer on
         Chopin and her work.

         Annotations of individual essays may be found in Section E.2, Edited
         Volumes.

D.137   Ruland, Richard. "Kate Chopin and *The Awakening*." *Essays on
         English and American Literature and a Sheaf of Poems.* Ed. J.
         Bakker, J. A. Verleun, and J.V.D. Vriesenaerde. Vol 63. Amsterdam:
         Rodopi, 1987.
         LOC: PE1 C66
         Ruland provides biographical information and argues that to focus
         on the heroic versus foolish suicide or other ambiguities of *The
         Awakening* is to turn it into a "problem novel" which will become
         outdated and therefore not endure. Paraphrasing Gabriel Marcel, he

states that "the best novels do not deal with problems and solutions, they dramatize mysteries." Citing an 1894 statement by Chopin that writing about social problems will not ensure a writer's survival, he argues that Chopin presents the "mystery of 20th century man."

Journal Articles

D.138   Elfenbein, Anna Shannon. "Kate Chopin's *The Awakening*: An Assault on American Racial and Sexual Mythology." *SoSt* 26 (1987): 304-12.
LOC: F366.L935
Elfenbein takes exception to the argument that a literary double standard was to blame for the critical reception of *The Awakening* and argues that the negative reception was based on the racist concept of passion as dark and purity as white. For example, W.M. Reedy accepted the "woman sinner" if she was a foreigner or of a lower-class, but not in a case such as Edna's. She argues that *The Awakening* subverts and exposes the gender and caste prejudices of both Creole society and American society at large. She also notes the alienation of Edna and other female characters from each other and argues that this alienation is largely based on class and established social roles. Yet, male control over women makes it impossible for Edna to ally herself with men. Edna betrays conventional attitudes of her class through her suicide, the socially correct response for a woman of her class and situation. The suicide indicts both racism and sexism because Edna alone of the characters in *The Awakening* awakens to the romantic and racist fictions of her society.

A bibliographical discrepancy exists in the *Southern Studies* volume in which this essay appears. The title given to the essay in the table of contents of the volume is "Kate Chopin's *The Awakening*: Matrix of Diversity," rather than the title that actually appears on the article. Elfenbein is also referred to in the journal by another surname, Shannon.

D.139   Jones, Suzanne W. "Place, Perception and Identity in *The Awakening*." *SoQ* 25.2 (1987): 108-119.
LOC: AS30.S658
See: E.1.6

D.140   Seyersted, Per. "Kate Chopin's Wound: Two New Letters." *ALR* 20.1 (1987): 71-75.
LOC: PS1 A65

Seyersted presents two new letters illustrating Chopin's depression and stifled creativity in the wake of the negative reviews of *The Awakening*.

D.141 Stepenoff, Bonnie. *Freedom and Regret: The Dilemma of Kate Chopin*. Columbia, MO: State Historical Society of Missouri, 1987.
LOC: F461.M59
Stepenoff offers information on the background and history of the regions in which Chopin lived.

D.142 Urgo, Joseph R. "A Prologue to Rebellion: *The Awakening* and the Habit of Self-Expression." *SLJ* 20.1 (1987): 22-32.
LOC: PS261.S527
Urgo argues that *The Awakening* is about Edna's need to express herself and that what awakens in her, along with her sensuality, is the ability to make her desires and emotions known. He views the narrative as not so much a story of rebellion, as one of developing the ability to rebel. He concludes that because what Edna has to say is unacceptable in her culture, she chooses suicide over silence or compromise.

D.143 Valentine, Kristin B. and Janet Larsen Palmer. "The Rhetoric of Nineteenth-Century Feminism in Kate Chopin's 'A Pair of Silk Stockings.'" *Weber Studies* 4.2 (1987): 59-67.
LOC: AS30.W38
Valentine and Palmer note the influence of the feminism of Stanton, Gage, Fuller, and Anthony and the absence of any biographically supported connection of Chopin to organized feminism. Chopin's writings reflect the struggle of women of her era to escape the self-sacrificing roles of wife and motherhood. Characters such as Mrs. Summers, Edna Pontellier, and Louise Mallard rebel against their proper roles, gaining momentary, but not long-term, freedom. The authors see Mrs. Summers and Louise Mallard as precursors to Edna because women should be active, not passive. They conclude that Chopin accepts a liberal, rather than a radical, feminist rhetoric because her narrators are balanced between "respect for self-sacrifice and endorsement of self-freedom."

D.144 Wershoven, C. J. "*The Awakening* and *The House of Mirth*: Studies of Arrested Development." *ALR* 19.3 (1987): 25 - 41.
LOC: PS1 A65
Wershoven points out that despite superficial dissimilarities, *The Awakening* and Edith Wharton's *The House of Mirth* contain a number of deep similarities, such as women searching for identity

through rebellion, renunciation, and isolation. In both novels, the woman's new self never emerges in the world. Thus, both comment on society's arresting of female development and become "cautionary tales" rather than "feminist manifestos." In this, they are unlike the work of both past and future female authors because they pose questions, but provide few answers.

D.145   Yaeger, Patricia S. "'A Language Which Nobody Understood': Emancipatory Strategies in *The Awakening.*" *Novel* 20 (1987): 197-219.
LOC: PN3311.N65
See: E.5.7, E.9.5

1988

Books and Book Chapters

D.146   Bauer, Dale M. *Feminist Dialogics: A Theory of Failed Community*.
Albany: State U of New York P, 1988.
LOC: PS374.F45 B38 1988
> Bauer states that Chopin articulates both Creole social norms and
> conflicting gendered voices through Edna's rebellion. *The
> Awakening* subverts the romantic structure because Edna denies the
> ideal of the mother-woman, even as her "fragmented, halting" voice
> speaks to the strength of the Creole culture. Drawing on Mikhail
> Bakhtin, Bauer notes a simultaneous cultural and personal dialogue,
> arguing that Edna's suicide demonstrates both the newfound
> consciousness of her physical desires and the limits of desire in her
> culture. Chapter 6 of *The Awakening* represents an attempt to retreat
> to an earlier, "pre-linguistic" time when she didn't have to "struggle
> with the social languages competing for control of herself." Bauer
> views speech as empowering but endangering, therefore, it marks
> selves as both subject and object. This dialogic subjectivity places
> language in the position of both power and chain.

D.147   Bonner, Thomas, Jr. *The Kate Chopin Companion*. Westport, CT:
Greenwood, 1988.
LOC: PS1294.C63 B6 1988
> Bonner's volume includes Chopin's translations of Guy de
> Maupassant's stories and a comprehensive dictionary of Chopin's
> characters. The volume also includes maps of the Cane River
> region.

D.148   Gehman, Mary and Nancy Ries. *Women and New Orleans: A History.*
2nd ed. New Orleans: Margaret Media, 1988.
LOC: F379 N553 A23 1988
Gehman and Ries suggest that *The Awakening* provides detailed
descriptions of upper-class Creole life because Chopin married a
Creole and lived in New Orleans between 1870-1880. They compare
Chopin to Grace King in terms of her use of Realism and New
Orleans regionalism. Their overall treatment of Chopin is very brief.

D.149   Gilbert, Sandra M. and Susan Gubar. *No Man's Land: The Place of
the Woman Writer in the Twentieth Century. Vol 1: The War of the
Words.* New Haven: Yale UP, 1988.
LOC: PR116 G5 1988
Gubar and Gilbert mention Chopin in passing, in the context of
"female aesthetic renunciation."

D.150   Goldman, Arnold. "Life and Death in New Orleans." *The American
City: Literary and Cultural Perspectives.* Ed. Graham Clarke. New
York: St. Martin's P, 1988.
LOC: PS169.C57 A44 1988
In the second half of this essay, Goldman argues that New Orleans is
split and diminished into two roles: masculine commerce and
feminine feeling (*eros*). He views *The Awakening* as Edna's attempt
to break away from compromise and a strict social order — an
attempt that is necessary to maintain the co-existence of the
masculine and feminine sides. He focuses largely on New Orleans
itself, using literary figures, such as Mark Twain and Kate Chopin,
to illustrate his points.

D.151   Koloski, Bernard, ed. *Approaches To Teaching Chopin's The
Awakening.* New York: MLA, 1988.
LOC: PS1294 C63 A6433 1988
Koloski's volume offers an evaluation of paperback editions of
Chopin's works, as well as works appearing in anthologies. He also
offers suggestions for further reading for both students and teachers,
including such topics as historical background, biography, critical
studies, and bibliographies. The bulk of the volume offers a variety
of critical approaches from noted Chopin scholars, organized into
four sections: Women's Experience, Backgrounds, Course Contexts,
and Patterns That Yield Meaning.

Annotations of individual essays may be found in the "Edited
Volumes" section, E.6.
See also: E.6.10

D.152   Mahlendorf, Ursula. "Der Weisse Rabe Fliegt: Zum Kunstlerinnenroman im 20. Jahrhundert." *Deutsche Literatur von Faruen, I: Vom Mittelalter bis zum Ende des 18. Jahrhunderts; II: 19. und 20. Jahrhundert.* Ed. Gisela Brinker-Gabler. Munich: Beck, 1988.
   LOC: PT167 D48 1988
   Mahlendorf argues that art theory is seldom addressed in feminist novels, and thus *The Awakening* was not viewed as a feminist novel until well into the 20th century. The author explores the psycho-social function of art for male and female poets, using a psychoanalytic approach. She explores the role of art in Edna's awakening and her relationship to other characters in the novel. The essay concludes that Chopin demonstrates the problems facing a feminist in a patriarchal society in "an almost classical manner."

   Annotated and translated by Jerry Erath, Northwestern State University.

D.153   Martin, Wendy, ed. *New Essays on the Awakening.* Cambridge: Cambridge UP, 1988.
   LOC: PS1294.C63 A6436 1988
   Martin offers a lengthy critical essay, presenting extensive biographical data that predates Emily Toth's biography. She provides a brief summary of other articles and a selected secondary bibliography. Martin views the primary concern of Chopin's fiction as a celebration of female sexuality and the tension between erotic desires and the demands of marriage, the family, and traditional society. She notes that Edna finds no support in either the domestic or romantic traditions of her time and views *The Awakening* as torn between "the poles of realism and romance."

   Annotations of individual essays may be found in the "Edited Volumes" section, E.7.

Journal Articles

D.154   Bell, Pearl K. "Kate Chopin and Sarah Orne Jewett." *Partisan Review* 55 (1988): 238-53.
   LOC: HX1.P3
   Bell argues that Chopin went beyond the mainstream gentility and Romanticism of her time, moving toward Realism. She provides a brief bio-critical essay comparing Chopin's life and work to that of Sarah Orne Jewett.

D.155 Matchie, Thomas. "The Land of the Free: Or, The Home of the
Brave." *Journal of American Culture* 11.4 (1988): 7-13.
LOC: E169.1.37
Matchie argues that the *bildungsroman* was especially important to
19th century literature because of the severe testing of social mores.
He examines Huckleberry Finn, Edna Pontellier, and Crazy Horse,
based on Sandoz's 1942 recreation. The three share several
commonalities: (1) economic circumstances, especially the notion
that people are property; (2) because of these shared circumstances,
they also shared an instinctive effort to form personal relationships;
(3) they fall into an impossible dilemma when these relationships
end. Edna awakens to the possibility of equality between persons
with her revolt against a society that sanctions sex, but allows people
to be property. Edna is "courageous" in the sense that her suicide
affirms the importance of being oneself, since one is not "alive if not
free."

D.156 Radcliff-Umstead, Douglas. "Chopin's *The Awakening*: The
Discovery of Eternity." *Zeitschrift fur Anglistik und Amerikanistik: A
Quarterly of Language Literature and Culture* 36 (1988): 62-67.
LOC: PR1.Z4
Radcliff-Umstead opposes Spangler's "Kate Chopin's *Awakening*: A
Partial Dissent" in *Novel* 3, 1970, stating that in denigrating suicide,
Spangler ignores ancient heroic suicides and martyrdom. He
compares Edna to protagonists in André Gide's novels *Les
Nourretures Terrestres* and *Immoralists*. He also makes reference to
Whitman's "Out of the Cradle Endlessly Rocking" and sees "suicide
as an affirmation of resolve" that comes from shedding all aspects of
conventionality to "discover one's true self" and "to know one's
aloneness." Thus, suicide "becomes the source of everlasting
beatitude for the brave soul."

D.157 Suárez-Lafuente, María S. "A Presupposition of Intertextuality in
Clarin's *La Regenta* and Chopin's *The Awakening*." *Romanic Review*
79 (1988): 492-501.
LOC: PC1.R7
Though the two texts seem superficially very different, each creates a
system of similarities and oppositions "that map out an intertext of
adultery which, regardless of time and space, points to the delicate
balance of human relationships." The article deals in depth with
biblical and religious images, classical allusions, and other image
schemas. The author ties Edna's growing knowledge and awareness
to the biblical Eve and the fallen woman who must be cast into the
abyss. She especially notes imagery involving the sea as serpents

and light as knowledge. Ultimately, Edna is represented as property which systematically loses its value as she awakens.

D.158   Toth, Emily. "Kate Chopin's New Orleans Years." *New Orleans Review* 15.1 (1988): 53-60.
LOC: AI21 T66 N49

Toth's essay provides a biographical sketch of Kate Chopin, which is more thoroughly explicated in her then-forthcoming biography. She also corrects several factual errors of early biographer Daniel Rankin. Drawing on copious evidence, she describes the Chopin's home in New Orleans, an account which supercedes Rankin's description.

1989

Books and Book Chapters

D.159   Ballenger, Grady, Karen Cole, Katherine Kearns and Tom Samet, eds. *Perspectives on Kate Chopin: Proceedings of the Kate Chopin International Conference*. April, 1989. Northwestern State University. Natchitoches, Louisiana. Natchitoches, LA: Northwestern State UP, 1990.
LOC: PS1294.C63 K383 1989

> This volume contains selected papers from the 1989 Kate Chopin International Conference held in Natchitoches, Louisiana at Northwestern State University.

> Annotations of individual essays may be found in the "Edited Volumes" section, E.1.

D.160   Elfenbein, Anna Shannon. *Women on the Color Line: Evolving Stereotypes and the Writings of George Washington Cable, Grace King, Kate Chopin*. Charlottesville: UP of Virginia, 1989.
LOC: PS266 L8E44 1989
Elfenbein examines the work of King, Cable and Chopin in terms of local color stereotypes, specifically, (1) "the tragic octaroon," (2) "the Louisiana milieu," and (3) "the genteel tradition." The chapter on Chopin deals in depth with "Désirée's Baby," "La Belle Zoraïde," "At the 'Cadian Ball," "The Storm," and *The Awakening*, along with a discussion of Chopin's women of color in her other works and their juxtaposition with white characters. She argues that both in

terms of sexuality and matters of race, Chopin's portrayals are both realistic and carefully depicted using stereotypes to critique and navigate the complex racial relations of Louisiana society. She also argues that Chopin's work was subtle, yet open in its treatment of the sexual, racial and class dimensions of her female characters, and that this tendency is most fully expressed in *The Awakening*.

D.161   Gilbert, Sandra M. and Susan Gubar. *No Man's Land: The Place of the Woman Writer in the Twentieth Century. Vol 2: Sexchanges.* New Haven: Yale UP, 1989.
LOC: PR116 G5 1988
This second of a three volume series includes an expansion of Gilbert's "The Second Coming of Aphrodite: Kate Chopin's Fantasy of Desire," as well as numerous references to Chopin in the context of other women writers of her era.

D.162   Goldman, Dorothy. "Kate Chopin's *The Awakening*: 'Casting Aside that Fictitious Self.'" *The Modern American Novella.* Ed. A. Robert Lee. New York: St. Martin's P, 1989.
LOC: PS379.M545 1989
Goldman argues that much of the early critical emphasis on sex in *The Awakening* was placed by male critics, but that recent female critics have realized that sex is only the catalyst to Edna's self-knowledge. In the context of her discussion of the identity theme in the novella, the author looks at plot, language, imagery, and narrative voice, analyzing ways in which they interact and mutually influence Edna's self-discovery.

D.163   Kouidis, Virginia M. "Prison into Prism: Emerson's 'Many-Colored Lenses' and the Woman Writer of Early Modernism." *The Green American Tradition: Essays and Poems for Sherman Paul.* Ed. H. Daniel Peck. Baton Rouge: Louisiana State UP, 1989.
LOC: PS15.G74 1989
Kouidis argues that Chopin uses Emerson as a representation of the system that Edna struggles to escape and "a judgement on the narrow vision by which Edna defeats herself." Edna's flood of memories at the end of the novel mark her suicide as a defeat. To the extent that the defeat involves her artistic limitations and her limits of vision, *The Awakening* serves as a starting point for works by Dorothy Richardson, Marianne Moore, and Mina Loy.

D.164   Lohafer, Susan. "Preclosure and Story Processing." *Short Story Theory at the Crossroads.* Ed. Susan Lohafer and Jo Ellyn Clarey. Baton Rouge: Louisiana State UP, 1989.

LOC: PN3373.S395 1989

In her study, Lohafer asked 180 subjects with educational backgrounds ranging from high school to Ph.D., to read "Aunt Lympy's Interference" and select "preclosure points," or places where the story could plausibly end. Her results demonstrate that readers have internalized conventions of narrative structure such that their preclosure points mirror the "superstructure-macrostructure rules" postulated by Teun A. van Dijk.

D.165   Taylor, Helen. *Gender, Race and Region in the Writings of Grace King, Ruth McEnery Stuart, and Kate Chopin.* Baton Rouge: Louisiana State UP, 1989.

LOC: PS266.L8T39 1989

Taylor's chapter on Chopin begins with a biographical sketch, placing her life and work in the historical and social context of the time. She argues that Chopin's fiction ignored the larger social, racial, and economic transitions of the Cane River region for the sake of preserving the unity and homogeneity of families, generations, races, classes, and genders. Taylor suggests that Chopin creates unity in the face of divisive social transformations through her use of repeated characters, place names, social activities, and natural elements to construct an atmosphere of harmonious rural relations. She argues that *The Awakening* and "The Storm" provide the logical conclusion to Chopin's writing about women, and that her departure from traditional themes was an aberration, as her work was firmly grounded in the conventions of local color and the "racist ideology" of authors such as King and Stuart. Chopin differs from the latter two only in her subtle, intertextual "reworkings" of European fiction.

Journal Articles

D.166   DeKoven, Marianne. "Gendered Doubleness and the 'Origins' of Modernist Form." *Tulsa Studies in Women's Literature* 8 (1989): 19-42.

LOC: PN471.T84

DeKoven argues that *The Awakening* is Modernist rather than Realist, citing its "decentered subjectivity, rupture of linearity in plot and temporal structure, foregrounding of the pre-Oedipal, presymbolic language, stylistic indeterminancy, multiplicity and fragmentation" as evidence for this categorization. Chopin, along with Charlotte Perkins Gilman, used Modernist techniques to create a feminist Modernism reflecting their fear of punishment for forbidden new desires. DeKoven emphasizes Chopin's ambivalence in empowering Edna and argues that *The Awakening* is "a characteristic work of early Modernist fiction by women."

D.167   Pitavy-Souques, Danièle. "Paysage langage ou l'impossible acces à la parole: une relecture de *The Awakening* de Kate Chopin." *Caliban* 26 (1989): 91-104.
LOC: PR1.C27
The essay examines the problem of language in *The Awakening*, arguing that Edna manages to rid herself of traditional societal representations of woman but fails to create and share a new language to express her new self. This failure is symbolized by the parrot in the opening scene of *The Awakening*. Chopin opposes women of two cultures, Adéle Ratignolle and Edna Pontellier, to examine how women use language to relate to men and to art. Adéle uses highly codified clichés because she has internalized social rules and relations, as opposed to the largely silent Edna. The author argues that after Edna learns to swim, the novel is composed of a series of paintings or vignettes that, with the exception of the symbolist party scene, are expressed as impressionistic marines. She further argues that Edna is defeated by the clichés that she rejects and walks into the sea as an act of feminine rebirth.

Translated by Marie Françoise Conin-Jones, University of North Texas.

D.168   Ryu, Chung-Eun. "Nature and Sexuality in the Fiction of Kate Chopin." *The Journal of English Language and Literature* 35 (1989): 131-47.
LOC: PE9 E53
Ryu argues that Chopin's work extends beyond the local color genre, and he focuses on her characterization, imagery, and themes. He argues that along with Walt Whitman and Theodore Dreiser, Chopin was the first American to focus on the relationship between sexual and social identity. He focuses on Chopin's use of natural settings as agents of enlightenment, her Naturalistic treatment of sexual relations, and the strain of biological determinism present in her works. He discusses both *The Awakening* and much of Chopin's short fiction in these terms.

D.169   Stange, Margit. "Personal Property: Exchange Value and the Female Self in *The Awakening*." *Genders* 5 (1989): 106 - 119.
LOC: NX1.G46
See: D.305, E.1.11, E.4.13, E.5.4, E.9.2, F.42

1990

Books and Book Chapters

D.170   Erickson, Jon. "Fairytale Features in Kate Chopin's 'Désirée's Baby':
        A Case Study in Genre Cross-Reference." *Modes of Narrative:
        Approaches to American, Canadian and British Fiction.* Ed. Reingard
        M. Nischik and Barbara Korte. Würzburg: Königshausen &
        Neumann, 1990.
        LOC: PS371 M63 1990
        In his analysis of the features of appearance and reality that are
        common to fairy tales, Erickson demonstrates how these elements
        contribute to the unexpected "surprise" second ending in "Désirée's
        Baby" that would "presumable be unnecessary" in a regular short
        story. He examines a variety of fairy tales, arguing that their
        similarity to "Désirée's Baby" illustrates "genre cross-reference" and
        intertextuality, thus explaining the power of the story.

D.171   Girgus, Sam B. *Desire and the Political Unconscious in American
        Literature: Eros and Ideology.* New York: St. Martin's P, 1990.
        LOC: PS169.S83 G57 1990
        Girgus compares *The Awakening* to Charlotte Perkins Gilman's
        Women and Economics and describes the exclusion of women from
        the rhetoric and ideology of consensus. He points out the texts'
        radically contrasting perspectives on how women can achieve
        freedom in the modern era. Gilman sees women's liberation coming
        only through major reform of the social and economic structures that
        influence behavior. For example, in "The Yellow Wallpaper"
        individual psychology and emotions are reflections of society. The

author views Chopin as equally radical in her insistence on the independence of women but argues that Chopin saw freedom as a process of relationships involving the psychology of desire and social ideologies. For Chopin, sexuality is a source of identity and strength; for Gilman, it is the major source of oppression of women. Girgus contrasts Gilman's emphasis on the reform-dominated feminist drive to equality with Chopin. He also argues that Gilman's book provides a social and economic context, which he contrasts with Chopin's work in terms of desire and consensus. The author provides an extended close reading of *The Awakening* from a Freudian perspective.

D.172   Horner, Avril and Sue Zlosnik. *Landscapes of Desire: Metaphors in Modern Women's Fiction*. New York: Harvester Wheatsheaf, 1990.
LOC: PS374.W6 H67 1990 or PR830.W6 H67 1990
Edna is contrasted with Adèle, the 19th century ideal mother, and Mlle. Reisz, the marginalized and eccentric artist, to illustrate the intangibility of social constraints. Léonce's remarks render the new woman both ludicrous and pretentious, while Dr. Mandelet's remarks marginalize Edna. Horner and Zlosnik examine the sea as a metaphoric "imaginary zone" where the socially-constructed self can be dissolved to reveal the true self. They view this metaphor as inherently unstable, allowing the reader to actively engage the text's dialogue. Chopin's work is compared to that of Charlotte Perkins Gilman and Edith Wharton in terms of its movement from enclosure to openness within metaphoric space and dialogue.

D.173   Papke, Mary E. *Verging on the Abyss: The Social Fiction of Kate Chopin and Edith Wharton*. New York: Greenwood, 1990.
LOC: PS1294 C63 Z85 1991
Papke includes a chapter on "the ideology of true womanhood" in the works of Chopin and Wharton. She includes chapters on their lives and art, as well as their social fiction. She further argues that while neither author is a feminist or even a feminist writer, their work provides a female discourse that both illustrates and challenges the marginalization and alienation of women in society and illuminates the boundaries of female desires.

Journal Articles

D.174   Dimock, Wai-chee. "Rightful Subjectivity." *Yale Journal of Criticism* 4 (1990): 25-52.
LOC: PN2 Y34
Dimock examines *The Awakening* in light of political theory,

focusing on the nature of constitutional rights and the evolution of 19th century contract law. The recognition of subjectivity in contracts — for example, with regard to fairness — mirrors the subjective and non-obligatory version of human rights demonstrated in *The Awakening*. This version seems superficially contradictory, as it invokes subjectivity to both validate and invalidate the terms of the wifely contract. Chopin negatively marks Léonce's subjectivity compared to Edna's, as demonstrated in the scene with the supposedly sick child. Edna's subjectivity gains weight as evidence — a partial victory — yet the rights of her children make her a slave. Therefore, suicide is logical as the only way to be free.

D.175 Michaels, Walter Benn. "The Contracted Heart." *New Literary History* 21 (1990): 495-531.
LOC: PR1.N44

D.176 Peel, Ellen. "Semiotic Subversion in 'Désirée's Baby.'" *AmLit* 62 (1990): 223-37.
LOC: PS1.A6
See: D.202

D.177 Radcliff-Umstead, Douglas. "Literature of Deliverance: Images of Nature in *The Awakening*." *SoSt* 1 (1990): 127-47.
LOC: F366.L935
Radcliff-Umstead argues that Chopin uses nature to demonstrate women's entrapment by a patriarchal system and their struggles to escape from it. Chopin's descriptions of nature are developed at the most basic levels of plot, character motivation, and point of view. Chopin focuses on nature images that convey both physical scenes and mental perceptions of those scenes by the actors in her narratives. He explores the use of nature in *The Awakening* because these images reveal the "semiotic complexities" of the novel. He concludes that the novel is built on the opposition between interiors and exteriors, spaces that Edna tries to escape because of their "imprisoning reality."

D.178 Ryu, Chung-Eun. "The Negro as a Serious Subject in Kate Chopin's Fiction." *The Journal of English Language and Literature* 36 (1990): 659-78.
LOC: PE9 E53
Ryu focuses on Chopin's treatment of race in the context of Louisiana society, especially New Orleans. He compares Chopin to George Washington Cable, Grace King, Ruth McEnery Stuart, and Lafcadio Hearn in their treatment of African-Americans. Ryu argues

that Chopin had a greater self-awareness in her treatment of race and Creole society than the other authors he mentions. He further argues that Chopin was neither a reformer nor a reactionary, and that she presented a realistic and dispassionate portrait of Louisiana racial relations.

D.179 Schweitzer, Ivy. "Maternal Discourse and the Romance of Self-Possession in Kate Chopin's *The Awakening.*" *Boundary 2: An International Journal of Literature and Culture* 17 (1990): 158-186.
LOC: PN2.B68
Schweitzer points out that the difference between male characters, such as Huckleberry Finn, and female characters, such as Hester Prynne and Edna Pontellier, is motherhood. The author raises the question of individualism and maturity versus its opposites, self-possession and masculine subjectivity. Even thought Edna achieves certain masculine attributes by the end of the novel, she is pulled back by maternity and can not reintegrate into society; therefore, she dies.

D.180 Shaw, Pat. "Putting Audience in Its Place: Psychosexuality and Perspective Shifts in *The Awakening.*" *ALR* 23.1 (1990): 61-69.
LOC: PS1 A65
See: E.5.3

D.181 Shaw, Patrick W. "Shifting Focus in Kate Chopin's *The Awakening.*" *SoSt* 1 (1990): 211-23.
LOC: F366.L935
Shaw's essay examines Chopin's management of point of view in *The Awakening*, arguing that an "internal/external shift in audience perspective" allows her to manipulate the narrative. Accordingly, he argues that the only time the reader is allowed to see Edna's thought processes is immediately before she dies. He praises Chopin for her adept handling of the "rhetoric and the craft of fiction."

D.182 Thomas, Heather Kirk. "'Development of the Literary West': An Undiscovered Kate Chopin Essay." *ALR* 22.2 (1990): 69 - 75.
LOC: PS1 A65
Thomas cites Chopin's newly discovered essay "Development of the Literary West," originally published in the *St. Louis Republic*, to show that contrary to biographical myth, Chopin was not bitter after the negative reviews of *The Awakening*. She saw the Western literary movement as vital, and herself as a working member of it and an

"able, even esteemed critic." Thomas also asserts that Chopin's log books for the years 1888-1902 show that she pursued her literary career just as actively as before the publication of *The Awakening*.

D.183   Toth, Emily. "The Shadow of the First Biographer: The Case of Kate Chopin." *Southern Review* 26 (1990): 285-292.
LOC: AP2.S8555
Toth's essay corrects mistakes made by early biographer Daniel Rankin and perpetuated by Per Seyersted. She argues that "Rankin was not a villain," despite one of Chopin's relatives calling him "that evil priest," but he shared the unacknowledged biases of countless biographers of women. Further, because of his vocation, he lacked "worldly insights which would have helped in understanding Chopin." She corrects further myths and biases that slowed the rediscovery of Chopin's work and also presents new data in anticipation of her then-forthcoming biography.

1991

Books and Book Chapters

D.184 Ammons, Elizabeth. *Conflicting Stories: American Women Writers at the Turn into the Twentieth Century*. Oxford: Oxford UP, 1991.
LOC: PS374.W6 A48 1991

Ammons argues that Eliot's *Mill on the Floss*, Theodore Fontane's *Effi Briest* and Chopin's *The Awakening* describe the conflict of traditional femininity with commitment to art. She argues that the central issue in *The Awakening* is Edna's realization of the fact that she is not a mother-woman and that being an artist and being erotic are mutually exclusive. Therefore, she can not truly have either. She concludes that the novel articulates female creativity.

Women of color made Edna's suicide possible because she could count on them to raise her children. The author argues that without black women, no awakening would have happened. Therefore, *The Awakening* is not universal, even though white feminists claim that it is. This lack of universality is "the great unexamined story." Ammons further argues that the novel is complicated and contradictory and that the oppression of women by other women goes across race and class.

D.185 Ammons, Elizabeth. "Gender and Fiction." *The Columbia History of
the American Novel.* Ed. Emory Elliott. New York: Columbia UP,
1991.
LOC: PS371.C7 1991
Ammons mentions Chopin in the context of 19th century women
writers.

D.186 Oriard, Michael. *Sporting with the Gods: the Rhetoric of Play and
Game in American Culture.* New York: Cambridge UP, 1991.
LOC: PS169.P55 O75 1991
Oriard's study of the cultural history of sport and gaming metaphors
makes passing reference to Chopin and *The Awakening.* He argues
that Edna is caught in a "play-oriented Catholic society" which
defines socially acceptable forms of both work and recreation. Since
holding a job outside of her home is not an option for Edna, she is
left with choices for play which she finds "pointless or oppressive."
This sense of the pointlessness of acceptable pursuits leads to her
dalliance with art and ultimately to her suicide.

D.187 Showalter, Elaine. *Sister's Choice: Tradition and Change in
American Women's Writing.* Oxford: Oxford UP, 1991.
LOC: PS147.S48 1991
Showalter argues that *The Awakening* broke new thematic and
stylistic ground and suggests that Maupassant's desire to escape
tradition and authority greatly influenced Chopin. She places *The
Awakening* in the context of contemporary domestic fiction, local
color, and the New Women writers. She demonstrates the influence
of this legacy, despite Chopin's break with these traditions. She
argues that much of the critical hostility leveled at *The Awakening*
was due to Chopin's defiance of conventional expectations in
women's writing. *The Awakening* is a transitional novel that
presages the move from the homosocial women's fiction of the late
19th century to the heterosexual fiction of Modernism.

Journal Articles

D.188 Anastasopoulou, Maria. "Rites of Passage in Kate Chopin's *The
Awakening.*" *SLJ* 23.2 (1991): 19-30.
LOC: PS261.S527
Anastasopoulou asserts that Edna's change of consciousness
necessitates the change in her life position and argues that Chopin
hints at two rites of passage which imply that Edna will ultimately
succeed, even as the ending suggests her failure. She uses
anthropological studies by Arnold van Gennet to explain the events

following Edna's awakening as a series of symbolic actions that serve as a ceremonial rite of passage. Edna can not take advantage of her new vision or complete the passage because she is trapped in "the patriarchal image of feminine identity."

D.189   Bender, Bert. "The Teeth of Desire: *The Awakening* and *The Descent of Man.*" *AmLit* 63 (1991): 459-73.
LOC: P51.A6
See: E.8.4

D.190   Brown, Pearl L. "Kate Chopin's Fiction: Order and Disorder in a Stratified Society." *University of Mississippi Studies in English* 9 (1991): 119-34.
LOC: PR5.M5A55
Brown points out the well-established critical connection between Chopin's themes in her short fiction and in *The Awakening*. The mixed reception *The Awakening* received suggests that its distastefulness to contemporary audiences is not because of "unfamiliar and exotic locations." Rather, the conventions of American local color, and the tentative or ambivalent rebellion against conventions, required that rebellion take place in the lower classes. In the short fiction, this rebellion is only against a single class or caste. In *The Awakening*, Edna defies not only her own class and culture, but her adopted one and its links to other subclasses and cultures. This disruption of a highly ordered society and its suggestion of disorder led to hostility. For example, some of the short stores were more sexually explicit than *The Awakening*. By applying these questionable morals to lower class women, Chopin was able to avoid criticism of her short fiction that was inevitable when a member of upper class society was presented in similar circumstances.

D.191   Daigrepont, Lloyd M. "Edna Pontellier and the Myth of Passion." *New Orleans Review* 18.3 (1991): 5-13.
LOC: AI21.T66 N49
The author argues that the sexual determinism shown in certain passages of *The Awakening*, along with the presence of a non-judgmental narrator, reveals a tendency toward Naturalism. Even so, the vision of Romanticism seen in her characters is also important. He states that *The Awakening* stands as a warning against pursuing passions often mistaken for love or transcendental fulfillment and mirrors the Naturalist warning against the pursuit of Romanticism and its conventions.

D.192   Foy, Roslyn Reso. "Chopin's 'Désirée's Baby.'" *Explicator* 49 (1991): 222-23.
LOC: PR1.E9
Foy postulates that the ruthlessness and cruelty of Armand in "Désirée's Baby" is more complicated than can be explained by 19th century racism. She states that a "repressed unconscious remembrance" of his mother and his own past are the well-spring of his cruelty. Reading his mother's letter purges Armand's past, "the dark side struggling to be set free," but leaves him to face an uncertain and tragic future.

D.193   Guidici, Cynthia. "Kate Chopin's 'Occasional' Women." *Conference of College Teachers of English Studies* 56 (1991): 25-34.
LOC: PN31.C65A
Guidici uses the concepts of "social domains" and "social occasions" as explained by Pierre Bourdieu and James C. Feris but expands on their definitions. She suggests that "death is also an occasion that suspends social rules." The essay looks at some of the short fiction as well as *The Awakening*, asserting that both revolve around a key event in the character's life. Guidici concludes that this approach offers a way for women to look at women's literature, as suggested by Elaine Showalter.

D.194   Kearns, Katherine. "The Nullification of Edna Pontellier." *AmLit* 63 (1991): 62-88.
LOC: PS1.A6
Kearns studies the awakening of the autonomous self and the problems that result from such awakenings. She argues that the "idealistic model of romantic transcendence" that Edna purses is at its core masculine and misogynistic, placing her in an "inescapable trap." She also examines the influence of Schopenhauer, Nietzsche and German Romanticism on both Chopin and late 19th century culture.

D.195   Malzahn, Manfred. "The Strange Demise of Edna Pontellier." *SLJ* 23.2 (1991): 31-39.
LOC: PS261.S527
Malzahn argues that there is no evidence that Edna intentionally killed herself, stating that views of both early reviewers and recent critics are equally likely to be blinkered. He views *The Awakening* as a psychological novel and Edna as unprepared for the exploration of her own psychology. He concludes that Edna may be pregnant by Alcée and kills herself in "rebellion against nature" and procreation.

D.196   Toth, Emily. "Kate Chopin on Divine Love and Suicide: Two
        Rediscovered Articles." *AmLit* 63.1 (1991): 115-21.
        LOC: PS1.A6
        Toth cites interviews in the *St. Louis Post-Dispatch* which appeared
        immediately prior to the publication of *The Awakening* to argue that
        Chopin, contrary to commonly held critical opinion, revised portions
        of the manuscript before its publication. One of the passages that
        Chopin revised dealt with the description of why Edna loved Robert.
        She also notes that Chopin was thinking deeply about love, the role
        of women in society, and suicide, however, her thoughts about
        suicide were unsympathetic. In this article, Chopin also spoke out
        against the sexual double-standard of her time.

1992

Books and Book Chapters

D.197   Boren, Lynda S. and Sara deSaussure Davis, eds. *Kate Chopin Reconsidered: Beyond the Bayou*. Baton Rouge: Louisiana State UP, 1992.
LOC: PS1294 C63 K385 1992

> Boren and Davis' volume focuses on Chopin's place as both a woman and a Southern writer. The volume includes 14 essays by major Chopin scholars, who write from biographical, new historicist, materialist, post-structuralist and feminist perspectives.
>
> Annotations of individual essays may be found in the "Edited Volumes" section, E.3.

D.198   Giles, Paul. *American Catholic Arts and Fictions: Culture, Ideology, Aesthetics*. New York: Cambridge UP, 1992.
LOC: PS153.C3 G55 1992
> In his study of Catholic influences on American culture, Giles describes Chopin as a Catholic apostate who was influenced by the dichotomy of a Catholicism which "constituted a native culture" for the 19th century Creole and one which provided "an interesting metaphorical concept" for the Modernist author. Catholics of the Modernist period were placed between two opposing tensions: the papal order to adhere to the standards of the church and the pressure to escape the restrictions of those standards. Pope Pius X declared Modernism, a movement of which Chopin was nominally a part, the

"heresy of all heresies." This proclamation did not stop Chopin, a Catholic herself, from playing with Modernism and pitting it against the conventions of Catholicism. He argues that she creates a "modernist ego and a Catholic id" by equating religion with other forms of oppression that enlightened individuals should reject.

D.199   Harris, Susan L. *Nineteenth Century American Women's Novels: Interpretive Strategies*. Cambridge: Cambridge UP, 1990, 1992.
LOC: PS374 W6 H37 1992
Harris briefly treats *The Awakening*, arguing that it builds on the 19th century female tradition. She notes that it is unique and significant because it highlights a woman for whom marriage is a dead end, yet offers no recourse in terms of a "magnetic male," a vocational goal or a daughter to offer hope for the future. Harris concludes that Edna is unable to define herself outside of her sexual awakening, and therefore uses suicide as an escape.

D.200   Harrison, Antony H. "Swinburne and the Critique of Ideology in *The Awakening*." *Gender and Discourse in Victorian Literature and Art*. Ed. Antony H. Harrison and Beverly Taylor. Dekalb, IL: Northern Illinois UP, 1992.
LOC: PR468 F46 G4 1992
Harrison asserts that "the Romantic ideology propounded by the conflicted political, philosophical and amatory values of Swinburne" provides the most important and pervasive subtext of *The Awakening*. He argues that *The Awakening* is a critique of capitalist social values, repressive patriarchal social mores, and the social and religious institutions that perpetuate them. Citing Swinburne copiously, he attempts to foreground "the unique Swinburnean lyricism of many descriptions in the novel."

D.201   Hoder-Salmon, Marilyn. *Kate Chopin's The Awakening: Screenplay as Interpretation*. Gainesville: UP of Florida, 1992.
LOC: PS1294.C63 A6434 1992
Hoder-Salmon presents a screenplay for *The Awakening* in an attempt to create a new critical methodology in which the objective is not the production of a movie but rather the use of film and stage techniques to illuminate the text. She argues that her method is the "ultimate step" to understand the mysteries of a text. The introduction to the volume states that the screenplay is an interpretive device, rather than a script to be filmed.

D.202   Peel, Ellen. "Semiotic Subversion in 'Désirée's Baby.'" *Louisiana Women Writers: New Essays and a Comprehensive Bibliography*. Ed.

Dorothy H. Brown and Barbara C. Ewell. Baton Rouge: Louisiana
State UP, 1992.
LOC: PS266.L8 L68 1992

Peel argues that semiotic and political approaches can be
productively combined to read "Désirée's Baby." She uses the term
political to refer to the power relations in society and argues that
Désirée problematizes the meaning of race, sex and class and
undermines the smugness that the empowered class demonstrated
when it categorized people by signifiers such as skin color. Peel
discusses the two major surprises that Armand encounters — that
Désirée is black, and then that the blackness revealed through the
infant is, in fact, his — the effect of which is to reveal not his wife's
race, but rather his weak ability to interpret symbols which denote
the race and power structures. She then questions whether these
surprises are as subversive as they first appear. She determines that
they are not subversive, for although they "may punish Armand for
his arrogance," they do not change anything in his subsequent
behavior. Peel further argues that the story focuses on Désirée
because she provides a disruption in the narrative by revealing the
flaws of the society. Chopin's story "criticizes, yet sympathetically
accounts" for the limits of Désirée's subversiveness, which consist of
three attributes — unconsciousness, negativity, and lack of group
solidarity.
See also: D.176

D.203   Rowe, Anne. "New Orleans as Metaphor: Kate Chopin." *Literary
New Orleans: Essays and Meditations.* Ed. Richard S. Kennedy.
Baton Rouge: Louisiana State UP, 1992.
LOC: PS267.N49 L58 1992

Rowe notes that New Orleans greatly influenced Chopin and that its
backdrop in *The Awakening* provided more than just local color
scenery. She argues that New Orleans serves as a metaphor for the
novel because Edna's growing knowledge and exploration of the city
represent her inner growth and awakening.

Journal Articles

D.204   Apthorp, Elaine Sargent. "Re-Visioning Creativity: Cather, Chopin,
Jewett." *Legacy* 9.1 (1992): 1-22.
LOC: PS149 L43

Apthorp compares *The Awakening* to Willa Cather's *Lucy Gayheart*,
arguing that they are ambiguous in similar ways. In each, "the
author struggles to represent, through manipulation of the linguistic
and representational conventions prescribed by patriarchal culture, a

possibility that can not be articulated in that language." The
strength of both novels is their capacity to suggest what Cather
termed "the presence of the things not named." Lucy and Edna
struggle to express that which has no language or models. The
models that *did* exist were stated explicitly at the end of "William's
Wedding" in Jewett's *The County of Pointed Furs*. Sensitive
reception and comprehension are acts of imagination and are
necessary to complete a work of art. Based on work by Nancy
Chodorow and Carol Gilligan, she argues that women's maternal
socialization encourages the development of this type of imagination.
This presents an "alternative model of creativity involving
receptivity and interaction with Other that is almost impossible to
articulate" because males dominate the standard models of language
and creativity.

D.205 Bendel-Simpso, Mary M. "Mothers, Women and Creole Mother-
Women in Kate Chopin's South." *SoSt* 3 (1992): 35-44.
LOC: F366.L935
This essay uses biographical data to support the argument that
Chopin's position in *The Awakening* was to perceive and comment
upon the hegemonic roles allowed Southern women. The Creole
mother's identity was "even more completely circumscribed by her
role as mother than American women as a whole." Edna's struggle
amounts to more than just conflict between her sexuality and societal
roles, and this yields the conflict present in *The Awakening*. The
more lax social structure of Grand Isle allows Edna "to recognize
and question" her position. The author concludes that the novel's
ending is not ambiguous because the contrasts between would-be
active agent and passive subject are not mutually exclusive.

D.206 Bender, Bert. "Kate Chopin's Quarrel with Darwin before *The
Awakening*." *Journal of American Studies* 26 (1992): 185-204.
LOC: E151.J6
See: E.8.3

D.207 Bonifer, M. Susan. "Hedda and Edna: Writing the Future." *Bulletin
of the West Virginia Association of College English Teachers* 14
(1992): 1-11.
Bonifer notes the frequent comparison of *The Awakening* with
Ibsen's *A Doll's House* and argues that a more subtle and
compelling comparison can be drawn with Ibsen's *Hedda Gabler*.
Both protagonists marry into foreign cultures in which they are
dominated both by the institution of marriage and by their inability
to communicate with the power structure of their new societies. She

notes the many similarities between both the two characters and the narrative structure of the two works. She argues that ultimately, both Edna and Hedda wish to believe that they have control over their lives, but each comes to realize that they only control their deaths and are thus led to suicide.

D.208   Cramer, Timothy R. "Testing the Waters: Contemplating the Sea in ED's Poem 520 and Kate Chopin's *The Awakening*." *Dickinson Studies: Emily Dickinson (1830-86)* 83 (1992): 51-56.
LOC: Z8230.5.E44
Cramer suggests that Chopin and Dickinson use sea imagery to give themselves freedom to treat topics such as sexuality, longing, and death. They also use the sea as a locale for soul searching. He points out similarities between Edna and the woman in Dickinson's poem 520 in terms of their search for freedom and self-awareness. These women also fear losing themselves in the process of this search.

D.209   Dawson, Melanie. "Edna and the Tradition of Listening: The Role of Romantic Music in *The Awakening*." *SoSt* 3 (1992): 87-98.
LOC: F366.L935
Dawson notes the late 19th century view of the music of the Romantic Period as being erotic and destructive, especially to young female listeners. *The Awakening* contains allusions to musical pieces and to both philosophical and literary examples of the erotic and the destructive. Edna's emotional and atypical behavior are reminiscent of these views, with Mademoiselle Reisz being the stereotypical Romantic musician and Edna being a typical young female listener. Drawing on similar contemporary literary examples of the same relationship, Dawson argues that *The Awakening* is not representing music in this stereotypical way because the characters do not fully live up to the stereotype. Instead, Chopin uses music and musical references as metaphors for all of Edna's emotions and presents music as a natural force that also has positive aspects.

D.210   Dressler, Mylène. "Edna Under the Sun: Throwing Light on the Subject of *The Awakening*." *AzQ* 48.3 (1992): 59-75.
LOC: AP2.A7265
Dressler counters criticism based on sexuality and standard feminist readings, arguing that the title is a trope for the "gazes" or "look" within the construct of Lacanian illumination. She charts a series of awakenings to "versions of experience as it is constructed within the sight/site of the gazes." Edna is cast in a masculine way of seeing, yet Edna's way of seeing is imbedded in these descriptions. Females

often function as the object of extended masculine social "gaze." Light imagery illustrates Edna's gradual opening of her eyes and demonstrates Chopin's manipulation of Lacanian "screens." She uses the screens to "slip the mask of her heroine onto her readers" so that they can see themselves in Edna.

D.211   Mitchell, Angelyn. "Feminine Double Consciousness in Kate Chopin's 'The Story of an Hour.'" *CEAMagazine* 5.1 (1992): 59-64.
LOC: PN2.C4
Mitchell asserts Chopin's relationship to Zora Neale Hurston's female double consciousness, which she defines as "a divided state of the female psyche engendered by the cultural constraints of gender and by the biological determinants of sex." She examines "The Story of an Hour" in terms of three complicating factors faced by Mrs. Mallard: biological determinism, patriarchal social conditioning, and the patriarchal institution of marriage. She also points out Chopin's use of irony, and compares her feminist themes to those of many contemporary women writers.

D.212   Winn, Harbour. "Echoes of Literary Sisterhood: Louisa May Alcott and Kate Chopin." *Studies in American Fiction* 20 (1992): 205-08.
LOC: PS370.S87
Winn argues that a comparison of Louisa May Alcott's *Little Women* and Chopin's *The Awakening* and "Charlie" illustrates Alcott's influence on Chopin as she and her characters "experience the struggle of the serious woman artist to break away from traditional and internalized obligations as well as to subvert patriarchal culture." She compares Jo, Edna, and Charlie to suggest their "literary sisterhood," as well as comparing Alcott to Chopin. She cites the reference to Emerson and the bird imagery in *The Awakening* to show the intertextuality. Alcott "provides Chopin with an important model in her artistic exploration to unmask the forms of conventional female identity."

1993

Books and Book Chapters

D.213   Bryan, Violet Harrington. *The Myth of New Orleans in Literature: Dialogues of Race and Gender*. Knoxville: U of Tennessee P, 1993.
LOC: PS267.N49 B78 1993
In the "woman question" and "Negro question," Kate Chopin, Grace King, and Alice Dunbar-Nelson add to the myth of New Orleans and serve as a counterpoint to male authors George Washington Cable and Charles W. Chestnut. The author looks at racial themes in *At Fault*, "La Belle Zoraïde," "Nég Créol," and "Désirée's Baby." She also examines the drive for "personal voice" in *The Awakening* and other Chopin works. New Orleans is examined as both a background and a catalyst in *The Awakening*.

D.214   Dimock, Wai-Chee. "Kate Chopin." Ed. Elaine Showalter, Lea Baechler and A. Walton Litz. *Modern American Women Writers*. New York: Collier Books, 1993.
LOC: PS151.M54 1993
Dimock offers a bio-critical essay dealing with Chopin and her works.

D.215   Griffith, Kelley. "Wagnerian Romanticism in Kate Chopin's *The Awakening*." *English Romanticism: Preludes and Postludes. Essays in Honor of Edwin Graves Wilson*. Ed. Donald Schoonmaker and John A. Alford. East Lansing: Colleagues P, 1993.
LOC: PR573.E54 1993
Griffith argues that Chopin's musical training and fondness for

Wagner invites the use of the "text" of *Tristan und Isolde* as a basis for determining Chopin's attitudes toward the ambiguity of Edna's suicide. Elements of plot, as well as scenes and themes present in *The Awakening* echo those of *Tristan und Isolde*, and suggest three particularly "Wagnerian" scenes in *The Awakening:* (1) the initial response of Edna to Mademoiselle Reisz's piano playing; (2) Mademoiselle Reisz's rendition of a piece from *Tristan und Isolde* at the evening recital at Grand Isle; (3) Edna's confession of her love for Robert to Mademoiselle Reisz at the pianist's apartment. Tying Wagner to the beginning of love affairs was a common trope during Chopin's era. The author concludes, based on views of other critics, that Chopin would have viewed Edna's "obsessive love" as a symptom of a "self-destructive psychosis."

D.216   Holditch, W. Kenneth. "The Broken World: Romanticism, Realism, Naturalism in *A Streetcar Named Desire*." *Confronting Tennessee Williams's A Streetcar Named Desire: Essays in Cultural Pluralism.* Ed. Philip C. Kolin. Westport, CT: Greenwood, 1993.
LOC: PS3545 I5365 S8 1993
Holditch argues that Chopin's *The Awakening* and William Faulkner's *The Wild Palms* discuss the "plight of the Romantic in an alien setting" in much the same way as Williams' *Streetcar*. Chopin's protagonist follows an "inevitable path to destruction" similar to that followed by Blanche Dubois. He further argues that New Orleans is the milieu in which the changes in the protagonists' lives take place. While he does not argue that Williams read Chopin's works, he points out that examining *The Awakening* helps to illustrate the same truth about the human condition with which his drama is concerned. The heros of Chopin, Faulkner, and Williams are each caught in the paradox of the spirit and the flesh which New Orleans symbolizes in these works.

D.217   Manning, Carol S., ed. *The Female Tradition in Southern Literature.* Urbana: U of Illinois P, 1993.
LOC: PS261 F46 1993
Manning's volume contains a wide-ranging collection of essays that place women writers in the Southern literary tradition. A number of the essays touch on Chopin and her work, placing them in the context of Southern women writers from the antebellum period to the present from both a revisionist and feminist perspective.

D.218   Moss, Rose. "Barriers of Reticence and Reserve." *Still the Frame Holds: Essays on Women Poets and Writers.* Ed. Sheila Roberts and Yvonne Pacheco. San Bernardino: Borgo, 1993.

LOC: PS151.S75 1993

Moss uses Louise Mallard in "The Story of an Hour" to illustrate how women experience barriers to speech and understanding because certain concepts and types of language are denied them by society. "Free speech," while not forbidden, was an experience denied Louise in both expression and experience until the "death" of her husband because of her duties and obligations as a wife. The author uses this insight to explore Doris Lessing's protagonist in "Letter from Home."

D.219 Scott, Anne Firor. "Women in the South: History as Fiction, Fiction as History." *Rewriting the South: History and Fiction.* Ed. Lothar Hönnighausen, Valeria Gennaro Lerda, Christoph Irmscher and Simon Ward. Tubingen: Francke, 1993.
LOC: PR261.R38 1993

Scott cites Chopin as one of a number of Southern writers whose work can be used to fill in historical gaps in the canon caused by contemporary racism and sexism.

Journal Articles

D.220 Castro, Ginette. "La Mere absente et/ou le manque a etre d'Edna Pontellier." *Q/W/E/R/T/Y: Arts, Litteratures & Civilisations du Monde Anglophone* 3 (1993): 133-38.
LOC: PR1.Q2

Castro argues that Edna's early loss of her mother prevents her from structuring her identity and relating to others normally. Her father's rejection of all sensuality worsens these problems and leads to a mind-body split. *The Awakening* is thus a narrative of Edna's attempt to overcome these parental limitations and to define herself as a woman and as a part of nature. Edna is symbolically reborn when Adèle bears her child. This rebirth forces Edna to realize that she must die if she refuses to sacrifice her freedom or ruins her children's future. She dies with dignity, however, not simply as a victim of the patriarchy. Through her death in the sea, she becomes one with the universe.

Translated by Marie Françoise Conin-Jones, University of North Texas.

D.221 Craft, Brigette Wilds. "Imaginative Limits: Ideology and *The Awakening.*" *SoSt* 4 (1993): 131-39.
LOC: F366.L935

Craft argues that the privileging of either the inner or outer selves noted in both Susan J. Rosowski's work on the "novel of awakening" and Franco Moretti's study of the *bildungsroman* is hazardous. The inner self of Edna Pontellier illustrates how social scripts imposed on the outer self can influence one's inner imagination. For example, Edna's fantasies of childhood infatuation are representative of the alternatives open to a young woman of her time — marriage and romance. Edna is never able to escape or even to gain a critical perspective on the constraints that society places on her and thus remains trapped by the romantic myth she has entertained since childhood. Neither is she able to become comfortable with rejecting socially-sanctioned alternatives, therefore, her suicide is not a victory as claimed by some feminist critics, but a failure of both her imagination and her spirit. The author also rejects Sandra Gilbert's argument that Edna creates a world outside of society with her death, since death as a form of protest is more limiting than the focus of the protest. In the end, Edna's awakening is simply the first step toward finding satisfactory options that were not available to her contemporaries.

D.222   Dingledine, Donald. "Woman Can Walk on Water: Island, Myth, and Community in Kate Chopin's *The Awakening* and Paule Marshall's *Praisesong for the Widow.*" *Women's Studies* 22 (1993): 197-216.
LOC: HQ1101.W77
Dingledine discusses the symbolism of *the Awakening* along with Paule Marshall's *Praisesong for the Widow*. He contrasts Edna's isolation with the married couple in the latter story and examines other literary works in terms of their readers' expectations.

D.223   Dyer, Joyce Coyne. *The Awakening: A Novel of Beginnings*. New York: Twayne, 1993.
LOC: PS1294.C63 A64336 1993
Dyer presents a chronology of Chopin's life and work, a detailed literary and historical background of *The Awakening*, an overview of its critical reception, a close reading of the novel, and a selected and briefly annotated bibliography of primary sources, secondary scholarship, and bibliographies.

D.224   Emmitt, Helen V. "'Drowned in a Willing Sea': Freedom and Drowning in Eliot, Chopin and Drabble." *Tulsa Studies in Women's Literature* 12 (1993): 315 - 332.
LOC: PN471 T8
Emmitt equates male drownings in literature to the Narcissus myth, but since women have no comparable mirror in society, she argues that drowning is different for them. In *The Awakening*, *The Mill on*

the Floss, and *The Waterfall*, the heroes' deaths are not viewed as suicides, as would be the case with male characters. Unlike their male counterparts, who have several choices of how to conduct their lives, Maggie and Edna have no choices, and metaphorically, neither does Jane. For the male, water becomes a devouring female; however, for women who can't find a mirror to reflect them, "the embrace of the water provides fulfillment."

D.225 Fourtina, Herve. "'Il etait une fois un moi': *The Awakening* de Kate Chopin." *Q/W/E/R/T/Y: Arts, Litteratures & Civilisations du Monde Anglophone* 3 (1993): 139-42.
LOC: PR1.Q2
This Lacanian study of *The Awakening* argues that Edna tries to avoid symbolization/castration, but fails. To regain a symbiotic fusion with the sea/Mother, she must commit suicide. Because she refuses symbolization, Edna remains outside of language, logic, and time and is subjected to the absolute law of the Father/phallus. Fourtina sees Edna's desire to escape alienation and become her own person not as a feminist project, but as a solipsistic failure to relate to the world and communicate with others. This failure robs Edna of any possible autonomy or identity, and this lack of a genuine self is what prevents her from becoming an artist.

Translated by Marie Françoise Conin-Jones, University of North Texas.

D.226 Franklin, Rosemary F. "Poe and *The Awakening*." *MissQ* 47 (1993): 47-57.
LOC: AS30.M58A2
Franklin points out that neither Emily Toth nor other critics offer a source for either the titles *The Awakening* or *A Solitary Soul* and asserts that the origin of both is "The Lake _____ to _____." In the context of this poem and four others having to do with sleeping, dreaming and waking, Franklin gives a general examination of Poe's influence on Chopin's tone, diction, imagery and theme. She argues that Chopin would have known of the second version of this poem, which was published in *The Raven and Other Poems* in 1845, since the first, *Tamerlaine* (1827) lacks the penultimate line "whose solitary soul could make." Poe presents a paradox similar to Chopin's in *The Awakening,* in that both prefer the "romantic dream-state." Edna's series of awakenings may be tied to passages in Poe's poems and notes that the two narrative voices of *The Awakening* represent "Poe-esque diction" in the indirect discourse between the objective "authority" and Edna's internal voice. Both

writers intertwine love and death in a Freudian manner. Franklin concludes that Chopin's aesthetic was the opposite of Poe's, due to the influence of Maupassant, but Edna was a Poe-esque character, and Chopin lures the reader into her Poe-esque world.

D.227 Pitavy-Souques, Daniele. "De G. Flaubert à K. Chopin, du Paraître à l'être: Notes sur Emma Bovary, Thérèse Lafirme, Edna Pontellier dans *The Awakening*." *Études Anglaises* 46 (1993): 477 - 86.
LOC: PR1.E8
This essay compares and contrasts Emma Bovary of *Madame Bovary* to Thérèse Lafirme in *At Fault* and Edna Pontellier in *The Awakening*. She argues that each novel deals with the problem of freedom, but each provides a very different analysis and solution. Flaubert's novel deals with Emma's social position rather than her inner self, in contrast to the two Chopin characters. She further argues that Chopin's work analyzes moral issues rather than social reality, especially the way in which 19th century American society uses morality to trap women. The essay also examines and contrasts the narrative strategies of Chopin and Flaubert.

Translated by Marie Françoise Conin-Jones.

D.228 Schulz, Dieter. "Notes Toward a *fin-de-siècle* Reading of Kate Chopin's *The Awakening*." *ALR* 25.3 (1993): 69-76.
LOC: PS1 A65
Schulz argues that *The Awakening* is an example of international trends in *fin-de-siècle* literature, specifically with regard to the question of solitude, and is thus similar to turn-of-the-century mood poetry and *art nouveàu*. Edna's combination of inwardness and alienation demonstrates the natural affinity between the female body and water that is expressed by Chopin and other contemporary authors. Chopin's sensibility is called "equally close to but also equally remote from Romanticism and Modernism" and is thus "a turn of the century sensibility that has an integrity of its own."

D.229 Seidel, Kathryn. "Art Is an Unnatural Act: Mademoiselle Reisz in *The Awakening*." *MissQ* 46 (1993): 199 - 214.
LOC: AS30.M58A2
Seidel argues that Edna and Mademoiselle Reisz's relationship shows many coded references to lesbianism which were common in 19th century society and its literary conventions. She argues that *The Awakening* presents lesbianism as "a reality to be faced, perhaps even embraced, not condemned."
See also: E.1.10

D.230   Shurbutt, Sylvia Bailey. "The Cane River Characters and Revisionist Mythmaking in the Work of Kate Chopin." *SLJ* 25.2 (1993): 14-23. LOC: PS261.S527
Shurbutt states that Chopin's fiction stepped outside of the Western patriarchal tradition to present women achieving fulfillment in roles considered inappropriate in 19th century American society. In so doing, she "overtly questioned accepted myths and attitudes" associated with women and marriage. Chopin's fiction deals with themes such as the "self-sacrificing mother-woman," the "fulfilled wife relinquishing self to husband," the "battered woman gritting teeth in ill-fortune," and "wisdom of church in determining moral right for women."

D.231   Skredsvig, Keri Meyers. "Chopin's Choices and Challenges: Language and Limits in 'A Point at Issue.'" *Revista de Filología y Lingüística de la Universidad de Costa Rica* 19.1 (1993): 77-85.
Skredsvig studies "A Point at Issue," using a sociolinguistic approach, and argues that the language of both Chopin and her characters illustrates a "feminist preoccupation with the relationship of self and society." Eleanor's verbal and non-verbal behavior unequivocally communicates the role of gender conditioning in her life. Skredsvig takes exception to critics who argue that the theme of the story is reason versus emotion in marriage and states that the story in fact represents both Chopin's and Eleanor's attempts to break through gender limitations.

1994

Books and Book Chapters

D.232   Bloom, Harold. *The Western Canon: The Books and School of the Ages*. New York: Harcourt Brace, 1994.
LOC: PN81.B545 1993
Bloom discusses what should, and should not, constitute the American literary canon. His extensive list of the revised canon, which appears as an appendix at the end of the volume, includes Chopin's *The Awakening*.

D.233   Fusco, Richard. *Maupassant and the American Short Story: The Influence of Form and the Turn of the Century*. University Park, PA: Pennsylvania State UP, 1994.
LOC: PS374.S5F87 1994
Fusco examines the impact of Maupassant's work on Ambrose Bierce, O. Henry, Kate Chopin, and Henry James. He argues that only Chopin and James, who both read Maupassant in French, fully appreciated his contribution to the short story, though critics tend to underestimate Maupassant's influence on their work. He devotes a chapter to Maupassant's influence on Chopin, especially as it relates to her growing frankness in depicting sexuality, the universal essence of human experience, and her tendency to eschew conventional plot. He treats Chopin's early stories, her translations of Maupassant's work and two structural classes of Chopin's later stories, which the author terms "descending helicals" and "sinusoidals," as well as briefly examining *The Awakening*.

D.234   Gilbert, Sandra M. and Susan Gubar. *No Man's Land: The Place of the Woman Writer in the Twentieth Century. Vol 3: Letters from the Front.* New Haven: Yale UP, 1994.
LOC: PR116 G5 1988
Gilbert and Gubar make passing references to Chopin and her work in the context of their study of 20th century women writers.

D.235   Heynitz, Benita von. *Literarische Kontexte von Kate Chopin's The Awakening.* Tubingen: Gunter Narr Verlag, 1994.
LOC: PS1294.C63 A6433 1994
Heynitz's study of *The Awakening* attempts to determine the proper placement of the novel in the American literary canon. Specifically, she examines whether Chopin should be designated as a Transcendentalist or as a local colorist. She further argues that Chopin was influenced by French Realism through the works of Maupassant, Flaubert, and Sand. The author troubles the notion of whether Edna Pontellier is a version of the concept of the "New Woman," determining that this paradigm does not fit Edna. The author draws parallels with the pre-Raphaelites, and Richard Wagner, concluding that *The Awakening* is a "total work in which prose, music, and art come together."

Translated and annotated by Jerry Erath, Northwestern State University.

D.236   Jarred, Ada D. *Kate Chopin: A Woman of Yesterday, Today and Tomorrow: A Manual.* Natchitoches, LA: Northwestern State U, 1990, 1994.
This manual offers information about the planning and production of a reading and discussion program led by Chopin scholars.

D.237   Keesey, Donald, ed. *Contexts for Criticism.* Mountain View, CA: Mayfield, 1994.
LOC: PN81 C745 1993
Keesey's volume is intended as a textbook, but includes reprints of numerous important critical essays on Chopin.

Annotations for individual essays appear in the "Edited Volumes" section, E.5.

D.238   Miller, James E., Jr., "Whitman's Multitudinous Poetic Progeny: Particular and Puzzling Instances." *Walt Whitman: The Centennial Essays.* Iowa City: U of Iowa P, 1994.
LOC: PS3238 W369 1994

This book refers to Chopin in passing, citing the important influence of Whitman on her work. "A Respectable Woman" is specifically mentioned because of its illusions to lines from sections 21-22 of *Song of Myself*: "Night of South Winds/Night of the large few stars! Still nodding night—"

D.239   Vlasopolos, Anca. "Staking Claims for No Territory: The Sea as Woman's Space." *Reconfigured Spheres: Feminist Explorations of Literary Space*. Ed. Margaret R. Higonnet and Joan Templeton. Amherst: U of Massachusetts P, 1994.
LOC: PN98.W64 R43 1994

Drawing on Chopin's *The Awakening*, Woolf's *A Room of One's Own*, and Austen's *Persuasion*, Vlasopolos argues that "the compulsory heterosexuality" of the time keeps Edna from realizing the mutual homoerotic attraction between herself and Mademoiselle Reisz. Edna's death in the sea "represents not only the amniotic fluid of her origin, but the promise of unfettered possibilities outside patriarchy." The author argues that *The Awakening* is Chopin's "first and only novel" and concludes that Edna's rebellion signals Chopin's "refusal to let her story be bound within the perimeters of male inscription." Chopin subverts a realistic ending by "denying finality" to Edna's death, pointing in the direction of post-modern indeterminacy.

D.240   Wheeler, Kathleen. *'Modernist' Women Writers and Narrative Art*. New York: New York UP, 1994.
LOC: PS374.W6 W44 1994

Wheeler views *The Awakening* as a continuation of the themes of self-discovery and self-creation seen in Chopin's short fiction. She argues that Chopin was influenced by, but rose to challenge, such male-dominated techniques as Realism and Naturalism through her use of irony and symbolism. Viewing *The Awakening* as Chopin's literary autobiography and a "tragic prognostication" of her future, Wheeler asserts that Chopin's fusion of Realism, irony, and symbolism is a unique literary style that is a step toward Modernism because of the resulting fragmentation of time sequences and literary structures. She suggests the existence of an alternative subtext, which designates Mademoiselle Reisz as the central character, and in which the "awakening" lacks the sexual liberation of Edna's surface text. She also argues that much of the romantic bantering between Edna and Robert is intended to "ironize" romantic fantasies in general. She notes a powerful feminist theme which exposes the destructiveness of viewing women as oceanic, primaeval beings. She concludes by stating that Sandra Gilbert's essay "The Second Coming of Aphrodite" falls prey to this fantasy.

Journal Articles

D.241   Baker, Christopher. "Chopin's 'The Storm.'" *Explicator* 52 (1994): 225-26.
LOC: PR1.E9
Baker analyzes flower imagery in "The Storm," making special note of the use of the lily to convey Calixta's beauty and her passion for Alcée. Calixta's name derives from the Greek *Calyx*, the outer protective covering of a flower, and Baker suggests that the name comes from Chopin's familiarity with biology. Calixta's name illustrates the parallel of her sexual receptivity to the opening of a flower. This parallel is reinforced by Calixta's presentation as a lily in her surroundings. Baker ties this flower imagery to other nature imagery in the story.

D.242   Birnbaum, Michele A. "'Alien Hands': Kate Chopin and the Colonization of Race." *AmLit* 66.2 (1994): 301-23.
LOC: PS51 A6
See: D.268

D.243   Branscomb, Jack. "Chopin's 'Ripe Figs.'" *Explicator* 52 (1994): 165-67.
LOC: PR1.E9
Branscomb emphasizes the importance of the church calendar in "Ripe Figs." For example, Toussaint may be either a place name or French for All Saint's Day. He argues that the story contains other religious imagery beyond the often-examined "youth and age" theme explored in this story. The time references reinforce other religious imagery in the story and allude to seasons beyond the seasons of nature, such as human growth and understanding.

D.244   Clemmen, Yves. "Photographic Politics: The Text and Its Readings in Kate Chopin's *The Awakening*." *SoQ* 32.4 (1994): 75-79.
LOC: AS30.S658
Clemmen argues that *The Awakening* is unfocused and elusive because it is a personal story and therefore narrowly focused, rather than a story about women's rights or adultery. He further postulates that *The Awakening* focuses and frames Edna at the visual level, thus leaving impressions on the reader but making no statements.

D.245   Cothern, Lynn. "Speech and Authorship in Kate Chopin's 'La Belle
        Zoraïde.'" *LaLit* 2.1 (1994): 118-25.
        LOC: PS 266 L8 L6
        Cothern examines "La Belle Zoraïde" in the context of the local
        color convention of reported speech as a narrative device. Drawing
        on the work of Mikhail Bakhtin and the Russian historical poeticist
        V.N. Vološinov, she illustrates the polyvocality and subversion of
        authorial context in Chopin's story. Cother also argues that
        Chopin's decision to create Manna Loulou, a character marginalized
        by race, gender and the institution of slavery, allows her to function
        as a critic both of society and of the Realist expectations of the
        contemporary literary community. This narrative strategy left
        Chopin less open to attack by critics, since her literary and social
        critique was embedded in the conventions of local color.

D.246   Cutter, Martha J. "Losing the Battle but Winning the War: Resistance
        to Patriarchal Discourse in Kate Chopin's Short Fiction." *Legacy* 11
        (1994): 17-36.
        LOC: PS149 L43
        Cutter compares Chopin's early works such as "At the 'Cadian
        Ball," "Wiser Than a God," and "Mrs. Mobry's Reason" to later
        ones such as "An Egyptian Cigarette," "Elizabeth Stock's One
        Story," and "Charlie." She notes that in the earlier fiction, women
        who overtly voice their desires and experiences are dismissed as
        meaningless or "insane." The later stories demonstrate the
        development of a covert voice which allows Chopin's characters to
        undermine patriarchal structures from within their own paradigms.
        This growth mirrors Chopin's experience as a writer, moving from
        "charming Creole stories with happy endings" to her more covert
        and subversive work as she tried to slip by the moral and literary
        censors of her day.

D.247   Dawson, Hugh J. "Kate Chopin's *The Awakening*: A Dissenting
        Opinion." *ALR* 26.2 (1994): 1-18.
        LOC: PS1.A65
        Dawson argues that *The Awakening* is undeserving of its high
        standing in American letters, stating that it is "over-cute," and lacks
        economy of expression. Chopin is pretentious and her language is
        inflated and juvenile. He argues that Transcendentalist themes are
        present in *The Awakening* but asserts that Chopin's treatment of
        them is shallow and lacks development. Dawson views Edna as a
        highly unsympathetic and selfish character; she is confused and self-
        destructive because she confides in Alcée rather than in Léonce or
        Dr. Mandelet. Robert is a "foppish parasite" whom Edna never

really loved, and Mademoiselle Reisz is intentionally cruel to Edna, her willing victim, perhaps because of feelings of guilt over her affairs. Chopin is not constructively critical of society, but instead, she allows Edna to simply insist on having her own way. The novel panders to the romantic childhood dreams of the audience, and *The Awakening* fails because of Edna's character. He concludes that the novel has been resurrected by late 20th century moralist critics and should be removed from the canon.

D.248   Day, Karen. "The 'Elsewhere' of Female Sexuality and Desire in Kate Chopin's 'A Vocation and a Voice.'" *LaLit* 2.1 (1994): 108-117.
LOC: PS 266 L8 L6
Day argues that five stories of feminine sexuality in *A Vocation and a Voice*, "An Egyptian Cigarette," "The White Eagle," "The Story of an Hour," "Two Portraits," and "Fedora" provide examples of how dreams and visions create a space for the feminine discourse of desire, which is repressed and unconscious, to encode itself in language. She argues that this analysis answers the questions posed in the work of Hélène Cixous, Luce Irigaray, Julia Kristeva and Jacques Lacan regarding the problem of feminine discourse in patriarchal Western culture.

D.249   Dyer, Joyce Coyne. "'Vagabonds': A Story Without a Home." *LaLit* 2.1 (1994): 74-82.
LOC: PS 266 L8 L6
Dyer notes with surprise that one of Chopin's best short stories, "Vagabonds," has seen print only twice: once in Seyersted's collected works, and once in 1932 when Rankin published it from manuscript. Both Seyersted and Toth see autobiographical influences in the story, and the story powerfully presents Chopin's central theme of recognizing our dual natures and listening to our dual voices. Dyer suggests the possible influence of Aristophanes' "The Frogs," and compares this story to *The Awakening*, "Loka," "Lilacs," and "Two Portraits." She also analyzes certain cancellations in the original manuscript and concludes that this story should be included in every collection of Chopin's work.

D.250   Ellis, Nancy S. "Sonata No. 1 in Prose, the "Von Stoltz": Music Structure in an Early Work by Kate Chopin." *LaLit* 2.1 (1994): 145-156.
LOC: PS 266 L8 L6
Ellis remarks on the importance of music in Chopin's life, along with her talent as both a performer and composer. Music provided Chopin with character types, motivations, conflicts, themes, and

symbols. More importantly, musical forms provide the narrative structure for many of her works. Ellis examines "Lilacs," "With the Violin," and "A Very Fine Fiddle" in terms of their musical forms. Ellis provides a detailed analysis of the musical structure of "Wiser than a God," Chopin's second published work, in terms of metaphor, social backgrounding, and narrative structure.

D.251 Ewell, Barbara C. "Making Places: Kate Chopin and the Art of Fiction." *LaLit* 2.1 (1994): 157 - 71.
LOC: PS 266 L8 L6
Ewell's interpretive essay studies Chopin's motives for writing: self-reflection, financial gain, and most importantly, her search for personal vision at mid-life. She concludes that Chopin used her fiction to construct her own story, and thereby to draw a connection between life and art that provided a space for both future readers and writers to invent their own lives.

D.252 Foata, Anne. "Aphrodite Redux: Edna Pontellier's Dilemma in *The Awakening* by Kate Chopin." *SoQ* 33.1 (1994): 27-31.
LOC: AS30.S658
Foata argues that Edna is a seeker of both the common or erotic and the celestial — absolute truth, love, beauty — but she sees the pitfalls of the erotic, and thus pursues the celestial more actively.

D.253 Goodwyn, Janet. "'dah you is, settin' down, lookin' jis' like w'ite folks!': Ethnicity Enacted in Kate Chopin's Short Fiction." *Yearbook of English Studies* 24 (1994): 1-11.
LOC: PE1.Y43
Goodwyn argues that Chopin's culture, and thus her fiction, is informed and biased by its roots in European arts and thought processes. Chopin privileges "the higher things derived from Europe," making any individual or group which is not privy to the aesthetics of European cultures natural outsiders. Goodwyn argues that Chopin's Creole stories are "stilted," using "self-conscious language which is typical of Chopin when not quite at ease with her material." Goodwyn further postulates that Chopin's depiction of Louisiana should be viewed as post-colonial rather than post-bellum, defining post-colonial as "all the culture affected by the imperial process from the moment of colonization to the present day."

D.254 Green, Suzanne D. "Fear, Freedom, and the Perils of Ethnicity: Otherness in Kate Chopin's 'Beyond the Bayou' and Zora Neale Hurston's 'Sweat.'" *SoSt* 5(1994): 105-124.
LOC: F366.L935

Green analyzes La Folle in Chopin's "Beyond the Bayou" and Delia in Hurston's "Sweat" as examples of the Other in terms of racial and gendered disempowerment. She argues that these characters exemplify the tendency of both authors to use women of color in their novels as symbolic representations of the universal problems faced by women in a hierarchical society. In "Beyond the Bayou," La Folle is enslaved both by her fear of crossing the bayou and her subservient social position in the aftermath of the Civil War. Both her symbolic fear and her literal powerlessness are embodied by "P'tit Maitre," her former master and the owner of the plantation on which she lives. As the story concludes, La Folle's passive-aggressive stance toward her former owner symbolizes the dawning of a new era of civil rights in which African-Americans would begin to slowly emerge from their state of Otherness.

D.255   Heath, Stephen. "Chopin's Parrot." *Textual Practice* 8 (1994): 11-32.
LOC: PN80.T49

Heath provides an in-depth comparison between Chopin's *The Awakening* and Flaubert's *Madame Bovary*, focusing on similarities in the thought and background of the two authors and their protagonists. He notes many similarities between both of the above and in the other characters in the two novels. He notes the influence of Darwin, Huxley, and Spencer, as well as music, on Chopin. He argues that Edna, Léonce, and their relationship presage Freud, given that Freud's work, especially *Studies on Hysteria* and *The Interpretation of Dreams*, were contemporaries of *The Awakening*. The essay examines the bird imagery in *The Awakening*, along with a few examples from Chopin's short fiction. He further notes Chopin's personal disgust with parrots. In *The Awakening*, the voice of the parrot combines with the voice of the sea, a coupling not uncommon in women's Modernist fiction. For example, Virginia Woolf's *To the Lighthouse* poses the problem of representation faced by Chopin in her cultural milieu and that she engaged in the text of *The Awakening*.

D.256   Hollister, Michael. "Chopin's *The Awakening*." *Explicator* 52.5 (1994): 90 - 92.
LOC: PR1.E9

Hollister argues that Chopin merges the techniques of Realism and Naturalism to present *The Awakening* from a Modernist perspective. He argues that Dr. Mandelet embodies Naturalism and that Mademoiselle Reisz embodies Realism. He concludes that Edna's suicide is due to her inability to embrace Modernism.

D.257   Hotchkiss, Jane. "Confusing the Issue: Who's *At Fault?*" *LaLit* 2.1
         (1994): 31-43.
         LOC: PS 266 L8 L6
         Hotchkiss provides a detailed analysis of *At Fault*. She cites Barbara
         Ewell's observation that many of its themes are derived from late
         19th century sentimental and domestic fiction, even as it critiques the
         intellectual and social conventions of the time and subverts the
         expected gender roles. The author applies Carol Gilligan's research
         on male and female moral development to Chopin's complex and
         confusing characters in order to address the question of who is "at
         fault" in the novel. Chopin addresses the issue of how moral
         decisions are made and in so doing challenges conventional
         opinions. *At Fault* thus takes the superficial form of the traditional
         sentimental novel, but hidden in the multi-layered text is a critique
         of moral judgement and the suggestion of a new order of moral
         thinking.

D.258   Koloski, Bernard. "The Anthologized Chopin: Kate Chopin's Short
         Stories in Yesterday's and Today's Anthologies." *LaLit* 2.1 (1994):
         18-30.
         LOC: PS 266 L8 L6
         Koloski provides a chronology of Chopin's anthologized work from
         1921 to 1992, along with the reasons editors cite for having included
         Chopin's works. His analysis is based on standard research tools,
         along with the works of major Chopin scholars. He discusses works
         in short story anthologies for general readers, paperback volumes of
         Chopin's works, and current textbooks.

D.259   Linkin, Harriet Kramer. "'Call the Roller of Big Cigars': Smoking
         Out the Patriarchy in *The Awakening*." *Legacy: A Journal of
         American Women Writers* 11 (1994): 130 - 42.
         LOC: PS149 L43
         Linkin argues that despite Freud's famous disclaimer, in feminist
         criticism a cigar always represents male power and that the smoking
         habits of Léonce, Robert, and Alcée represent emblems of patriarchal
         domination. Their smoking habits also represent the "essential
         framework" for understanding Edna's relations to both men and
         Creole society.

D.260   Lundie, Catherine. "Doubly Dispossessed: Kate Chopin's Women of
         Color." *LaLit* 2.1 (1994): 126-144.
         LOC: PS 266 L8 L6
         Lundie addresses the questions of race in Chopin's work raised by
         Helen Taylor and Anna Elfenbein. She also addresses the argument

of bell hooks that white feminists tend to draw analogies between black men and white women to the exclusion of black women. The author argues that, in fact, Chopin often gives black women and their concerns center stage, as illustrated in "Désirée's Baby" and "La Belle Zoraïde," noting the complexity of Chopin's treatment of race. She applies Elizabeth Ammons' analysis of racial issues in *The Awakening* to Chopin's other fiction and concludes that Chopin's treatment of race in these two stories is both sensitive and disturbing, a fact of which white female critics must be aware.

D.261 Menke, Pamela Glenn. "Fissure as Art in Kate Chopin's *At Fault*." *LaLit* 2.1 (1994): 44-58.
LOC: PS 266 L8 L6

Menke provides a close reading of *At Fault*, using Hélène Cixous' binary and oppositional definition of discourse and Julia Kristeva's theory of the semiotic. She also draws on the work of Joanne Dobson to reveal the subversive subtext that commonly runs through sentimental 19th century fiction, arguing that *At Fault* contains "an inverted demonic text with narrative movement." The demonic text moves toward dissolution while the main text moves toward resolution. The major theme of the main text, the "mistress narrative," is "natural accommodation" and the disastrous consequences of behavior contrary to it. The demonic text encompasses the fantasies and evils, such as the ghost of Old McFarlane, that reflect repressed plantation violence that the "mistress narrative" can not contain. This disjunction is the operative metaphor of *At Fault*, reflecting the disjunction in Chopin's artistic and personal life.

D.262 Padgett, Jacqueline Olson. "Kate Chopin and the Literature of the Annunciation, with a Reading of 'Lilacs.'" *LaLit* 2.1 (1994): 97-107.
LOC: PS 266 L8 L6

Theologian Elisabeth Schüssler Fiorenza's has observed that the myth of the Virgin Mary "sanctions a deep psychological and institutional split" among women in the Catholic tradition. Thus, according to Padgett, secular and religious women are divided by both the question of chastity and by the convent. She argues that "Lilacs" plays out this division, drawing on the Annunciation story of St. Luke. This story, along with *The Awakening* and "The Story of an Hour," presents a failed Annunciation, in which the promise of redemption and salvation becomes renunciation and denunciation. This failure places Chopin's work in the tradition of Meridel Le Sueur and Zora Neale Hurston.

D.263   Saar, Doreen Alvarez. "The Failure and Triumph of 'The Maid of Saint Phillippe'": Chopin Rewrites American Literature for American Women." *LaLit* 2.1 (1994): 59-73.
LOC: PS 266 L8 L6
Saar analyzes Chopin's essay "In the Confidence of a Story-Writer" and her short story "The Maid of Saint Phillippe" to illustrate Chopin's struggle to become a recognized author and the conditions under which women's literature could gain critical acceptance. The essay reveals more about Chopin's thoughts on the nature of literature than any of her other work. The story, despite Chopin's firm insistence that she intended it to be her greatest literary achievement, has been dismissed as a failure by critics and readers, both contemporary and modern. Chopin seemed to take this failure more personally than other, more pronounced rejections of her short fiction. Saar argues that Chopin presented some of her most radical ideas about the condition of women while employing one of the most conventional of 19th century literary genres – the historical tale. She concludes that the story's rejection convinced Chopin that such a mixture of male literary conventions could not be combined with female history to the satisfaction of either the male or the female audience. This realization greatly influenced Chopin's later work, especially *The Awakening*, and allowed her to find her own distinctive voice.

D.264   Sempreora, Margot. "Kate Chopin as Translator: A Paradoxical Liberation." *LaLit* 2.1 (1994): 83-98.
LOC: PS 266 L8 L6
Sempreora argues that Chopin's bilingualism and the apparent influence of Maupassant have become conventions of Chopin criticism due to the work of Seyersted, Toth, and Taylor. She asserts that critics have overlooked the effect that translating Maupassant's morbid, misanthropic, and misogynistic work had on Chopin's own writing. She observes this influence in "At the 'Cadian Ball," written in the tradition of classic American local color and its sequel, "The Storm," an iconoclastic work in a truly feminine voice. She attributes the many differences in these closely related tales to the six years and eight Maupassant translations that elapsed between them.

D.265   Steiling, David. "Multi-Cultural Aesthetic in Kate Chopin's 'A Gentleman of Bayou Têche.'" *MissQ* 47.2 (1994): 197 - 200.
LOC: AS30. M58A2
Steiling examines "A Gentleman of Bayou Têche" to demonstrate Chopin's narrative strategy of deconstructing the conventions of local color to transcend the limits of the genre.

D.266   Toth, Emily. "A New Generation Reads Kate Chopin." *LaLit* 2.1
         (1994): 8-17.
         LOC: PS 266 L8 L6
         This introduction to the 1994 special edition of *Louisiana Literature*
         exposes many long-held Chopin myths and provides a history of
         recent Chopin scholarship. Toth mentions some of the leading
         figures in the field, as well as introducing the essays that follow.

D.267   Weatherford, K. J. "Courageous Souls: Kate Chopin's Women
         Artists." *American Studies in Scandinavia* 26 (1994): 96-112.
         LOC: E11.A38
         Weatherford looks at "Wiser than a God" and *The Awakening* to
         examine Chopin's personal struggle to attain equal status with male
         writers. Her first story is the only one in which she presents female
         artistic success "so confidently and without compromise." The
         author compares Paula von Stoltz to Mademoiselle Reisz and sees
         her as an "empowering wish fulfillment of what the woman with
         artistic ambition might accomplish." Weatherford asserts that Paula
         was Chopin's alter-ego and appears to have been a personal
         inspiration for Chopin at the stage of her career in which she was
         publishing with a flurry. Chopin is compared to Edna Pontellier and
         Mademoiselle Reisz as artists, in the context of Edna's late start as
         an artist and her role as a mother, and Mademoiselle Reisz's search
         for national recognition. Weatherford argues that "she could identify
         with neither character completely, and in the inconsistency of her
         portrayal, Chopin lays bare her own dilemma." She never resolved
         the ambiguity and deep-seated anxiety about her place and future as
         an artist.

1995

Books and Book Chapters

D.268   Birnbaum, Michele A. "'Alien Hands': Kate Chopin and the Colonization of Race." *Subjects and Citizens: Nation, Race and Gender from Oroonoko to Anita Hill.* Ed. Michael Moon and Cathy N. Davidson. Durham, NC: Duke UP, 1995.
LOC: PS169.N35 S83 1995
   Birnbaum argues that Edna's sleepiness throughout *The Awakening* represents her attempt to dispose of her "fictitious self" and that her *ennui* represents an "out of culture experience." She feels caged by the expectations of domestic life, and as a result, claims moral and erotic freedom. Edna's liberation is "narcoleptic, a movement in and out of consciousness" because she is "pressed into slumber by her husband's demands." Birnbaum also points out that Edna is repeatedly visited by a foreign presence, and it is this "alien touch" that leads her to discover the "erotic frontiers of the self." Birnbaum concludes that Edna explores the visible sexual difference around her that is associated with Blacks, quadroons and Acadians in the novel.
   See also: D.242

D.269   Fluck, Winfried. "Kate Chopin's *At Fault*: The Usefulness of Louisiana French for the Imagination." *Transatlantic Encounters: Studies in European-American Relations, Presented to Winfried Herget.* Ed. Udo J. Hebel and Karl Ortseifen. Trier: W.V.T. Wissenschaftlicher Verlag Trier, 1995.
LOC: PS159.E85 T73 1995
   Fluck challenges the assertion of Elaine Showalter that *The*

Awakening stands apart from the three major stages of 19th century American literature — the domestic novel, local color fiction, and "New Woman fiction." He argues that Chopin's earlier work is very much in line with the conventions of these three traditions and that these traditions were transformed and carried on by literary Realists. He notes the influence of early Realists, such as Maupassant, on Chopin and that *The Awakening* is itself an example of literary Realism. He argues that rather than representing a radical break with tradition, as many contemporary critics argue, *The Awakening* represents the logical progression of both Chopin's career as a writer and the American woman's literary tradition in general. To support his argument, the author presents an in-depth analysis of *At Fault*, arguing that it combines elements of all three earlier traditions, and also reexamines the French influence on the novel.

D.270   Hochman, Barbara. *"The Awakening* and *The House of Mirth*: Plotting Experience and Experiencing Plot." *The Cambridge Companion to American Realism and Naturalism: Howells to London.* Ed. Donald Pizer. Cambridge: Cambridge UP, 1995.
LOC: PS374.N29 C36 1995
Hochman explores the relationship of the above authors to their characters and also to each other but argues that Chopin and Wharton are separated from their characters by their articulation of the characters' conflicts versus the characters' failed artistic aspirations. She places both authors in the Naturalist camp, and especially notes their isolation. She also compares the characters' storytelling to the novelists' narrative voices and notes "fairy-tale motifs." Hochman concludes that reading fiction is itself phenomenologically similar to the liminal states experienced by the characters in the works of Chopin and Wharton.

D.271   Karur, Iqbal, ed. *Kate Chopin's The Awakening: Critical Essays.* New Delhi: Deep & Deep, 1995.
LOC: PS1294 C63 A64355 1995

Karur's volume offers numerous brief personal essays about *The Awakening.*

Annotations of individual essays may be found in the "Edited Volumes" section, E.4.

D.272   Lyons, Mary E. *Keeping Secrets: The Girlhood Diaries of Seven Women.* New York: Holt, 1995.
LOC: PS409.L96 1995

Lyons offers an interpretive examination of Chopin's diaries, documents which sporadically cover her life from age ten until shortly before her death. The article also makes reference to Chopin's novels and selected short fiction in the context of her journal entries.

D.273   Walker, Nancy A. *The Disobedient Writer: Women and Narrative Tradition*. Austin: U of Texas P, 1995.
LOC: PS152.W35 1995

Walker's volume gives a limited discussion of Chopin, describing her as a writer who altered the course of women's writing. Unlike her contemporaries, many of whom could find no "point of entry" into the literary scene, Chopin was, and remains, widely read and influential. Walker reminds readers that Chopin was widely renounced for her "unladylike" fiction, and that she "drew criticism of a morally indignant kind." She describes "Elizabeth Stock's One Story" as a model for the plight of women writers of Chopin's generation, making Chopin a foil to the other female writers of her era. She speculates on the influence that Chopin's work would have exerted on later writers — especially women writers — had the bulk of her work not been out of print for over five decades.

Journal Articles

D.274   Brightwell, Gerri. "Charting the Nebula: Gender, Language and Power in Kate Chopin's *The Awakening*." *Women and Language* 18.2 (1995): 37-41.

Brightwell argues that women are not limited only by their subordinate role in society. She uses *The Awakening* to illustrate that language is an indirect tool of female oppression because of a lack of appropriate feminine registers to express women's desires in the male dominated language.

D.275   Buckman, Jacqueline. "Dominant Discourse and the Female Imaginary: A Study of the Tensions Between Disparate Discursive Registers in Chopin's *The Awakening*." *English Studies in Canada* 21 (1995): 55-76.
LOC: PS374.N29 C36 1995

Buckman argues that the dominant patriarchal discourse, which makes possible myths of motherhood, romance, and seduction, is accompanied by a marginalized subtext which seeks to subvert and transform that discourse. The tension between these two discourses produces the novel's ambiguity. The essay explores the relationship between Edna's subjectivity and language, as the reader must find alternative discourse strategies in the subtext. She also argues that the above opposition exists in Edna's subjectivity at both the symbolic and semiotic levels in the text, as expressed by the dual trajectories of Edna's gaze.

D.276   Camfield, Gregg. "Kate Chopin-hauer: Or, Can Metaphysics Be Feminized?" *SLJ* 27.2 (1995): 3-22.
LOC: PS261.S527
Although the influence of Arthur Schopenhauer on Kate Chopin is mentioned prominently in her diaries and noted in both of her major biographies, few critics have examined his impact on her works. Chopin began her career because of the inspiration of Schopenhauer's idealistic aesthetic of renunciation. Her novel, *The Awakening*, was written near the end of her life and shows both the influence of Idealism and Chopin's artistic growth beyond the narrow constraints of that philosophy. Chopin's growing resistance to Idealism and its latent objectification of women illustrates her incipient feminism. Many critics have noted the ambiguity present in *The Awakening*, especially in its ending, but the novel's ambiguity derives from the inevitable tension between German Idealism and 19th century American feminism. Examples taken from both *The Awakening* and from Chopin's works of short fiction illustrate the evolving influence of these two major philosophies as her career progressed. In addition, the history of Western Idealism is outlined, as exemplified in the works of Schopenhauer, and the tenets of early American feminist thought are shown to provide an original basis for studying Chopin's work.

D.277   Corum, Carol S. "Music in *The Awakening*." *Mount Olive Review* 8 (1995-96): 36-44.
Corum discusses Chopin's musical background and the influence of this background on *The Awakening*. She focuses on the four pieces of semi-classical and classical music mentioned in the novel: the overtures to *Zampa* by Joseph Herold and *Poet and Peasant* by Franz von Suppe, "*Impromptu*" by Frédéric Chopin, and "Isolde's Song" by Richard Wagner. Not only does music excite Edna's senses and contribute to her sensual and spiritual awakening, it is used to define the two social spheres in which she moves, symbolized by Adèle Ratignolle and Mademoiselle Reisz. Chopin's knowledge of the aesthetic qualities of music allows her to reinforce the contrast between the social realms represented by these two women.

D.278   Gunning, Sandra. "Kate Chopin's Local Color Fiction and the Politics
        of White Supremacy." *AzQ* 52.3 (1995): 61-86.
        LOC: AP2.A7265
        Gunning examines the Southern family in "A No-Account Creole"
        and *At Fault* with respect to the resulting tensions as Southern
        society struggled with ethnic, class, gender, and economic power
        shifts at the turn of the century. She argues that the issue of white
        supremacy serves not only as a subject for social commentary but as
        a structural element in Chopin's fiction. She asserts that because of
        birth and marriage, Chopin would have been well-steeped in the
        elements of white supremacy, regardless of her opinions. Thus,
        these elements must be an undercurrent in her fiction. She states
        that Chopin subverts elements of white supremacy just enough to
        loosen the social constraints of her female characters. She examines
        class and ethnic divisions between whites, especially Americans and
        Creoles, and also examines "A Lady of Bayou St. John" and "La
        Belle Zoraïde" to present a playful subversion of white attitudes
        toward sexual repression and miscegenation without unduly
        offending her white audience. The author states that Chopin's work
        is as much a response to racial stereotypes as it is a reaction to
        patriarchal domination and provides a hitherto neglected site from
        which to consider the racialization of gender within turn of the
        century women's fiction.

D.279   Menke, Pamela Glenn. "Chopin's Sensual Sea and Cable's Ravished
        Land: Sexts, Signs, and Gender Narrative." *Cross Roads: A Journal
        of Southern Culture* 3.1 (1994-95): 78-102.
        LOC: F206.C76
        Menke presents a detailed comparative analysis of land and water
        signs in Chopin's *At Fault* and *The Awakening* and also looks at
        Cable's *The Grandissimes* and *John March, Southerner*. Using the
        approach of Hélène Cixous, she argues that Chopin allows the reader
        to construct the "gender narratives" which exist in the metaphorical
        patterns of the text and reflect the author's perceptions regarding
        cultural values, traditions and other social circumstances. Menke
        also draws on the work of Annette Kolodny, Patricia Yeager, Joanne
        Dobson, and Myra Jehlen. The author concludes that Chopin
        privileges water and flexibility while Cable privileges social
        hierarchy. Both Chopin and Cable note that women's position and
        ultimate happiness is dependent on male definitions.

D.280   Platizky, Roger. "Chopin's *The Awakening*." *Explicator* 53 (1995):
        99-102.
        LOC: PR1.E9

Platizky argues that Edna suffers from a "repressed post-traumatic memory" from either having witnessed or having been the victim of sexual molestation, although, as he states, "there is no direct evidence of such violation." He supports his diagnosis with evidence of Edna's mood swings, her lack of voice early in the novel, and textual allusions to the Philomela myth.

D.281   St. Pierre, Ronald. "Kate Chopin's *The Awakening* and American Literary Tradition." *Shoin Literary Review* 28 (1995): 17-24.

D.282   Thomas, Heather Kirk. "Kate Chopin's Scribbling Women and the American Literary Marketplace." *Studies in American Fiction* 23.1 (1995): 19 - 34.
LOC: PS370.S87
Thomas charts Chopin's career and attitudes based on three female writers in her fiction. Miss Witherwell in "Miss Witherwell's Mistake" illustrates Chopin's abhorrence of traditional women's subjects although she produced women's fiction for over a decade. Miss Mayblunt illustrates the tension of the writer's public persona when it is trapped between commercialism and serious art. The protagonist of "Elizabeth Stock's One Story" represents the failed literary woman who loses her reputation and dies alone in silence. The three characters serve as negative foils to Chopin herself, illustrating her ambivalence toward her own career.

D.283   Yonogi, Reiko. "The Struggle Toward Self-Realization: Gustave Flaubert's *Madame Bovary*, Kate Chopin's *The Awakening*, and Arishima Takeo's *Aru onna*." *ICLA '91 Tokyo: The Force of Vision, II: Visions in History; Visions of the Other*. Ed. Earl Miner, Toru Haga, Gerald Gillespie, Margaret Higonnet and Sumie Jones. Tokyo: ICLA, 1995.

1996

Books and Book Chapters

D.284   Koloski, Bernard. *Kate Chopin: A Study of the Short Fiction*. New York: Twayne - Simon and Schuster, 1996.
LOC: PS1294.C63K65 1996
Koloski argues that Chopin's biculturalism, bilingualism and immersion in the world of ideas from an early age led to her unique literary vision. The volume is divided into three sections. "The Short Fiction" provides a brief introduction to the literary influences and historical setting of Chopin's work, along with a detailed analysis of selected works from her three short story collections, some of her children's fiction, and some uncollected stories. "The Writer," presents selected criticism written by Chopin dealing with regionalism, local color and the major authors and literary topics of the day. "The Critics," presents essays or excerpts from the work of major Chopin scholars, including: Anna Shannon Elfenbein, Barbara C. Ewell, Susan Lohafer, Mary E. Papke, Peggy Skaggs, and Emily Toth. The volume also includes a selected bibliography of primary works, biographies, critical studies, articles and parts of books, and bibliographies.

D.285   Petry, Alice Hall. *Critical Essays on Kate Chopin*. New York: G.K. Hall, 1996.
LOC: PS1294.C63 C75 1996
This volume contains selected reviews of *Bayou Folk*, *At Fault*, *A Night in Acadie* and *The Awakening*. Also included are a 1994 biographical sketch, three critical essays published before 1969,

seven published after 1969, and seven original essays. The introduction provides a biographical sketch of Chopin's life and career along with a summary of both the contemporary and modern critical responses to the work.

Annotations of individual essays may be found in the "Edited Volumes" section, E.8.

D.286   Tuttleton, James W. *Vital Signs: Essays on American Literature and Criticism.* Chicago: Ivan R. Dee, 1996.
LOC: PS121 T88 1996
Tuttleton offers a generally favorable review of Toth's biography, calling it a detailed and substantial portrait with much information. He states that "it repays a close reading." Tuttleton also takes strong exception to feminist readings of *The Awakening* and claims that Chopin was never a "lost author," but that her work has been "ransacked" by feminist critics. He concludes by asserting that connections made between Chopin's life and her work, and especially that she had an affair, as Toth states, are incorrect.

Journal Articles

D.287   Fleissner, Jennifer L. "The Work of Womanhood in American Naturalism." *Differences: A Journal of Feminist Cultural Studies* 8.1 (1996): 57-93.
LOC: HQ1101 .D54
Fleissner provides a long discussion of Naturalism and the main critical approaches to it, especially feminism and new historicism. She asserts that the male Naturalist canon, with writers such as Dreiser, Norris, and Crane, is incomplete without incorporating female non-sentimentalists, such as Chopin, Gilman, Jewett and Freeman. This essay provides a comprehensive overview of Naturalism and other turn of the century literary movements and is especially useful for pedagogical purposes.

D.288   Fluck, Winfried. "'The American Romance' and the Changing Functions of the Imaginary." *New Literary History* 27 (1996): 415-58.
LOC: PR1 .N44
Fluck argues that despite its Realism in terms of narrative structure, *The Awakening* should be included in discussions of the Romantic search for self. *The Awakening* begins as a Realistic novel, but then radically subverts the genre through Edna's assertion and expansion of herself and her severance of all social ties. Despite its superficial Realism, *The Awakening* is a romance because of its lack of balance

between the individual in society, the use of fairy-tale motifs, and Edna's quest for an unreachable goal. The author briefly discusses "The Story of an Hour" in the same light.

D.289 Hermes, Liesel. "Frauenbilder in der amerikanischen Literatur: Kate Chopin, EdithWharton, Carson McCullers."
Fremdsprachenunterricht: Die Zeitschrift fur das Lehren und Lernen Fremder Sprachen 6 (1996): 445-50.

D.290 Johnson, Rose M. "A Ratio-nal Pedagogy for Kate Chopin's Passional Fiction: Using Burke's Scene-Act Ratio to Teach 'Story' and 'Storm.'"
Conference of College Teachers of English Studies 60 (1996): 122-28.
LOC: PN32.C65a
Johnson points out that many college freshman are as critical and judgmental of "The Story of an Hour" and "The Storm" as many 19th century critics. She suggests the use of Kenneth Burke's scene-act ratio as a teaching tool to lead students into more literary and less psychological and moralistic readings of literary works.

D.291 LeBlanc, Elizabeth. "The Metaphorical Lesbian: Edna Pontellier in *The Awakening.*" *Tulsa Studies in Women's Literature* 15 (1996): 289-308.
LOC: PN471.T84
LeBlanc argues that *The Awakening* must be read not only as a feminist text, but as a lesbian text. She draws on the work of Showalter and Seidel to support her argument, along with the work of numerous lesbian and feminist theorists. LeBlanc argues that "Edna herself illuminates strategies for reconstructing a lesbian identity, both within and apart from the heterosexual economy" and that the ambiguous ending of *The Awakening* "allows for speculation that Edna (as far as was possible for a woman of her ability and emotional makeup in her particular historical period) realized the ultimate 'lesbian moment.'"

D.292 Lloyd, Caryl L. "Voix Étrangères/Voix Féminines." *L'Ouest Français et la Francophonie Nord-Américaine.* Ed. Georges Cesbron. Angers: Presses de l'Université d'Angers, 1996.
Lloyd argues that Chopin was doubly marginalized both as a woman and as a feminist at the end of the 19th century and as part of the Creole minority at a time when the French influence in North America was in decline. Thus, she had to deal with the weight of a mythical past, along with a sometimes difficult present. As a writer, she had to deal with being bi-lingual and bi-cultural, and as a result was long considered merely a regionalist, and thus the strength and

originality of her works was overlooked. Yet, these handicaps ultimately became her main strengths, and her deep knowledge of French literature enabled a dialogue with American culture and traditions even as her personal voice grew to transcend all of these influences.

Translated by Marie Françoise Conin-Jones, University of North Texas.

D.293 Pontuale, Francesco. "*The Awakening*: Struggles Toward *l'Ecriture Feminine*." *MissQ* 50.1 (1996): 37-50.
LOC: AS30.M58A2
Pontuale argues that *The Awakening* anticipated features of *l'ecriture feminine*, in that it considers women's portrayals of the body, motherhood, and bisexuality. *The Awakening* does not employ linguistic deviations such as marked syntax, but reading the book as a feminist text "offers the possibility of applying feminist and female issues" to Chopin's text.

D.294 Taylor, Walter and Jo Ann B. Fineman. "Kate Chopin: Pre-Freudian Freudian." *SLJ* 29 (1996): 35-46.
LOC: PS261.S527
Taylor and Fineman's essay offers a Freudian analysis of *The Awakening*, arguing that Chopin illustrates an understanding of subconscious motivation as it was later articulated by Freud. They illustrate Chopin's understanding of depth psychology by focusing on Edna's adjustment to the loss of her mother. The scene in which Edna remembers walking through the meadow is a "screen memory" which masks her wish to return to her mother's arms. This longing influences her relationships with Adèle Ratignolle and Mademoiselle Reisz and her fixation in the oceanic state in which the boundaries between self, mother, and environment are erotically blurred.

D.295 Wolff, Cynthia Griffin. "Un-Utterable Longing: The Discourse of Feminine Sexuality in *The Awakening*." *Studies in American Fiction* 24 (1996): 3-22.
LOC: PS370.S87
See: D.303

1997

Books and Book Chapters

D.296   Beer, Janet. *Kate Chopin, Edith Wharton and Charlotte Perkins Gilman: Studies in Short Fiction.* London: Macmillian and New York: St. Martin's P, 1997.
LOC: PS374.S5B44 1997
Beer examines Chopin's short stories, focusing on several key issues. She argues that in Chopin's work, Louisiana should be viewed as a post-colonial society rather than an American post-bellum society and examines her works dealing with ethnicity in this light. In contrast to her ethnic literature, Chopin's more exotic short fiction lacks the sense of place that served as a screen for her more controversial stances. She examines the strategies that Chopin uses in her erotic fiction to distance herself from Louisiana society while maintaining conventional American forms in order to make these works acceptable to 19th century editors. Beer also examines Chopin's "micro-fiction" – works of less than two pages or of approximately 1,000 words – in order to shed light on the thematic and structural aspects of her work as a whole.

Chapter 2 of this volume is a reprint of D.253.

D.297   Benfey, Christopher. *Degas in New Orleans: Encounters in the Creole World of Kate Chopin and George Washington Cable.* New York: Knopf, 1998.
LOC: ND553.D3B46 1998
Benfey examines the socio-cultural history of New Orleans during

the 1870's, when Edgar Degas visited his American relatives who operated as cotton factors next door to Oscar Chopin. He views New Orleans through the interconnected lives, friendships, and family ties of Degas, George Washington Cable, and Kate Chopin. He examines both the French-Creole culture of Louisiana and its "little-known mirror image" in France – *notre petite colonie Louisianaise* or the "Louisiana colony" – which constituted a transatlantic axis freely traveled in both directions by prominent individuals and families, both black and white. He discusses how these cultural influences affected the work of all three artists and specifically addresses Chopin's "After the Winter," *At Fault*, *The Awakening*, "La Belle Zoraïde," "Désirée's Baby," "Emancipation: A Life Fable," "The Locket," "The Maid of St. Phillippe," "A Matter of Prejudice," "The Return of Alcibiade," "A Sentimental Soul," "The Story of an Hour" and "A Wizard From Gettysburg."

This volume was published in 1998, but copyrighted in 1997. *See also D.304*

D.298   Den Tandt, Christophe. "Oceanic Discourse, Empowerment and Social Accommodation in Kate Chopin's *The Awakening* and Henrik Ibsen's *The Lady from the Sea.*" *Union in Partition: Essays in Honour of Jeanne Delbaere.* Ed. Gilbert Debusscher and Marc Maufort. Liege, Belgium: L3 – Leige Language and Literature, 1997.

Journal Articles

D.299   Cole, Karen. "A Message from the Pine Woods of Central Louisiana: The Garden in Northrup, Chopin, and Dormon." *LaLit* 14 (1997): 64-74.
LOC: PS 266 L8 L6
Cole compares the symbolism of gardens along the "River Road" in Eastern Louisiana to that of the Pine Hills of Central Louisiana. She argues that the symbolism of the latter reflects a more frank appreciation of the hardships of land and climate along with the complexity of human interactions with each other and with nature. She draws evidence from Solomon Northrup's narrative *Twelve Years a Slave*, Carolyn Dormon's *Bird Talk* and Kate Chopin's *At Fault*. She argues that in these works the garden mediates between the harsh realities of the natural and social realms. Thus, gardens provided a place where humanity and nature could meet in harmony as an escape from their mutual harshness.

D.300   Ewell, Barbara C. "Regions of the Spirit: Nature vs. Dogma in Chopin's Religious Vision." *Performance for a Lifetime: A Festschrift Honoring Dorothy Harrell Brown: Essays on Women, Religion, and the Renaissance.* New Orleans: Loyola U, 1997.
Ewell notes the influence of Chopin's early religious training , especially Catholicism's affirmation of nature as an inspirational force. Despite her ultimate rejection of organized religion and her embrace of scepticism and critical scientific thought, Chopin retained Catholicism's sacramental vision of nature. Ironically, the influence of her early religious training proved to be the source of Chopin's later affirmation of human sexuality. The essay examines Chopin's novels and short fiction, arguing that her religious vision led her to reject the patriarchal dogmas of her time as self-divisive and alienating.

D.301   Giorcelli, Cristina. "'Charlie': Travestimento e Potere." *Abito e Identita: Ricerche di Storia Letteraria e Culturale, II.* Ed. Cristina Giorcelli. Rome: Assoiciate Editrice Internazionale, 1997.

D.302   McCoy, Thorunn Ruga. "Chopin's *The Awakening.*" *Explicator* 56 (1997): 26-27.
LOC: PR1.E9
McCoy examines the importance of Edna's clothing in *The Awakening* as symbolic of socially-defined gender roles. When Edna sheds her clothing, she is symbolically embarking on the traditionally male journey of self-discovery and discarding traditional female roles.

D.303   Wolff, Cynthia Griffin. "Un-Utterable Longing: The Discourse of Feminine Sexuality in *The Awakening.*" *The Calvinist Roots of the Modern Era.* Ed. Aliki Barnstone, Michael Tomasek Manson and Carol J. Singley. Hanover, NH: UP of New England, 1997.
LOC: PS228.C34 C35 1997
Wolff argues that the exotic and non-communicative chatter of the parrot in *The Awakening*'s opening is representative of larger themes, such as: (1) the suppression of female sexuality and freedom of expression by the medical establishment and (2) the established religion of the mid-to-late 19th century. She argues that Edna is not only torn by these conflicts but also by a conflict of culture. Edna's absence of speech, especially at the beginning of the novel, is an effort to gain control of her self. Since Edna can find neither a vernacular nor an audience, her dilemma presents a study of female

nature, distorted and constricted by society. Wolff argues that Edna herself was a failure, but that Chopin's presentation of her situation was a success.
See also: D.295

1998

Books and Book Chapters

D.304   Bentey, Christopher. *Degas in New Orleans: Encounters in the Creole World of Kate Chopin and George Washington Cable.* New York: Knopf, 1998.
LOC: ND553.D3B46 1998

See D.297

D.305   Stange, Margit. *Personal Property: Wives, White Slaves, and the Market in Women.* Baltimore: Johns Hopkins UP, 1998.
LOC: PS374.W6 S74 1998

See: D.169, E.1.11, E.4.13, E.5.4, E.9.2, F.42

Journal Articles

D.306   Mahon, Robert Lee. "Beyond the Love Triangle: Trios in *The Awakening.*" *Midwest Quarterly* 39 (1998): 228-36.
LOC: AS30 .M5
Mahon argues that *The Awakening* presents Edna Pontellier's journey of self-discovery. The novel begins with, and is based upon, a love triangle, which can only exist because of "natural tensions among the three points." Edna is "pulled in three directions, yet caught between two extremes."

D.307   Toth, Emily and Per Seyersted, eds. Cheyenne Bonnell, assoc. ed.
        Kate Chopin's Private Papers. Bloomington, IN: Indiana UP, 1998.
        LOC: PS1294.C63A6 1998
          See also: A.6

1999

Books and Book Chapters

D.308   Toth, Emily. *Unveiling Kate Chopin.* Jackson, MS: UP of
Mississippi. Forthcoming 1999.
    See: B.4

Journal Articles

D.309   Bonner, Thomas, Jr. and Judith H. Bonner. "Kate Chopin's New
Orleans: A Visual Essay." *SoQ*, Forthcoming 1999.
    LOC: AS30.S658
    This illustrated essay describes a variety of structures and other
settings in and around New Orleans that play a role in Chopin's
fiction.

D.310   Dickson, Rebecca. "Kate Chopin, Mrs. Pontellier, and Narrative
Control." *SoQ*, Forthcoming 1999.
    LOC: AS30.S658
    The author notes that prior to the 20th century, most fiction written
by women revolved around an ingenue who was totally under male
control. She argues that a handful of 19th century women writers,
such as Austen, Sand, Brontë, and Jewett attempted to give their
female characters some control over their lives and stories.
However, these efforts were hindered by the rules of Western society
and the expectations of their readers. Dickson takes the example of
The Awakening and Edna Pontellier to argue that Chopin envisioned
and portrayed women in control of both their lives and narratives to

an extent unimaginable to her predecessors. By extending previous efforts to decenter the cult of the virgin, Chopin shifted the literary focus from woman's sexual status to her exploration of life and transformation of herself.

D.311   Ewell, Barbara C. "Unlinking Race and Gender: *The Awakening* as a Southern Novel." *SoQ*, Forthcoming 1999.
        LOC: AS30.S658
        Ewell examines the influence of Southern society and regional literary conventions on Chopin and *The Awakening*. Despite the fact that Chopin is not "technically a Southerner" and that "*The Awakening* doesn't always 'feel' like a Southern novel," they were both shaped by the Southern literary tradition. She argues that the fundamental instability of race and gender in Southern literature explains why Chopin and her novel appear disconnected from that tradition. Ewell examines the conventions of antebellum society, local color literature, and women's domestic fiction to explore the difficulty that Chopin would have had in untangling her tale of a woman's search for fulfillment from these cultural influences, even as she succeeded in undermining and criticizing a number of these influences.

D.312   Menke, Pamela Glenn. "The Catalyst of Color and Women's Regional Writing: *At Fault*, *Pembroke*, and *The Awakening*." *SoQ*, Forthcoming 1999.
        LOC: AS30.S658
        Menke argues that many critics have underestimated the influence of local color and women's regional writing on Chopin and her work. She examines *The Awakening* in the context of Chopin's recorded comments on local color, the influence of local color conventions on *At Fault*, and the relationship of *The Awakening* to women's regional writing, especially Mary E. Wilkins Freeman's *Pembroke*. She states that such an analysis provides a basis for reinvigorating critical discussions of other 19th century women writers, such as Freeman and Jewett. She also argues that critics who view *The Awakening* as a singular work or who "cleverly invent or discover heritages for it" understate Chopin's achievement and ignore her true literary heritage.

D.313   Taylor, Helen. "Walking through New Orleans: Kate Chopin and the Female Flâneur." *SoQ*, Forthcoming 1999.
        LOC: AS30.S658
        Taylor argues that critics tend to overlook Chopin's contributions to the literature of urban life, overemphasizing her rural and regionalist

influences. She notes the importance of New Orleans in *The Awakening* as well as in Chopin's other works, one-sixth of which are set in that city. She emphasizes that most of Chopin's life was spent in urban areas and discusses the problems that city life presented for 19th century women. She also notes that New Orleans has long been renowned as a center of sensuality and eroticism and that Chopin frequently walked — both alone and accompanied by her husband — both there and in the many other cities that she visited. Taylor also notes the importance of walking in Chopin's works and its often ambiguous and erotic nature. She states that the importance of the city of New Orleans and walks are most pronounced in *The Awakening*.

D.314   Toth, Emily. "Kate Chopin's Secret, Slippery Life Story." *SoQ*, Forthcoming 1999.
LOC: AS30.S658

This biographical essay addresses and seeks to correct the numerous myths that surround Chopin's life and works. She argues that Chopin's life and times were much more complex than is often recognized and that the influence of other women on Chopin's life is often underestimated. She concludes that the traditional focus on Chopin in terms of traditional female roles — wife, mother, extramarital lover — misses the far more important role of her intense drive and ambition in her life and literary work.

Essays in Edited Volumes

E.1 Ballenger, Grady W., Karen Cole, Katherine Kearns, and Tom Samet eds. *Perspectives on Kate Chopin: Proceedings of the Kate Chopin International Conference.* April, 1989. Northwestern State University. Natchitoches, Louisiana. Natchitoches, LA: Northwestern State UP, 1990.
LOC: PS1294.C63 K383 1989

Contents of Volume

E.1.1 Bardot, Jean. "French Creole Portraits: The Chopin Family from Natchitoches Parish."
See: E.3.1

E.1.2 Davis, Doris. "*The Awakening*: The Economics of Tension." Davis demonstrates the connection between Chopin's personal economic experience and knowledge and Edna's experience in seeking her independence. The author also points out the cultural influence of the Gilded Age on both Chopin and Edna. Edna's dilemma is a lack of understanding. She loves money "as much as any woman," but her attraction to Robert is based in part on his lack of economic drive. Davis notes the lack of female models for economic independence as a partial reason for Edna's ultimate failure to gain independence and her resulting suicide.
See also: E.3.6

E.1.3   Greer, John Thomas. "Dialogue Across the Pacific: Kate Chopin's *Awakening* and the Short Fiction of Zhang Jie."
Greer notes the increasing popularity of *The Awakening* in both the People's Republic of China and Taiwan in the 1980s. He also points out the popularity of the term "awakening" in contemporary Chinese fiction by female authors and the dual Chinese meaning of the word. The first meaning is "to rise to a higher spiritual state," and the second is "to come to realize something." Greer draws a comparison between *The Awakening* and the short fiction Zhang Jie. For example, "Love Must Not Be Forgotten," "Emerald," and "The Ark" share common themes with *The Awakening*. He also addresses the double role of women in love and marriage and the imagery common to both authors, specifically the use of birds and the sea. He suggests the possibility of common sources.

E.1.4   Gremillion, Michelle. "Edna's Awakening: A Return to Childhood."
Gremillion analyzes *The Awakening* in terms of Piaget's theory of childhood eccentricity and examines Edna's childhood reminiscences. She emphasizes Edna's false sense of power regarding the ocean, Robert, and her relationship with Léonce. She especially focuses upon the importance of the final scene of the novel and Edna's recollection of her childhood.

E.1.5   Jacobsen, Cheryl L. Rose. "Dr. Mandelet's Real Life Counterparts and Their Advice Books: Setting a Context for Edna's Revolt."
In this excerpt from her dissertation, Jacobsen analyzes 25 health manuals written for women by women during the ten-year period before and after *The Awakening* was published. Half of the writers were physicians or other health professionals. She notes that Dr. Mandelet is most understanding of Edna and places him between the traditional female-male advisors and counselors of the time. She argues that Adèle's childbirth scene and Dr. Mandelet's advice both subvert the 19th century cult of domesticity and sexual Romanticism. She also places other scenes in the novel in their historical context.

E.1.6   Jones, Suzanne W. "Place, Perception, and Identity in *The Awakening*."

Jones argues that the dichotomy of settings in *The Awakening* — for example Grand Isle and Chênière Caminada versus New Orleans — reflects two different ways of life: the spontaneous and sensual as opposed to the structured and refined. This contrast represents the conflict between Edna's social role and her personal identity. It also reflects the conflict between the Creole paradox of openness and covertly strict social roles versus the overtly constrained Kentucky Presbyterianism. These two settings allow Chopin to focus on the turn-of-the-century dilemma faced by women who attempted to deal with the psychological costs of accepting socially defined roles, as opposed to the social cost of attempting to create new roles. This conflict is shown by Edna's inability to reconcile the two divergent patterns characterized by her freedom on Grand Isle and her childish behavior in New Orleans.
See also: D.139

E.1.7   LeFew, Penelope A. "Edna Pontellier's Art and Will: The Aesthetics of Schopenhauer in Kate Chopin's *The Awakening*."
LeFew notes that both Rankin and Seyersted refer to Chopin's knowledge of Schopenhauer. She argues that the strongest evidence of this knowledge is two direct references in *At Fault* that suggest more than a passing knowledge of Schopenhauer's philosophy. She argues that *The Awakening* shows a very subtle and sophisticated understanding and expression of the major themes in Schopenhauer's *The World as Will and Representation*, which most critics regard as his major work. These themes allow a resolution of Edna's ambiguous and unfocused search for the unknown, the strange and evocative power of Mlle. Reisz's art, and Edna's suicide. These three themes represent Chopin's presentation of Schopenhauer's concept of the will.

E.1.8   Manders, Eunice. "The Wretched Freeman."
Manders argues that Chopin's progressive depiction of her female characters did not extend to her black characters. She cites Starling Brown's stereotype of the "wretched freeman" in her analysis of "The Bênitou's Slave," "Odalie Misses Mass," "Tante Cat'rinette," and "Nég Créol." She notes, however, that despite Chopin's acceptance of post-bellum stereotypes in place in the sub-genre of plantation fiction, she more well developed intricate black characters than did George Washington Cable, Grace King or Ruth McEnery

Stuart. By primarily investigating human nature, especially in the latter two stories mentioned above, Chopin adds a psychological dimension unusual in this genre.

E.1.9   Rowe, John Carlos. "The Economics of the Body in Kate Chopin's *The Awakening*."
See: E.3.12

E.1.10   Seidel, Kathryn Lee. "Art is an Unnatural Act: Homoeroticism, Art and Mademoiselle Reisz in *The Awakening*."
See: D.229

E.1.11   Stange, Margit. "Personal Property: Exchange Value and the Female Self in *The Awakening*."
See: D.169, E.4.13, E.5.4, E.9.2

E.1.12   Vanlandingham, Phyllis. "Kate Chopin and Editors: 'A Singular Class of Men.'"
Vanlandingham examines Chopin's relationship with her editors in terms of her naïveté and amateur's enthusiasm, arguing that the independence resulting from this flawed relationship led to her originality, especially as evidenced in *The Awakening*. This originality stands in contrast to her better-connected contemporaries, such as Grace King.

E.2 Bloom, Harold, ed. *Kate Chopin: Modern Critical Views*. New York: Chelsea, 1987.
LOC: PS1294.C63 K38 1987

Contents of Volume

E.2.1   Dyer, Joyce Coyne. "Gouvernail, Kate Chopin's Sensitive Bachelor."
Dyer analyzes recurring characters in Chopin's short fiction and *The Awakening*, especially Gouvernail, and takes what is known of him from the short stories to explain the significance of his appearance at the final dinner party in *The Awakening*. She notes that the importance of the Swinburne lines quoted are only apparent in light of Gouvernail's appearance in the short fiction. Dyer argues that Gouvernail highlights themes, establishes moods, subtly indicates the

direction of Chopin's art and philosophy, and then disappears
from the later fiction, which usually concludes with happy
endings.
See also: D.73

E.2.2   Dyer, Joyce Coyne. "Kate Chopin's Sleeping Bruties."
         Dyer discusses the abundance of female awakenings in both
         the short fiction and *The Awakening* but also notes Chopin's
         sensitivity to her male characters. She argues that Chopin's
         true subject was human nature, not just women's nature.
         See also: D.74

E.2.3   Eble, Kenneth. "A Forgotten Novel." Rpt. from *Western
         Humanities Review* 10.3 (1956).
         Eble argues that *The Awakening* was advanced in theme and
         technique for its day and cites it as evidence that regional
         writers can go beyond the limits of regional material. He
         regards Edna as "an American Bovary" and praises the
         "insightful questioning" of Rankin's biography. Eble
         examines the symbolism of the sea, the sand, the sun, and the
         sky. He concludes by calling for the recovery and
         preservation of this work.

E.2.4   Gardiner, Elaine. "'Ripe Figs': Kate Chopin in Miniature."
         Gardiner deals with a single brief sketch to show how in 300
         words, Chopin demonstrates the three major techniques that
         culminate in *The Awakening*: establishing contrasts, using
         nature imagery, and using cyclical plot patterns.
         See also: D.83

E.2.5   Gilbert, Sandra. "The Second Coming of Aphrodite: Kate
         Chopin's Fantasy of Desire."
         Gilbert notes that the dinner party near the end of *The
         Awakening* has been largely ignored by critics, yet argues that
         the scene is structurally complex and that its symbolism
         provides insight into the novel as a whole. She argues that
         Chopin presents a feminist and matriarchal myth of the
         second coming of Aphrodite/Venus as an alternative to the
         masculinist and patriarchal myth of Jesus. The dinner party
         plays a crucial role in this new mythology. She also argues
         that *The Awakening* mingles Naturalism and Symbolism in
         the same way and because of the same continental influences
         seen in the works of Moore and Joyce. This combines with
         the Realistic technique and feminist perspective with which

she is more commonly associated, reminiscent of the works of Virginia Woolf. She further argues that the tension between Realistic and mythic elements in the novel serves to complicate and illuminate the work.
See also: D.95, E.5.1

E.2.6   Lant, Kathleen Margaret. "The Siren of Grand Isle: Adèle's Role in *The Awakening*."
Rather than describing Edna's awakenings in the context of her relationships with the men in her life, Lant argues that it is Adèle who initially awakens Edna, and who also sends her to her death when Edna realizes that she will never be able to reconcile the "inner life which questions" with the "outward existence which conforms." Adèle is identified with the classical sirens, as she both "lures and imperils Edna, a human counterpart to the seductive sea that beckons to Edna's soul." She first awakens Edna near the sea, enticing her to speak of her childhood and recognize the missing elements in her life. Adèle's lying-in seals Edna's fate, reminding her that while she may be able to escape from societal expectations, she can not escape the fact that she is a biological mother with all of the accompanying responsibilities. Her remaining choice is to reject her biological ties by also renouncing her physical self, thus leading to her swim into the Gulf.
See also: D.110

E.2.7   Ringe, Donald A. "Cane River World: Kate Chopin's *At Fault* and Related Stories." Rpt. from *Studies in American Fiction* 3 (1975): 157-66.
LOC: PS370.S87
Ringe examines *At Fault* and Chopin's short fiction in terms of their presentation of the social and historical world of Northwest Louisiana during the post-Civil War/Reconstruction period, rather than in terms of the 20th century or themes from *The Awakening*. He argues that the Cane River World that Chopin created was a "coherent one."

E.2.8   Rosowski, Susan J. "The Novel of Awakening."
Rosowski looks at the female "novel of awakening," contrasting it with male *Bildungsroman*. She defines the "awakening" novel in terms of numerous 19th-and-20th century works from both sides of the Atlantic, including *The Awakening* in her analysis. Rosowski argues that prior to her

study, the "definitions and examples that follow the [examination of the *bildungsroman*] are notably masculine, omitting developments of this theme in literature by and about women." She suggests that the *bildungsroman* has been used in literature in two distinctly different ways: the "novel of apprenticeship" which largely applies to male protagonists, and the "novel of awakening" which is more relevant to female characters. She argues that these two types of *bildungsroman* share common traits: they recount the "attempts of a sensitive protagonist to learn the nature of the world, discover its meaning and pattern and acquire a philosophy of life." The end result of awakening for female protagonists is that they have in fact awakened "to limitations." Edna Pontellier experiences this "reality of limitation" and finds it unacceptable. She then "completes the process of awakening by placing her romantic dreams for escape in the context of time and change," and she makes a "final attempt to escape."
See also: D.55, D.93

E.2.9   Wolff, Cynthia Griffin. "Kate Chopin and the Fiction of Limits: 'Désirée's Baby.'"
Wolff examines "Désirée's Baby" in terms of its ambiguity and the scattered critical response it received. She concludes that in the context of Chopin's complete work, the piece is her most "vivid and direct."
See also: D.43

E.2.10   Ziff, Larzer. "An Abyss of Inequality."
Ziff compares Chopin's techniques, for example, sudden reversal of situation, to the works of Guy de Maupassant. He also relates Edna's situation in the novel to Chopin's life.
See also: D.46

E.3   Boren, Lynda S. and Sara deSaussure Davis, eds. *Kate Chopin Reconsidered: Beyond the Bayou*. Baton Rouge: Louisiana State UP, 1992.
LOC: PS1294 C63 K385 1992

Contents of Volume

E.3.1   Bardot, Jean. "French Creole Portraits: The Chopin Family from Natchitoches Parish."
Bardot draws on new biographical sources from Louisiana

and France to shed light on Oscar Chopin's family before and during the American Civil War. He draws predominantly on letters beginning with the immigration of Oscar Chopin's father to America. He observes that characters reminiscent of Kate Chopin's in-laws are represented in *At Fault* and her Cane River short stories.
See also: E.1.1

E.3.2   Barker, Deborah E. "The Awakening of Female Artistry." Barker cites numerous critics in arguing that the painting of the nude female form represents the artistic appropriation and commodification of women. She states that in *The Awakening*, Chopin explores the artistic, sexual, social, and religious appropriation of women. Edna's attempts to paint Adèle without objectifying her bring forth Edna's growing sensuality and dissatisfaction with the social and religious restrictions placed on her as a wife and mother, leading directly to her moment of awakening. Edna views Adèle as both a sensual/sexual figure and as a religious icon – the Madonna. As the tension between Edna's roles as mother and artist increase, her growth as an artist mirrors her personal growth.

E.3.3   Black, Martha Fodaski. "The Quintessence of Chopinism." Black takes exception to Fox-Genovese's argument that Chopin had little interest in the "woman question" or other social problems. She cites textual evidence from *The Awakening* to show Chopin's challenge to conventional assumptions about women's sexuality and gender roles. She also argues that the works of Henrik Ibsen, George Bernard Shaw, and Elizabeth Cady Stanton exerted an influence on Chopin's writing. Black states that *The Awakening* provides a new feminist heroine on which women could model their lives. *The Awakening* exposes the gulf between the illusions and realities of Chopin's characters, thus presenting Shaw's arguments in fictional form.

E.3.4   Blythe, Anne M. "Kate Chopin's 'Charlie.'" Blythe argues that "Charlie" is not only one of the longest, but also one of the strongest and most moving of Chopin's short stories. She asserts that the piece has been either ignored or misread since its appearance in 1969, particularly by Per Seyersted and Freudian critics who have followed. She attacks both Seyersted's reading and Freudian interpretations of the story in general, arguing that the tale is one of the growth of a young woman of unusual potential who succeeds in life. Blythe also argues that Chopin wrote much of herself into this character, and that the story deserves a place of honor in pre-World War I American fiction.

E.3.5   Boren, Lynda S. "Taming the Sirens: Self-Possession and the Strategies of Art in Kate Chopin's *The Awakening*."
Boren notes Chopin's musical interest and talent and argues that music dictates the moods, themes, and structure of *The Awakening*. She also argues, recounting the end of the novel, that Edna drowns in a sea of sensations, sound being the one that finally overwhelms her. The incongruous mixture of sounds of the end of the novel represent a resolution of discord with harmony between Edna's birth into a patriarchal world and her conflict with the forces of nature, neither of which could confine her passionate soul. She also explores the musical themes and symbolism of the novel in detail.

E.3.6   Davis, Doris. "*The Awakening*: The Economics of Tension."
Davis notes that Chopin skillfully handled economic issues in *The Awakening*, making them a vital part of the novel. She contrasts *The Awakening* with Dreiser's *Sister Carrie*, arguing that Edna's search for independence involves an abandonment of economic status rather than a pursuit of acquisitions. The author suggests that the economic tenor of *The Awakening* may derive from Chopin's own economic concerns as the young widow of a failed business man. She also notes Seyersted's argument that Chopin began writing primarily for financial reasons and concludes by examining economic issues in *At Fault* and some of Chopin's shorter fiction.
See also: E.1.2

E.3.7   Davis, Sara deSaussure. "Chopin's Movement Toward Universal Myth."
Davis examines *A Vocation and a Voice* as a collection and argues that it demonstrates Chopin's shift in style from the bayou myth toward a more universal one, reminiscent of Greek mythology. She notes Chopin's difficulty in publishing these stories individually and argues that the difficulty was due to the similar themes, symbols, and psychological realities that led to the negative reception of *The Awakening*. She notes the mythic quality developed in

these stories that is fully realized in *The Awakening*, which allow escape from 19th century social and literary restrictions. She also notes the importance of dreams in the stories from this collection and argues that they develop themes of force versus relaxation that are important in *The Awakening*.

E.3.8   Ellis, Nancy S. "Insistent Refrains and Self-Discovery: Accompanied Awakenings in Three Stories by Kate Chopin." Ellis notes the power of music to trigger emotional awakenings as seen in *The Awakening* and examines "With the Violin" in which music saves a man from suicide. She also examines "After the Winter" and "At Chênière Caminada," in which notes from an organ awaken and transform the lives of two men. She concludes that music is both ordinary and extraordinary, secular and sacred, playing thematic and symbolic roles in Chopin's male and female characters.

E.3.9   Ewell, Barbara C. "Kate Chopin and the Dream of Female Selfhood." Ewell argues that Chopin viewed her writing as an exploration of life. As a woman writer, she had to confront the selfless nature of women in a patriarchal society, and Chopin's fiction is an attempt to show what it is to be a female self and how that self is defeated by what Emerson termed "the least authentic and true forces in society." Ewell describes *The Awakening* as an ambivalent triumph – combining the impossibility of the American dream for woman as Other, with the hope for a self not wholly the subject or object of desire.

E.3.10   Jacobs, Dorothy H. "*The Awakening*: A Recognition of Confinement." Jacobs argues that *The Awakening* is a novel of painful self-recognition in which Edna realizes that a world apparently open to her potential is in fact closed to her strongest desires and to her will. She compares Edna's situation to that of Lear and Oedipus and finds analogues to Edna in Ibsen's *A Doll's House*, *Ghosts*, and *Hedda Gabler*. The protagonists of Ibsen's domestic fiction share with Edna a questioning and defiance of male ordained duties which is carried out in solitude. Edna is a tragic hero, as she pursues her solitary vision of life to its conclusion and to her own destruction.

E.3.11 Joslin, Katherine. "Finding the Self at Home: Chopin's *The Awakening* and Cather's *The Professor's House*."
Joslin argues that Cather's *The Professor's House* is an unacknowledged literary response to *The Awakening*, but Cather's work reverses the gender roles in the conflict of the search for self versus domestic obligations. The primary difference between the protagonists is that Cather provides a *deus ex machina* to prevent the suicide of her protagonist. The author argues that both authors are skeptical of romance and that neither offers much hope of escape from the depression, alienation, and despair of domesticity. Both novels suggest we must find ourselves at home, if at all.

E.3.12 Rowe, John Carlos. "The Economics of the Body in Kate Chopin's *The Awakening*."
Rowe presents a Marxist analysis of *The Awakening*, focusing on Edna's moments of lethargy as evidence of her alienation from herself and her labor. He especially focuses on references to Edna's hands in terms of Friederic Engels analysis of labor and society. He also draws on the works of Marx and Scarry. He focuses on Léonce's role as a speculator to highlight the socioeconomic theme underlying the novel. He also uses Gilbert's analysis of the Aphrodite myth to tie patriarchal, economic, and ecclesiastical domination together. Robert and Alcée are the same as Léonce in the sense that their lives are focused on economic piracy, gambling, and speculation. Edna's resulting alienation from herself and her labor support either of the conventional views regarding the ambiguous final scene of the novel.
See also: E.1.9

E.3.13 Thomas, Heather Kirk. "'What Are the Prospects for the Book?': Rewriting a Woman's Life."
Thomas attacks a long-standing biographical myth – that the harsh critical reception of *The Awakening* led to a depression that ended Chopin's literary career. Circumstantial evidence supports the claim that increasingly poor health ended Chopin's prolific literary production. She notes correspondence indicating a physical decline beginning in the summer of 1899 and provides evidence of migraine headaches and eye problems prior to that time. The focus on illness in Chopin's post *Awakening* literary production mirrored her own declining health, and after *The Awakening*, Chopin reverted to her earlier, more market-oriented style in

an attempt to regain her literary position as she anticipated death.

E.3.14   Toth, Emily. "Kate Chopin Thinks Back Through Her Mothers: Three Stories by Kate Chopin."

Toth disputes claims that Chopin's work is either objective or non-autobiographical and especially takes exception to male critics of the early 1970's who claim that Chopin's work was universal rather than feminist. She notes that Rankin missed Chopin's irony and critical statements and in general, sugar-coated her life. Toth also points out that Seyersted was hampered by his New Critical training in his analysis of Chopin. She discusses the autobiographical nature of the characters in Chopin's short fiction and the influence of Chopin's female ancestors on her fiction. Toth especially notes Chopin's use of irony and her feminist perception of marriage to demonstrate these autobiographical characteristics.

E.4   Kaur, Iqbal, ed. *Kate Chopin's The Awakening: Critical Essays.* New Delhi: Deep & Deep, 1995.
LOC: PS1294 C63 A64355 1995

Contents of Volume

E.4.1   Amin, Amina. "Kate Chopin's *The Awakening*: Sex-role Liberation or Sexual Liberation?"

Amin examines *The Awakening* in the context of women's right to passion. The author cites examples from Ovid to Mary Wollstonecraft and notes the many women writers who dealt frankly with the theme of adultery. Amin argues that Chopin was the first American female writer to awaken to a sense of her own identity and to create a female protagonist who not only awakens to her sexuality, but boldly states it.

E.4.2   Bande, Usha. "From Conflict to Suicide — A Feminist Approach to Kate Chopin's *The Awakening*."

Bande applies the theories of Karen Horney and Marcia Weskott to *The Awakening* and also examines the novel's contemporary social background. She concludes that neither Kate Chopin nor Edna Pontellier can be described as feminists, but that both may be considered path-finders for future generations of women.

E.4.3   Battawala, Zareen. "The Long and Winding Road: An
         Analysis of Kate Chopin's *The Awakening*."
         Battawala argues that *The Awakening* was among the earliest
         feminist novels and that its issues remain valid even a century
         later. The author argues that Edna fails in her search for her
         own identity not only because of social and cultural
         constraints but because of her own failures of character and
         her irresponsibility. She argues that Edna's awakening is
         incomplete, and that she fails to realize her potential, thus her
         experiences in the novel should be viewed as an incomplete
         journey.

E.4.4   Bharathi, V. "The Existential Dilemma of Edna Pontellier in
         Kate Chopin's *The Awakening*."
         Bharathi examines *The Awakening*, drawing on the
         framework described by Rita Felski in "The Novel of Self-
         Discovery: A Necessary Fiction?" and existential philosophy,
         especially the work of Heidegger and Sartre. She describes
         Edna's progress from a state of frustration and despair to a
         sense of alienation and total acceptance of responsibility for
         her actions. Edna's suicide then becomes the ultimate act of
         self expression in a restrictive and oppressive society. She
         notes Sartre's observation that death is the only thing that can
         be done by oneself, and she refers to Heidegger's notion of the
         "moment before death," a time at which "past, present and
         future are gathered into the unity of the resolute self."
         Bharathi ties these existential notions to Edna's steady
         withdrawal from social interaction, then sexual interaction,
         and finally from life itself, leading to what she calls "a fresh
         interpretation of the novel."

E.4.5   Block, Tina. "Self-Reflexive and Impressionistic Feminism of
         Edna Pontellier in Kate Chopin's *The Awakening*."
         Block argues that Edna is neither entirely the victim of
         patriarchal oppression nor of her own socially constructed
         consciousness. Her failure to find a place to enjoy her
         contradictory desire for both social autonomy and social
         relations thus leads to her alienation and death. She argues
         that Edna's predicament illustrates a situation common to
         women in the late 19th century.

E.4.6   Gopalan, Rajalakshmi. "Kate Chopin's *The Awakening*: The
         Complexity of Edna Pontellier."
         Gopalan argues that the central issue of *The Awakening* is the

same as that of *At Fault* — how does anyone, especially a woman, achieve personal integrity in a world of constraints? Chopin examines this question in the figure of Edna, illustrating both compromise and failure in the effort to establish the relationship between the self and society. Chopin does this using familiar and conventional motifs and styles.

E.4.7   Gosh, Nibir K., "Kate Chopin and *The Awakening* of Eve." Gosh notes the similarity of *The Awakening* to Ibsen's *A Doll's House* and argues that *The Awakening* anticipated attitudes later articulated in *The Feminine Mystique* by Betty Friedan and *Sexual Politics* by Kate Millet. The author argues that this prophetic quality is the novel's true significance and explains its popularity in the late 20th century.

E.4.8   Jacob, Susan. "Fate and Feminism in Kate Chopin's *The Awakening*." Jacob notes the contradictory readings of *The Awakening* seen in previous critical works and argues that they arise from Chopin's contradictory portrayal of Edna — sympathetic on the one hand, yet portraying her as often insensitive to herself and others and often out of her depth. She notes the resemblance of *The Awakening* to George Eliot's *The Mill on the Floss* in the circumstances and fates of their protagonists.

E.4.9   Juneja, Punim. "Suicide as Metaphor: Edna's Search for Identity." Juneja argues that the question of Edna's suicide is too complex to be answered by previous critics and places it in the context of the search for identity. She notes Chopin's positive approach to Edna's drives and aspirations, making the comparison to Tolstoy's *Anna Karenina*. She argues that because of her place in society, Edna's only means to preserve her selfhood is to destroy it.

E.4.10   Paul, Premila. "The Sea Holds No Terrors: Search and Beyond in *The Awakening*." Paul notes that Chopin's work revolved around women who were unconventional and ahead of their time in terms of social codes and female behavior. She argues that *The*

Awakening is not a "mere" feminist novel, but that it presents a non-gender specific view of the need and struggle for self-realization.

E.4.11   Poovalingam, N. "Artist's Unrest and Arrested Growth: Edna Pontellier in *The Awakening*."
Poovalingam argues that Edna's awakening is not the dawning of a new consciousness but a realization of the futility of her search for ever-illusive sexual gratification. The author also argues that the ambiguous ending of the novel is an arbitrary and inadequate attempt to bring it to a rapid close.

E.4.12   Ramamoorthi, Parasuram. "The Self that Dares and Defies: A Study of Kate Chopin's *The Awakening*."
Ramamoorthi argues that Edna's suicide is not escapist but is a final act of assertion based on the self-knowledge she gains after "falling in love with Arobin." She states that Edna's quest for self-realization "unravels the pleasure of the soul through the sensual pleasures of the body." Edna's knowledge forces her to journey into a world of her own through suicide.

E.4.13   Stange, Margit. "Personal Property: Exchange Value and the Female Self in *The Awakening*."
Stange bases her argument on the sexual meaning of the term self-ownership as used by 19th century American feminists such as Elizabeth Cady Stanton. The essay focuses on the symbolism of ownership and wealth in *The Awakening*, arguing that the only way for Edna to exercise self-ownership, given the structure of society, was to become a free agent in the sexual marketplace and to withhold herself from motherhood. Chopin's novel suggests that what a woman owns in owning herself is her sexual exchange value and the resulting freedom to either withhold or give herself sexually. In this context, Adèle Ratignolle serves as an example of how a woman can be both sensual and motherly simultaneously, thus highlighting Edna's inability to reconcile those roles in the context of Creole society.
See also: D.169, E.1.11, E.5.4, E.9.2, F.42

E.4.14   Trikha, Manorama. "Kate Chopin's *The Awakening*: A Quest of 'Sybil.'"
Trikha states that *The Awakening* is noteworthy for its poetic

style and regional flavor. She argues that the novel has a dual structure: (a) one based on the temporal succession of external events and (b) an internal structure of symbols and metaphors that contributes to the central themes of the novel. These elements convey Edna's successful quest for identity to Chopin's readers.

E.4.15   Vevaina, Coomi S. "Puppets Must Perform or Perish: A Feminist Archetypal Analysis of Kate Chopin's *The Awakening*."
Vevaina argues that since women are puppets of the patriarchy, only Feminist Archetypal Theory and analysis can disentangle female psyches from the larger male-dominated culture. She argues that *The Awakening* is an archetypal novel and examines it and its female characters by means of Feminist Archetypal Theory.

E.4.16   Viswanath, Ganga. "To Your Own Self Be True: A Study of Edna Pontellier in *The Awakening*."
Voswanath argues that the novel depicts the feminist leanings of the author and compares the lives of Kate Chopin and Edna Pontellier. She offers a brief critical history of the novel, and states that it is autobiographical in both its characterization of Edna and in her ultimate fate.

E.4.17   Wasson, Leslie. "*The Awakening* and 'The Yellow Wallpaper': Misunderstood and Rediscovered."
Wasson examines the backgrounds and motives of the authors, the content of the works, and contemporary critical reviews to study their reception. She argues that both were misunderstood for a variety of reasons and thus were not widely read, having only recently met with favor.

E.5   Keesey, Donald, ed. *Contexts for Criticism*. Mountain View, CA: Mayfield, 1994.
LOC: PN81 C745 1993

Contents of Volume

E.5.1   Gilbert, Sandra. "The Second Coming of Aphrodite: Kate Chopin's Fantasy of Desire."
See: D.95, E.2.5

E.5.2   May, John R. "Local Color in *The Awakening*." Rpt. from
         Southern Review 6 (1970): 1031-40.
         May argues that the critical focus on Edna's sexual
         awakening misses the larger point: the universal themes of
         human desire for freedom and the resistance of externally
         imposed limits. Ironically, these themes are conveyed by the
         local color elements which are generally dismissed by critics.
         He sees the local color novel as one, such as *The Awakening*,
         in which the setting is integral to thematic development, not
         incidental to it.

E.5.3   Shaw, Pat. "Putting Audience in Its Place: Psychosexuality and
         Perspective Shifts in *The Awakening*."
         Shaw argues that the key to *The Awakening* is in subtle shifts
         of point-of-view. As the novel moves from "scientific" to
         "poetic" reality, readers increasingly identify with Edna's
         psychological and physical states. Chopin's narrative
         technique is similar to that of James Joyce and William
         Faulkner in its perhaps unconscious sophistication. Edna's
         suicide becomes positive not only because it is a symbolic
         rebirth, but because the reader accompanies Edna on her final
         swim and because of the paradoxical irony of juxtaposing
         Edna's complex character with Robert's simplistic one.
         See also: D.180

E.5.4   Stange, Margit. "Personal Property: Exchange Value and the
         Female Self in *The Awakening*."
         See: D.169, E.1.11, E.4.13, E.9.2, F.42

E.5.5   Walker, Nancy. "Feminist or Naturalist: The Social Context of
         Kate Chopin's *The Awakening*."
         Walker argues that *The Awakening* is not a feminist novel
         and that Edna simply awakens to her sensual nature, unaware
         of and unconcerned with the reasons for her actions. The
         Louisiana Creole setting and Naturalistic conventions explain
         Edna's development without necessitating a resort to
         feminism or psychoanalytic analysis.
         See also: D.57

E.5.6   Wolff, Cynthia Griffin. "Thanatos and Eros: Kate Chopin's
         The Awakening." Rpt. from *American Quarterly* 25 (1973):
         449-71.
         Wolff argues that the power of the novel is not in its
         anticipation of feminism or its anticipation of later authors as

many would argue, but in its "ruthless fidelity to the
disintegration of Edna's character." She then proceeds with a
psychological evaluation of Edna based on the works of
Sigmund Freud, R.D. Laing and Helenè Deutsch.
See also: E.9.4

E.5.7   Yaeger, Patricia S. "'A Language Which Nobody Understood:'
Emancipatory Strategies in *The Awakening*."
"Rather than the usual feminist analysis," this essay focuses
on Edna's sexual awakening. Yaeger looks at the language
in *The Awakening*, indicating that Edna seeks but does not
possess. Using Lyotard's *Les Differend* as a tool to analyze
Chopin's work, Yaeger applies his idea that "something that
asks to be put into sentences and suffers the wrong of not
being able to be at that moment." Edna's relationships with
men are productive as she seeks a language register of her
own. Even in her own death, relationships point to
discrepancies in the existing social orders as well as other
possible orders.
See also: D.145, E.9.5

E.6 Koloski, Bernard, ed. *Approaches To Teaching Chopin's The Awakening.*
New York: MLA, 1988.
LOC: PS1294 C63 A6433 1988

Contents of Volume

E.6.1   Bauer, Dale Marie and Andrew M. Lakritz. *"The Awakening*
and the Woman Question."
Bauer and Lakritz look at *The Awakening* in terms of
Bakhtinian social and cultural dialogue, engaging students in
a discussion of Chopin's themes and philosophical and
scientific views of women and their place in society. They
also suggest having students examine what Chopin's era and
the modern era have in common, how they differ, and how
newly-emerging attitudes affect the reading of her works.

E.6.2   Bonner, Thomas, Jr. *"The Awakening* in an American
Literature Survey Course."
Bonner gives a brief history of trends in teaching American
literature. He examines *The Awakening* in terms of local
color, Realism, and Romanticism, examining it as a bridge
between Romanticism and Realism. He lists passages for
discussion and relates them to other major American authors

and works. He suggests discussing Chopin's treatment of
Southern and Creole women in order to raise feminist themes.

E.6.3 Dyer, Joyce. "Symbolism and Imagery in *The Awakening*."
Dyer focuses on psychological symbolism as the key to
understanding *The Awakening*. She compares Chopin's work
to that of Melville, Ibsen, and Whitman and also examines
the importance of Chopin's musical references.

E.6.4 Ewell, Barbara C. *"The Awakening* in a Course on Women in
Literature."
Ewell relates Chopin's fiction to her ten years of experience
teaching women's studies to a variety of students. She
provides lists of other texts for use in such a course and
discusses what different types of students can gain from *The
Awakening*.

E.6.5 Fox-Genovese, Elizabeth. *"The Awakening* in the Context of
the Experience, Culture, and Values of Southern Women."
Fox-Genovese examines the historical influences on both
Chopin and the novel, in particular, Southern views as
opposed to Northern sensibilities about the Civil War, race,
class, and women's rights. She focuses these issues in terms
of the personal, rather than the larger sociological
perspective.

E.6.6 Franklin, Rosemary F. "Edna as Psyche: The Self and the
Unconscious."
Franklin examines *The Awakening* in terms of the Eros and
Psyche myth, as interpreted by Jungian theorist Erich
Neumann to broaden Edna's individual struggle to the
universal and tragic. She includes an appendix with an
archetypal interpretation of the myth and outlines how
Chopin's novel follows this myth.

E.6.7 George, E. Laurie. "Women's Language in *The Awakening*."
George's essay is geared to introductory courses and courses
for non-majors. She provides an outline for teaching *The
Awakening* in five days and suggests summarizing review
essays and research articles that reflect both American and
French feminisms, along with linguistic theory. She
examines male and female language in *The Awakening* along

with female-to-female language and male-to-female language. She provides numerous examples of resources for these topics.

E.6.8   Jacobs, Jo Ellen. "*The Awakening* in a Course on Philosophical Ideas in Literature."
Jacobs discusses Chopin's work in the context of a course for advanced English and philosophy majors. She outlines a four week schedule of background reading, along with other novels. She suggests that authors such as Plato, Sartre, or Wilson may be used. She provides an example, based on Rollo May's *Love and Will* and provides a detailed outline of how to read *The Awakening* and examine its characters in terms of May's ideas.

E.6.9   Jones, Suzanne W. "Two Settings: The Islands and the City."
Jones attempts to focus on Chopin's ambivalence of character, narration and language. Using chapters 1-16, set on Grand Isle and the surrounding islands, and the rest of the novel, set in New Orleans, she demonstrates the dichotomy between the inhibited Victorian woman and the liberated woman, who is a victim of her own impulsiveness. Edna represents the inhibited woman while she is on the islands but becomes the liberated woman when she returns to New Orleans. Jones also examines the conflict between societal roles and personal identity.

E.6.10   Koloski, Bernard. "Materials, Including Editions, Further Reading for Students, Further Reading for Teachers, and Aids to Teaching."
See: D.152

E.6.11   Lattin, Patricia Hopkins. "Childbirth and Motherhood in *The Awakening* and in "Athénaïse."
Lattin suggests studying *The Awakening* out of isolation and teaching it along with "Athénaïse" to provide a reference point for the themes of childbirth and motherhood. She introduces the social context of Chopin's fiction and discusses the recurrent characters. She also gives an introduction to the concept of intertextuality, focusing specifically on how to read fiction in an intertextual context.

E.6.12   Morris, Ann R. and Margaret M. Dunn. "*The Awakening* in an Introductory Literature Course."

The essay illustrates how to place *The Awakening* into a three-week segment dealing with a literary research paper for a first-year literature course. They use the Norton Critical Edition of *The Awakening* and the essays included in it as sources for assignments. They also provide a week-by-week outline of topics and assignments for the course.

E.6.13   Papke, Mary E. "Chopin's Stories of Awakening."
Papke suggests teaching the short fiction first, in order to show how to read Chopin and to introduce the themes that occur in *The Awakening*. She discusses using "The Story of an Hour," "Regret," "Athénaïse," "A Pair of Silk Stockings," "Her Letters," and "An Egyptian Cigarette." The author discusses how these works relate to each other and to *The Awakening*.

E.6.14   Rankin, Elizabeth. "A Reader-Response Approach."
Rankin suggests having students stop reading halfway through the novel and predict its end. She then suggests charting these predictions in terms of a tree diagram, and using the diagrams as a springboard for discussion. She then uses a close reading to show the extent to which the predictions are in the reader, as opposed to in the text.

E.6.15   Rogers, Nancy. "Stylistic Categories in *The Awakening*."
Rogers outlines a course for advanced undergraduates in textual linguistics or stylistics. She focuses on chapter 1, but also includes passages from the rest of the novel. She notes that *The Awakening* is superficially simple and uninteresting. She specifically examines Chopin's use of lexical and grammatical categories, figures of speech, narrative point of view, and speech acts. She draws largely on the work of Leech and Short for background information in discourse analysis and stylistics.

E.6.16   Rosowski, Susan J. "*The Awakening* as a Prototype of the Novel of Awakening."
Rosowski presents *The Awakening* as the prototypical novel of awakening and compares and contrasts it with the traditional *bildungsroman*. She also examines the fairy-tale qualities of *The Awakening* and ties it to other literature about women.

E.6.17   Skaggs, Peggy. "*The Awakening's* Relationship with American Regionalism, Romanticism, Realism, and Naturalism."

Skaggs examines Chopin's fiction in terms of the American literary traditions indicated in the essay's title. She places Chopin's short fiction in the context of representative authors and critics of these movements. She also provides a list of suggested topics for discussion, and suggestions for further reading.

E.6.18   Solomon, Barbara H. "Characters as Foils to Edna."
Solomon looks at Adèle and Mademoiselle Reisz as foils to Edna who serve three purposes. They allow the reader to compare and contrast Edna to other women. She uses these comparisons to show the range of female possibilities at a time when all women were viewed as being similar in instinct and interests. Solomon uses the exhortations of Adèle and Mlle. Reisz to Edna to show her problems as unsolvable, given her environment, era, and newly-discovered identity.

E.6.19   Sweet-Hurd, Evelyn. "*The Awakening* in a Research and Composition Course."
Sweet-Hurd suggests *The Awakening* as a topic in research and composition courses, so lectures and discussion can enhance student work. She suggests that *The Awakening* may be used for either an extensive library research project or to teach close readings of a text. She provides a list of topics from historical and psychological to contrastive character studies.

E.6.20   Thornton, Lawrence. "Edna as Icarus: A Mythic Issue."
Thornton attempts to provide critical distance in the study of *The Awakening*, noting that students usually identify too strongly with Edna. He uses the Icarus myth as context for a psychological study of Edna and ties Chopin's novel to the tradition of psychological Realism, in terms of Edna's romantic desires.

E.6.21   Toth, Emily. "A New Biographical Approach."
Toth provides a thorough biography of Chopin, focusing on how the biographical data relates to *The Awakening* and the short fiction.

E.6.22   Walker, Nancy. "The Historical and Cultural Setting."
Walker provides the historical background of the Creole culture, New Orleans, Grand Isle, and Catholicism versus other Southern religions and cultures. She also examines the

politics of place in order to frame Edna Pontellier in the proper social context.

E.7   Martin, Wendy, ed. *New Essays on The Awakening.* Cambridge: Cambridge UP, 1988.
       LOC: PS1294.C63 A6436 1988

Contents of Volume

E.7.1   Delbanco, Andrew. "The Half-Life of Edna Pontellier."
          Delbanco argues that one reason *The Awakening* has found a modern audience is its appeal to the leftist "subversive" and the rightist "curatorial" that are both current expressions of antipathy toward centralized authority and power. He argues that *The Awakening* thus could be reduced to neither a feminist critique of patriarchal authority nor a reactionary renunciation of cultural change, though it might be read as either. He examines the question of "male attenuation" in both *The Awakening* and other contemporary women's fiction. The author compares *The Awakening* to "Désirée's Baby," in the sense that Edna's attempts to "pass as a male" are similar to those of racial passing in the works of authors such as Charles W. Chestnutt.

E.7.2   Gilmore, Michael T. "Revolt Against Nature: The Problematic Modernism of *The Awakening*."
          Gilmore argues that Edna's "revolt" must be viewed in the context of the American cultural crisis related to changes in the perception of nature. He notes that society viewed the "New Woman" as symptomatic of a loss of "natural values" tied to the close of the frontier and the growth of urbanization and industrialization. The title, *The Awakening,* would have been taken by Chopin's contemporaries as promising a traditional, religious theme. *The Awakening* marks a turn toward the anti-Naturalist, self-referential agenda of Modernism. The author also asserts the similarity of Chopin's work to that of the impressionists and its conflict with the *laissez-faire* ideology of the time. He examines similar trends in literature and other arts along with the approach of Modernist themes, but emphasizes Chopin's ultimate deference to nature and Realism.

E.7.3   Giorcelli, Cristina. "Edna's Wisdom: A Transitional and Numinous Merging."

Giorcelli notes the ambiguity of the ending of *The Awakening* in the sense that it is both "open" and "technically circular" and that it escapes easy classification in terms of Realism, Naturalism, or Symbolism. These and other dichotomies derive from Edna's liminal psychology that expresses both sides of a contrasting pair, for example, between sleep and wakefulness. Thus, neither Edna, nor the novel itself, fit into traditional structural categories. Giorcelli also explores the relationship of *The Awakening* to the myths of Persephone, Artemis, and Athene as aspects of femininity. She concludes with an examination of the possible influences of Nietszche and Emerson.

E.7.4   Showalter, Elaine. "Tradition and the Female Talent: *The Awakening as a Solitary Book.*"

Showalter notes the influence of Maupassant on Chopin and argues that *The Awakening* is an account of Edna's journey from "romantic fantasies of fusion with another person to self definition and self reliance." She views *The Awakening* as a revolutionary work between the Romantic past and Modernist future, but notes that it did not influence literary conventions as it might have because of its disappearance from print. She argues that we should read the novel in the context of its transitional place in the American female literary tradition. She explores *The Awakening*'s place in this tradition, but notes the novel's unfortunate lack of influence on Chopin's contemporaries and later authors.
See also E.9.1

E.8   Petry, Alice Hall. *Critical Essays on Kate Chopin.* New York: G. K. Hall, 1996.
LOC: PS1294.C63C75 1996

Contents of Volume

E.8.1   Arner, Robert D. "Pride in Prejudice: Kate Chopin's 'Désirée's Baby.'" Rpt. from *MissQ:* 25 (1972):131-40.
Arner asserts that most critics consider *The Awakening* flawed to some degree but argues that they misjudge the complexity of the story in its theme, structure, and imagery. Both the structure and theme originate in the racial caste system of the South which is reinforced by two major patterns of imagery: the contrast of light and shadow/whiteness and blackness, and the opposition between God or Providence and

Satan. The combination of racial and seduction themes draws from the traditions of *Uncle Tom's Cabin* and *Clarissa* to form what he calls "one of the best of its kind in American literature."

E.8.2   Bauer, Margaret D. "Armand Aubigny, Still Passing After All These Years: The Narrative Voice and Historical Context of 'Désirée's Baby.'"

Bauer argues that contrary to the readings of most critics, Armand is aware of his mixed heritage at the beginning of the story and has been passing for white all of his life. He chose the foundling Désirée as his wife to insure that his secret could not be revealed through his children. The author cites textual evidence and the story's unreliable narrator, along with copious historical data and references to other passing literature to support her argument. She argues that this analysis subtly and subversively shifts the "blame" from Armand himself to society.

E.8.3   Bender, Bert. "Kate Chopin's Quarrel with Darwin before *The Awakening*."

Bender argues that Chopin thought of Darwin as something of a mentor, but that while she accepted the major theses of *The Origin of Species*, she rejected his argument on the subject of sexual selection. Chopin vehemently disagreed with Darwin's argument that women were by nature passive in sexual encounters and inferior to men in that arena. He argues that *The Awakening* is a study of Darwin's theory of sexual selection which attempts to disprove his views concerning female sexuality.
See also: D.206

E.8.4   Bender, Bert. "The Teeth of Desire: *The Awakening* and *The Descent of Man*."

Bender states that Chopin's fiction is a "darkening meditation" of Darwinian thought. He cites the influence of Darwin's *The Descent of Man and Selection in Relation to Sex* and argues that following *At Fault*, "all of Chopin's courtship plots during the next ten years are studies in natural history according to the logic of sexual selection." He speculates on Chopin's reading of *Descent* and its influence on her work and also notes the influence of Whitman and *Song of Myself*. The reference in chapter 13 of *The Awakening* when Edna tears the bread with "her strong white

teeth" is a reference to the canines referred to in the second edition of *Descent*.
See also: D.189

E.8.5   Berkove, Lawrence I. "'Acting Like Fools': The Ill-Fated Romances of 'At the 'Cadian Ball' and 'The Storm.'"
Berkove argues that rather than a moral or realistic depiction of passion and adultery, "At the 'Cadian Ball" and "The Storm," are ironic, especially as evidenced by the final line of "The Storm." He argues that Chopin's well-drawn characters and sympathetic portrayal tend to obscure the conventional morality that a careful analysis of these stories reveals.

E.8.6   Dyer, Joyce Coyne. "The Restive Brute: The Symbolic Presentation of Repression and Sublimation in Kate Chopin's 'Fedora.'"
Dyer examines "Fedora," which she calls one of Chopin's finest symbolic stories of suppression and sublimation. She examines how Chopin uses symbolism rather than direct narration or explanation to demonstrate theme, plot, and Fedora's emotional confusion.
See also: D.76

E.8.7   Leder, Priscilla. "Land's End: *The Awakening* and 19th Century Literary Tradition."
Leder argues that *The Awakening* incorporates elements of such 19th century literary movements as Romanticism, Transcendentalism, Realism, local color, and Naturalism, demonstrating both their influence and their limitations. She sees *the Awakening* as a true turn-of-the-century work in the sense that it both concludes the literary movements of the 19th century and foreshadows those of the 20th. Thus, Edna's suicide is symbolic of both her personal triumph and failure, along with the failure of 19th century literary traditions to do justice to women's experience and the triumph of a 19th century novel that exceeds them.

E.8.8   Seidel, Kathryn Lee. "Picture Perfect: Painting in *The Awakening*."
Seidel examines Edna's development as an artist in light of the restrictions on women. The author argues that her growth as an artist mirrors her growth as a person, and that both proceed in three stages: (1) a mimetic, early conventional work represents her place in the patriarchal culture, (2) her

rebellious portraits as she begins to break out and explore possibilities, and (3) her daring original drawings after she moves into her own house.

E.8.9   Skaggs, Peggy. "The Boy's Quest in Kate Chopin's "A Vocation and a Voice."
Skaggs argues that Chopin's work goes beyond feminist advocacy and female themes. She compares "A Vocation and a Voice" to *The Awakening* to show that the characters' conflicting needs are universal, transcending sexual limitations. Chopin is concerned with the identity problems of human beings rather than just those of women and notes that many of Chopin's characters and perspectives are male. Similar themes of loss of innocence, and the search for place, love, and self may be found in both Chopin's male and female characters.
See also: D.56

E.8.10   Sullivan, Ruth and Stewart Smith. "Narrative Stance in Kate Chopin's *The Awakening*." Rpt. in *Studies in American Fiction* 1 (1973): 62-75.
LOC: PS370.S87
Sullivan and Smith state that previous critics' statements on *The Awakening*'s theme and narrative point of view are inaccurate. They argue that Chopin presents two contradictory views of Edna, one critical and one sympathetic, making it impossible to identify Chopin with Edna. They state that readers tend to identify too much with the sympathetic view and therefore miss the novel's "sober Realism." In addition, they argue that Edna is nether a "feminist heroine" nor a "somewhat shallow self-deceiver." They argue that readers project their own fantasies onto the novel while the "realistic narrative" appeals to the adult self and the "partisan" to the child.

E.8.11   Thomas, Heather Kirk. "'The House of Sylvie' in Kate Chopin's 'Athénaïse.'"
Thomas notes that Seyersted views "Athénaïse" as among Chopin's most influential works and that Helen Taylor views it as a precursor to *The Awakening*. Both the title character and the story have received much critical attention, however, it is ironic that Sylvie, the mature and self-sufficient African-American woman has received very little critical attention. Sylvie is a better surrogate mother than the three more

traditional female foils who council Athénaïse on her marriage, and tl author notes possible biographical inspirations for this character. Thomas places Chopin's work in the context of Zora Neale Hurston's campaign for stories of "everyday" people of color "above the servant class" and notes that Chopin was ahead of her time in this regard. She also argues that this story contributed greatly to Chopin's development as a writer.

E.8.12   Thornton, Lawrence. *"The Awakening: A Political Romance."*
Thornton makes the comparison of *The Awakening* to *Madame Bovary* but argues that Edna recognizes the political implications of her position, while Bovary uses society only as a mirror for her romantic fantasies. Edna recognizes the "dilequescent" nature of Romanticism, affecting her view of personal freedom and leading directly to the conflict between a would-be independent woman and Creole society. *The Awakening* goes beyond *Madame Bovary* because Edna's search for independence forces consideration of freedom and oppression in society, while the latter is limited to sentimentality and narcissism.
See also: D.67

E.8.13   Wagner-Martin, Linda. "Kate Chopin's Fascination with Young Men."
Wagner-Martin argues that Chopin's fiction is notable for the "healthy sexual passion" of her positive characters, both male and female. She also argues that this tendency predates the influence of Maupassant, to whom it is often credited. The heroism of her early heroines is in their repression of sexuality. Her earlier fiction also presents loving, yet realistic portraits of young men and the author argues that these portraits are expressed in *The Awakening* in the form of Robert, Victor, and Edna's sons. Chopin's talent for expressing the passion of believable yet loveable young men was perhaps due to her five sons who were of a similar age to many of her male characters during her career as an author.

E.8.14   Walker, Nancy A. "Her Own Story: The Woman of Letters in Kate Chopin's Short Fiction."
Walker notes the importance of the written word in Chopin's fiction and writing as a metaphor for empowerment, or lack thereof, citing "Charlie" and "La Belle Zoraïde" as examples. She examines "Athénaïse," using reading and writing to

show young women's distance from the intellectual world. Walker demonstrates that "Miss Witherwell's Mistake" juxtaposes the small town writer with her niece, who writes her own life script and "Elizabeth Stock's One Story" illustrating Chopin's awareness of cultural barriers to women in literature.

E.9 Walker, Nancy A., ed. *The Awakening* by Kate Chopin, with critical essays. Boston: Bedford Books - St. Martin's P, 1993.
LOC: PS1294.C63 A6435 1993

Contents of Volume

E.9.1   Showalter, Elaine. "Tradition and the Female Talent: *The Awakening* as a Solitary Book."
See: E.7.4

E.9.2   Stange, Margit. "Personal Property: Exchange Value and the Female Self in *The Awakening*."
See: D.169, E.1.1, E.4.13, E.5.4, F.42

E.9.3   Treichler, Paula A. "The Construction of Ambiguity in *The Awakening*: A Linguistic Analysis."
Treichler argues that the central theme in *The Awakening* is Edna's attempt to define herself as an active subject rather than a passive object. Treichler examines grammatical voice and also looks at formal grammatical patterns and how they shape our understanding of Edna. The author notes that, for example, the verb awaken, which appears in both the title and as the central metaphor of the novel, can be both a transitive and an intransitive verb. She also examines the evolution of personal pronouns throughout the novel. No unambiguous reading of the novel is possible because of its language and the author argues that Edna's situation is genuine and can not be fully resolved.
See also: D.63

E.9.4   Wolff, Cynthia Griffin. "Thanatos and Eros: Kate Chopin's *The Awakening*." Rpt. from *American Quarterly* 25 (1973): 449-71.
See: E.5.6

E.9.5   Yaeger, Patricia S. "'A Language Which Nobody Understood': Emancipatory Strategies in *The Awakening*."
See: D.145, E.5.7

Dissertations

1976

No dissertations dealing with Chopin were written during this year.

1977

F.1   Lattin, Sarah Patricia Hopkins. "Method and Vision in Kate Chopin's
       Fiction." Diss. U of Kentucky, 1977. *DAI-A* 38.10 (1978): 6133.
       Lattin argues that in addition to the elements of 19th century Realism
       present in Chopin's work, her focus on romantic alienation reflects a
       form of late-19th century Transcendentalism. This combination of
       influences culminates in *The Awakening*.

1978

F.2   Dyer, Joyce Ann. "Kate Chopin's Use of Natural Correlatives as
       Psychological Symbols in Her Fiction." Diss. Kent State U, 1977.
       DAI-A 31.11 (1978): 6723.
       Dyer argues that Chopin should be labeled a "psychological
       symbolist" rather than as a local colorist because of her symbolic use
       of nature in her work. She also argues that had Chopin lived longer
       and received more critical praise, she likely would have developed a
       richer and more ambiguous symbolism, just as her later work is more
       complex than her earlier fiction.

F.3   Garitta, Anthony Paul. "The Critical Reputation of Kate Chopin."
       Diss. U of North Carolina at Greensboro, 1978. *DAI-A* 39.6 (1978):
       3579.
       Garitta focuses on the impact of reviewers and critics on Chopin's
       career from the publication of *At Fault* to the present and reassesses
       the merit of her work in light of modern scholarship. He notes the
       great influence of reviewers on Chopin's career and includes an
       overview of her critical reputation, past and present.

F.4   Roumm, Phillis G. "Portraits of Suffering Womanhood in
       Representative Nineteenth-century American Novels: The
       Contribution of Kate Chopin." Diss. Kent State U, 1977. *DAI-A*
       38.10 (1978): 6133.
       Roumm examines the portrayal of suffering women characters from
       1799-1899 and argues that they were generally stereotyped, but that
       even among the less stereotypical characters, Edna Pontellier is
       unique in her realistic complexity. She also studies the roles of real
       women from colonial times to the 1920s as they relate to Chopin's
       life and work.

1979

F.5   Butler, Harry Scott. "Sexuality in the Fiction of Kate Chopin." Diss.
       Duke U, 1979. *DAI-A* 40.12 (1980): 6277.
       Butler examines Chopin's treatment of human sexuality, arguing
       that it combines elements of both Naturalism and Romantic-
       Transcendentalism. Sexuality is portrayed both positively and
       pessimistically, combining these visions ambiguously in *The
       Awakening*.

F.6   Clatworthy, Joan Mayerson. "Kate Chopin: The Inward Life Which
       Questions." Diss. State U of New York at Buffalo, 1979. *DAI-A* 40.4
       (1979): 2059.
       Clatworthy argues that Chopin's fiction sought to resolve her inner
       and outer beings. The study examines the narrative patterns,
       images, and ideas in her work and explores Chopin's relationship to
       her characters and readers.

1980

F.7   Gaudet, Mary Marcia Gendron. "The Folklore and Customs of the
       West Bank of St. John the Baptist Parish." Diss. U of Southwestern
       Louisiana, 1980. *DAI-A* 41.4 (1980): 1710.
       Gaudet's study examines the folklore and customs of St. John the

Baptist Parish's west bank and argues that the area has an
indigenous folklore tradition. This tradition is simultaneously
Southern, indicating the influence of folklore on the Southern mind
and oral tradition, and resulting in the body of Southern work. The
primary focus of the study is on holiday customs such as rituals of
birth, marriage and death, as well as river and levee lore. Other
aspects explored include the Catholic church, superstition, folk
medicine, and tales of slavery and the Black experience. These folk
traditions exert a great influence on the works of writers such as
Ernest Gaines, George Washington Cable, Kate Chopin and Walker
Percy.

F.8   Glenn, Ellen Walker. "The Androgynous Woman Character in the
        American Novel." Diss. U of Colorado at Boulder, 1980. *DAI-A*
        41.11 (1980): 4713.
        Glenn argues that androgyny is a useful role model for examining
        gender-defined traits because it allows the androgynous character to
        choose behaviors freely without regard to sex-role appropriateness.
        She points out that androgyny clarifies the definition of womanhood
        because it creates an awareness that is not possible within traditional
        gender roles. Her study extends the work of Carolyn Heilbrun in
        Toward a Recognition of Androgyny, which focuses on the
        androgynous characteristics of Hawthorne's Hester Prynne. Glenn's
        study seeks the potentially androgynous woman over the history of
        the American novel, arguing that androgynous qualities are absent
        from the Realistic novel, but possible in the speculative novel. She
        argues that *The Awakening* explores the extent to which androgenous
        potential is thwarted by society. She further argues that Chopin,
        unlike Henry James, rejected these norms. Thus, Chopin's novel
        shows the incompatability of an androgenous woman in a realistic
        setting. Glenn also studies the work of Ellen Glasgow, Sarah Orne
        Jewett, Willa Cather, Charlotte Perkins Gilman, Joanna Russ and
        June Arnold.

F.9   St. Andrews, Bonnie Anne. "Forbidden Fruit: The Relationship
        Between Women and Knowledge." Diss. Syracuse U, 1980. *DAI-A*
        41.6 (1980): 2620.
        St. Andrews argues that both sacred and secular literature offer
        protagonists who acquire knowledge and are changed as a result.
        Confrontations leading to knowledge are considered positive when
        experienced by males, but in similar situations, females are
        disparaged. She first describes the literary tradition of vilifying
        women who seek knowledge, pointing out that in both sacred and
        secular tales women are warned against the pursuit of knowledge.

This act is perceived as willfully disobedient, and the choice of self-rule is thus equated with evil. Chapter 2 concentrates chiefly on *The Awakening*, analyzing religious and fairytale images in the novel and many of Chopin's short stories. She offers in-depth analyses of the works of Lagerlof, Atwood, Lessing, as well discussions of Ibsen, Woolf, Joyce, and Sachs.

1981

F.10   Huf, Linda. "Portrait of the Artist as a Young Woman: The Female *Kunstlerromane* in America." Diss. U of Maryland, College Park, 1981. *DAI-A* 42.8 (1982): 3600.
Huf disputes the argument that women rarely write *Kunstlerromane*, the autobiographical novels depicting their struggles to become artists. Her study offers a detailed analysis of several *Kunstlerromane* by American women novelists. Her study includes analyses of the following works: Fanny Fern's *Ruth Hall,* Elizabeth Stuart Phelps' *The Story of Avis*, Kate Chopin's *The Awakening*, Willa Cather's *The Song of the Lark*, Carson McCullers' *The Heart Is a Lonely Hunter*, and Sylvia Plath's *The Bell Jar*.

F.11   Keyser, Jeanette Parker. "Character Mediation: Reference, Recognition, Context Retrieval, and Generation." Diss. U of Wisconsin, 1981. *DAI-A* 42.3 (1981): 1137.
Keyser's study articulates a "theory of character" that explains intuitions and biases on the part of the reader. Readers draw inferences about characters, granting them "extensional properties," and then store these inferences in memory to be recalled long after we have forgotten the text that caused us to draw such inferences. She argues that the coherence of a narrative is the result of locating and retrieving "abilities of character." Each chapter of the dissertation investigates a "character activity" and suggests "theory-constitutive models." She draws her evidence from literary texts that highlight the particular character activity under scrutiny. Chopin's *The Awakening* is examined because it "overdetermines the ability of character to be a focal event in an event chain."

F.12   Kimbel, Ellen. "Chopin, Wharton, Cather and the New American Fictional Heroine." Diss. Temple U, 1981. *DAI-A* 42.2 (1981): 703.
The appearance of *The Awakening*, along with Edith Wharton's New York novels and Willa Cather's frontier novels, marked a departure from 19th century depictions of the American female hero. The female protagonists created by 19th century novelists were rigidly stereotyped in terms of gender roles. Kimbel's study examines the

female hero in several major 19ᵗʰ century novels and then turns to individual studies of the female characterization in *The Awakening*, as well as works by Wharton and Cather. These characters demonstrate numerous departures from previous traditions. She concludes the discussion with the observation that the "powerfully delineated heroine" disappears from American fiction as both a literary and cultural phenomenon.

F.13   Leder, Priscilla Gay. "'Snug Contrivances': The Classic American Novel as Reformulated by Kate Chopin, Sarah Orne Jewett, and Edith Wharton." Diss. U of California, Irvine, 1981. *DAI-A* 42.9 (1982): 4000.
Leder's dissertation draws on the works of Kate Chopin, Sarah Orne Jewett, and Edith Wharton to illustrate the ways in which women writers continue the tradition of the American novel. Edna Pontellier, in Chopin's *The Awakening*, is bound by her domestic roles and obligations, and she seeks to escape from her confinement in the sea. Edna's contact with Creole culture both instigates and limits her search for identity.

F.14   Levy, Elaine Barbara. "The Unconscious and Existentialism: A Dialectic in Modern Fiction." Diss. New York U, 1981. *DAI-A* 43.8 (1983): 2659.
Levy's study examines the relationship of the unconscious mind to the existential search for freedom. She devotes a chapter to exploring the discontented woman in the latter 19ᵗʰ century, focusing on Flaubert's *Madame Bovary* and Chopin's *The Awakening*. She focuses on the rise of the self as religious and cultural constraints begin to weaken. The study also includes analyses of works by Jane Austen, D. H. Lawrence, and Fyodor Dostoevsky.

F.15   Panaro, Lydia Adriana. "Desperate Women: Murderers and Suicides in Nine Modern Novels." Diss. New York U, 1981. *DAI-A* 42.7 (1982): 3150.
Panaro examines the causes of the destructive behavior of women in nine novels, drawn from America, France, Italy and England. The novels she studies include: *The Awakening* by Kate Chopin, *The House of Mirth* by Edith Wharton, *Therese Desqueyroux* by Francois Mauriac, *Adrienne Mesurat* by Julien Green, *The Sheltered Life* by Ellen Glasgow, *To The North* by Elizabeth Bowen, *Le Ambizioni Sbagliate* by Alberto Moravia, *L'Invitée* by Simone de Beauvoir, and *E'Stato Cos'i* by Natalia Ginzburg. Each of the novels are from the modern period and come from the Western literary tradition. Based on psychological theory, she postulates that perceptions of female

inferiority and dependence lead to self destructive behavior. She argues that female heroes are perceived as "female satellites" to male characters, and that none successfully create their own identity. This fatal dependency leads to either murder or suicide.

1982

F.16   Lant, Kathleen Margaret. "Behind a Mask: A Study of Nineteenth-Century American Fiction by Women." Diss. U of Oregon, 1982. *DAI-A* 43.9 (1983): 2993.

Lant's study examines the 19th century American literary tradition, demonstrating the coping strategies of women who possessed limited power. She examines the theme of "feminine dishonesty" in women's writing, pointing out that in domestic fiction, heroines lie to make their lives easier. In later works by women, dishonesty is employed when other means are not available to the characters. In the works of Louisa May Alcott, Fanny Fern and Harriet Beecher Stowe, dishonesty undermines the status quo in the institutions of marriage and slavery. By the end of the century, a tone of pessimism and disillusionment is present in women's writing. The female heroes in fiction by Chopin and Freeman realize that dishonesty has become a destructive part of their character. Thus, they become aware of the need to live two lives. Chopin's characters resolve this conflict through death, and Freeman's choose isolation.

F.17   Levy, Helen Fiddyment. "No Hiding Place on Earth: The Female Self in Eight Modern American Women Authors." 2 vols. Diss. U of Michigan, 1982. *DAI-A* 43.10 (1983): 3356.

Levy looks at eight American women writers – Chopin, Wharton, Glasgow, Cather, Porter, McCullers, McCarthy and Didion – in the context of their social and literary backgrounds. Each of the works that she selects has a female protagonist. Levy plots each respective authors' evolving definition of the female through their respective careers, arguing that women writers draw from two different traditions. These predecessors created an alternative emotional world through their characters. Women writers were able to address imaginative and intellectual societal issues after the institution of the home had been eroded. The woman writer walked a difficult line between providing a realistic treatment of society while providing freedom and emotional escape for her female hero. If she falls too close to either extreme, the hero risks disgrace, madness, or death.

F.18   Parker, Pamela Lorraine. "The Search for Autonomy in the Works of Kate Chopin, Ellen Glasgow, Carson McCullers, and Shirley Ann

Grau." Diss. Rice U, 1982. *DAI-A* 43.2 (1982): 454.

Parker's study tracks the Southern female character's search for autonomy in Kate Chopin, Ellen Glasgow, Carson McCullers, and Shirley Ann Grau. She describes the historical and sociological factors which influence the Southern female and describes the qualities and searches of these character. Parker argues that Chopin's Southern females reveal the origins of this character. She concludes that these writers demonstrate the tragedy of the myth of the Southern Belle.

F.19   Williams, Patricia Ann Owens. "Self-Made and Unself-Made: The Myth of The Self-Made Man and the Ideologies of the True Woman, New Woman, and Amazon, 1820-1920." Diss. U of New Mexico, 1982. *DAI-A* 43.5 (1982): 1597.

Williams studies the self-made man, and his counterparts, found in the dying breed of the True Woman, and the evolving New Woman who worked outside of the home, yet was somewhat dependent on a man. A category of women that Williams classifies as Amazons declined both the role of True Woman and New Woman. She argues that cultural systems such as marriage, law, and education provided the basis for power and authoritarian hierarchy in the home and in the business world. The westward movement and industrialization led to the breakdown of these authoritarian relationships, and protagonists such as Edna Pontellier offer literary representations of these changing relationships.

1983

F.20   Hoder-Salmon, Marilyn. "A 'New-born Creature', the Authentic Woman in *The Awakening*: Novel to Screenplay as Critical Interpretation." Diss. U of New Mexico, 1983. *DAI-A* 45.8 (1985): 2567.

Hoder-Salmon's dissertation consists of a screenplay of *The Awakening* and two essays. The first of the essays offers biographical data, cultural and historical data, and literary and film theory. The second essay offers a critical interpretation of the screenplay. She argues that her interpretation of *The Awakening* is part of a scholarly and societal movement toward a more balanced perspective on women's culture and experience.

F.21   Huh, Joonok. "Shifting Sexual Roles in Selected American Novels, 1870-1920." Diss. Indiana U, 1983. *DAI-A* 44.3 (1983): 752.

The American novel from 1870 until 1920 presented images of awakened females, and these images necessitated the reformulation of the images of male characters as well. Male characters changed in a variety of ways: their dominance was lessened, and their undisputed authority was subverted. Male characters were increasingly limited to the domestic and social sphere while women rebelled against these very traditions, seeking independence. Huh argues that this shift took place in two stages. The first was a transitional stage which tested established stereotypes. This stage was exemplified by the works of Louisa May Alcott, Frank Norris and Kate Chopin. The second stage of the change involved a more radical transformation of the fabric of society, and this change is seen in the work of Henry James and Edith Wharton. By the end of this shift in gender roles, women ceased to compromise themselves, and men became prisoners of their own refined self-consciousness.

F.22   Gupta, Linda Roberta. "Fathers and Daughters in Women's Novels." Diss. American U, 1983. *DAI-A* 44.6 (1983): 1783.
       Gupta's dissertation studies father-daughter relationships in a variety of 19th and 20th century novels by women, including Kate Chopin's *The Awakening*. She compares these novels to European *marchen*, in which fathers are shown as tyrannical or possessive. To attain maturity and independence, a young female protagonist must outwit her father and challenge his authority." Gupta argues that this theme of challenging male authority is also present in the other novels she studies.

F.23   Papke, Mary Elizabeth. "'Abysses of Solitude': The Social Fiction of Kate Chopin and Edith Wharton." Diss. McGill U, 1983. *DAI-A* 44.5 (1983): 1451.
       Papke argues that the fiction of both Kate Chopin and Edith Wharton provides a link between the 19th and 20th centuries in terms of literary and cultural attitudes and criticizes social practices. The literary forms that each author chose were defined by the male discourses of psychological Realism, local color fiction, and the novel of manners. However, both authors subverted these traditions to their own ends. They also realistically portrayed American women and their search for selfhood. Their work is important because it is a part of the first modern female literary discourse in America.

1984

F.24   Bair, Barbara. "'Ties of Blood and Bonds of Fortune': The Cultural Construction of Gender in American Women's Fiction–An Interdisciplinary Analysis." Diss. Brown U, 1984. *DAI-A* 45.7 (1985): 2153.

Bair's study analyzes the development of a feminist canon of American literature during the 19th and 20th centuries. She examines the influence of women authors on one another, placing special emphasis on the use of symbol and metaphor, and also questioning social constructs and control. She draws on a variety of disciplines, including anthropology, history, sociology, psychology and women's studies, using them to critique traditional social constructs. She considers themes of: (1) feminist thought as it relates to literature, (2) anti-modernism, (3) female friendship, and (4) the use of the life cycle as a political metaphor in fiction. Bair studies a wide variety of authors, including Kate Chopin.

F.25   Jones, Suzanne Whitmore. "Myths and Manners in the Southern Novel." Diss. U of Virginia, 1984. *DAI-A* 45.8 (1985); 2528.
        Jones disputes the traditional assimilation of the Southern novel into the American romance. She argues that the preoccupation with manners of such writers as George Washington Cable, Kate Chopin, Ellen Glasgow, William Faulkner, Eudora Welty, and Walker Percy. She examines people as members of a community, demonstrating the peculiarly Southern myth that separates the traditions of the Southern novel and the American romance.

F.26   Payerle, Margaret Jane. "'A Little Like Outlaws': The Metaphorical Use of Restricted Space in the Works of Certain American Women Realistic Writers." Diss. Case Western Reserve U, 1984. *DAI-A* 45.9 (1985): 2876.
        Payerle analyzes the focus on the environment and material objects of five American women Realist writers, arguing that they use physical restriction as a metaphor for social and cultural restrictions. She suggests that in *The Awakening,* Edna learns to manipulate her physical surroundings to demonstrate her rejection of her constrained social role.

1985

F.27   Lenarcic, Faye Mertine. "The Emergence of the Passionate Woman in American Fiction, 1850-1920." Diss. Syracuse U, 1985. *DAI-A* 46.9 (1986): 2693.
        The 19th century American tradition acknowledges the power and danger of both male and female sexuality. While men fear the *femme fatale*, women fear seduction and the fate of the fallen woman. Many feminist writers portray the intelligent woman as the one who subdues her passion, while a few portray the sexually awakened woman for whom no acceptable mate exists. By 1900, the latter

becomes more prominent, in contrast to the sexless New Woman seen in the fiction of writers such as Elizabeth Stuart Phelps, Mary Wilkins Freeman, Sarah Orne Jewett, and Charlotte Perkins Gilman. Writers such as Gertrude Atherton, Kate Chopin and Edith Wharton portray women who embrace their sexuality and search for the ideal mate.

F.28   Shapiro, Ann R. "A Separate Sphere: The Woman Question in Selected Fiction By Nineteenth-century American Women, 1852-1899." Diss. New York U, 1985. *DAI-A* 46.8 (1986): 2294.
This study examines fiction that elucidates the Woman Question as it was perceived in 19th century America. The Woman Question, for the purposes of Shapiro's discussion, is defined as widespread concern over women's roles in both the domestic and the larger social spheres. The dissertation studies six novels – *Uncle Tom's Cabin, The Silent Partner, Work, A Country Doctor, Pembroke*, and *The Awakening* – and examines plot, setting and iconography to determine the differences in novels written by men and those written by women of the era. She concludes that the same themes are frequently reiterated, regardless of the writer's gender. She finds that both male and female authors have the "same urge to break with tradition, reject conventional values, and pursue adventure." The Woman question becomes a universal question as both male and female characters question conventions of marriage, work, and religion. Female characters also reject True Womanhood in the quest for freedom and equality. The study also argues that the canon of American literature is neither accurate nor representative. The critical history of the novels reveals that the perceived value of each has fluctuated with shifting perceptions of women in society.

1986

F.29   Dearbone, Moselle Arnetta Williams. "'Discordant Sound': The Search for 'The Harmony of an Undivided Existence' in Kate Chopin's Fiction." Diss. U of Houston, 1986. *DAI-A* 48.1 (1987): 126.
Dearbone argues that Chopin was a product of the 19th century ideal in which the "man's world" and the "woman's world" were clearly delineated. She points out that Chopin was largely compliant with social expectations, but that her fiction demonstrates nonconformity with a rigid social system. Chopin's characters can not consistently reconcile these disparate elements. However, because she realizes that reconciling the inner life with outward appearances was not possible in 19th century society, she denied most of her characters her own insights.

F.30   Swigart, Margaret Jane Bugas. "The Mother in Modern Literature."
        Diss. State U of New York at Buffalo, 1986. *DAI-A* 47.7 (1987):
        2581.
        Swigart explores the literary themes and images of motherhood and
        the psychological conflicts inherent in child bearing. Kate Chopin,
        Tillie Olsen, Doris Lessing, Anne Sexton, Grace Paley, and Sylvia
        Plath reveal the transformation of the role of caregiver brought about
        by both the emotional and economic impact of industrialization. In
        chapter four, she examines the process of emotional separation of
        mothers from their children, as depicted in the fiction of Chopin and
        Lessing. She draws on the theories of psychoanalyst Margaret
        Mahler to examine the effect of the child's separation from the
        mother.

F.31   Young, Margaret Mary. "Exposing the Myth of Bliss: Marriage and
        The Female Adam in the Fiction of Kate Chopin." Diss. Saint Louis
        U, 1986. *DAI-A* 48.4 (1987): 966.
        Young's study focuses on the cultural depiction of marriage and the
        resulting negative consequences for women, as illustrated in
        Chopin's fiction. She discusses biographical data from Chopin's life
        to demonstrate the shaping of the author's personal and artistic
        assessment of marriage and self-definition. Using the "myth of bliss"
        as a backdrop, she argues that the "myth of the American Adam"
        shows Chopin's female characters to be self-defined, self-directed,
        and self-justified. The remainder of the study looks at specific
        examples of marriage relationships, which are drawn from *At Fault*,
        the short fiction, and *The Awakening*. The study concludes by
        looking at Edna Pontellier in the context of Chopin's other female
        characters and their association with their literary sisters, Hester
        Pryne and Isabel Archer. Young describes the goal of her study as
        offering an analysis of the marriage and its effect on women by
        exploring one artist's respone.

1987

F.32   Dielman, Dorothy Eloise Reynolds. "Realism and the Shadow of
        Emile Zola in Chopin's Fiction." Diss. U of Oregon, 1987. *DAI-A*
        48.3 (1987): 649.
        Dielman classifies Chopin's fiction as part of the Realist school
        because of her treatments of region, character and dialect. These
        attributes are especially notable in the novels and stories set in
        Natchitoches Parish, New Orleans, and Grand Isle. Her stories
        progress, through her use of Realism, from themes of romance to the

rejection of marriage and the raising of social consciousness. She further argues that *At Fault* and *The Awakening* are thematically tied to Emile Zola's *L'Assommoir, Therese Raquin*, and *Une Page d'Amour*.

F.33   Merideth, Eunice Mae. "Stylistic Gender Patterns in Fiction: Curricular Concern." Diss. Iowa State U, 1987. *DAI-A* 48.7 (1988): 1644.

Merideth's research attempts to identify gender patterns in fiction through the use of a computer program which identifies syntactic patterns ranging from frequency of questions, imperatives, and exclamations to the use of universals, negatives, adverbs, and comparisons. She draws her data from Henry James' *Daisy Miller, The Portrait of a Lady*, and *The Bostonians*, along with Kate Chopin's *The Awakening* and focuses on a male and a female character from each novel. She postulates that the dialogue of male characters denotes strength and power, while the dialogue of female characters denotes polite and uncertain speech. She demonstrates that gender patterns are embedded in language, and that these patterns can be identified in this type of study. She concludes that this identification can lead to unmarked communication in terms of gender and stereotypes.

F.34   Woodland, James Randal. "'In That City Foreign and Paradoxical': The Idea of New Orleans in The Southern Literary Imagination." Diss. U of North Carolina, Chapel Hill, 1987. *DAI-A* 48.7 (1988): 1772.

Woodland examines the "New Orleans literary tradition." Drawing on the work of a host of American writers, including Kate Chopin, Woodland demonstrates that the dialect, the exotic and romantic nature, and the sensuality of the city have made it an attractive setting for American writers to set their work in.

1988

F.35   Thomas, Heather Kirk. "'A Vocation and a Voice': A Documentary Life of Kate Chopin." Diss. U of Missouri, Columbia, 1988. *DAI-A* 50.4 (1989): 949.

Thomas' dissertation sets out to dispel many of the myths that have inaccurately haunted Chopin's critical reputation. She provides a "documentary life" which allows the reader to examine its creative and historic context. The dissertation also provides new material that

Chopin wrote and new material about the author's life. It also
contains biographical notes on Chopin's acquaintances and a
selection of sources for her work.

1989

F.36   Carvill, Caroline. "The Stereotype of Spinsters in Southern Fiction."
        Diss. U of Arkansas, 1989. *DAI-A* 51.11 (1991): 3741.
        Carvill studies the role of spinsters in both Southern society and
        literature, categorizing spinsters into four groups: saints, victims,
        ridiculous, or dangerous. She argues that Chopin's fiction employs
        all four types. Although these types of characters are never perceived
        in positive roles, they are treated better in antebellum and late 19th
        century literature than they were in later works. She also discusses
        the role of unmarried women in the writing of Eudora Welty and
        Carson McCullers.

F.37   Gaard, Greta Claire. "Anger Expressed/Repressed: Novels by White,
        Middle-class, American Women Writers, 1850-Present." Diss. U of
        Minnesota, 1989. *DAI-A* 50.9 (1990): 2895.
        Psychological theories have often described women's anger as
        unfeminine, destructive, and ugly. Gaard's study of Harriet Beecher
        Stowe, Elizabeth Stuart Phelps, Louisa May Alcott, Kate Chopin,
        and Rebecca Hill argues that their writings exemplify the positive
        aspects of women's anger. These writers use anger to criticize the
        oppression of others in the face of social attitudes that dub women's
        anger as illness or insanity. Gaard argues that women's anger is
        dangerous to the hegemony of the white male system because once
        one oppressed group begins to struggle against such attitudes others
        are soon to follow, causing the intertwined systems of oppression
        such as capitalism, Christianity, and patriarchy to unravel. These
        writers use anger as a tool to empower and instigate social change.

F.38   Hadella, Charlotte Cook. "Women in Gardens in American Short
        Fiction." Diss. U of New Mexico, 1989. *DAI-A* 50.11 (1990): 3588.
        Hadella uses three of Hawthorne's "Eve" stories – "Young Goodman
        Brown," "Rappaccini's Daughter," and "The Snow-Image" to create
        a paradigm for the study of the American Eve. Hawthorne's three
        stories establish the themes, plot elements and characterization
        which appear repeatedly in the "woman-in-the-garden motif." Her
        study then moves to an analysis of these elements in fiction by
        Alcott, Jewett, Gilman, Steinbeck, Chopin, Welty, and Walker.

F.39   MacDonald, Alan. "Saying Something for Nothing: Attitudes of Some
        American Women Writers to the Romance of Open Space." Diss. U
        of York, UK, 1989. *DAI-A* 51.2 (1990): 505.
        MacDonald's study addresses the aesthetic problem that American
        authors face when dealing with open space and its connotation of a
        void. The contradictions of trying to deal with open space within the
        necessarily closed space of fiction is an issue that is dealt with by
        women authors such as Kate Chopin, Marilynne Robinson, Rachel
        Ingalls, Edith Wharton, Sylvia Plath, Willa Cather and Bobbie Ann
        Mason.

F.40   Mizrahi, Joan Berman. "The American Image of Women as
        Musicians and Pianists, 1850-1900." Diss. U of Maryland, College
        Park, 1989. *DAI-A* 50.7 (1990): 1843.
        Mizrahi's dissertation studies the late 19th century connection
        between women and the piano, specifically as it relates to the
        popular perceptions of women in the art and literature of the period.
        Women were perceived as angelic, the defenders of morality and
        culture on the one hand, and as dangerous and sinister on the other.
        Mizrahi studies works from music periodicals, as well fiction by
        Kate Chopin, Harold Frederic, and Henry James. She analyzes the
        fictional references to female musicians and identifies five common
        images of women in that role.

F.41   Morris, Paula J.K. "Magnolias and Rattlesnakes: The Southern Lady
        in Fiction." Diss. U of York, UK, 1989. *DAI-A* 51.9 (1991): 3074.
        Morris' dissertation explores the archetype of the Southern lady and
        the way this archetype is represented in fiction. She studies a variety
        of Southern authors, beginning with representations of the lady in
        the fiction of Edgar Allan Poe and Sir Walter Scott. She then moves
        to the four women writers on whom she focuses the bulk of her
        study: Kate Chopin, Ellen Glasgow, Lillian Hellman, and Eudora
        Welty. She discusses the impact of the ideal of the lady on Chopin's
        life, self-perception, and work. She addresses this representation in
        three of Chopin's short stories and in *The Awakening*. She makes
        similar analyses of the other three authors included in her study.

F.42   Stange, Margit Knowlton. "Personal Property: Exchange Value and
        the Female Self in Turn of the Century American Texts." Diss. U of
        California, Berkeley, 1989. *DAI-A* 51.5 (1990): 1614.
        Stange's study focuses on the late 19th century, a period during
        which women entered the labor market and the consumer society,
        rather than devoting themselves to domesticity. During this age of
        industrial and market growth, value exchange became emphasized in

interpersonal economics. When women entered the market, they had to overcome their status as the property of men. This discourse is articulated in the relationship of women to contemporary markets. Stange points to Chopin's fiction as indicative of these attitudes. In turn-of-the-century American texts, women became alienated and debased as they were forced to relinquish self-ownership and market their femininity. Women authors thus market and circulate their narratives of ownership and femininity.

F.43   Yonogi, Reiko. "The Struggle Towards Self-fulfillment in Perspective: The Theme of Woman's Awakening in Three Realist Novels – Gustave Flaubert's *Madame Bovary*, Kate Chopin's *The Awakening*, and Arishima Takeo's *Aru Onna*." Diss. U of Illinois at Urbana-Champaign, 1989. *DAI-A* 51.2 (1990): 501.

Yonogi examines the female struggle for self-fulfillment in the novels studied, arguing that each of the female protagonists is a victim of a society that confines them to traditional female roles, without allowing them the freedom to explore other possibilities. She also argues that their self-destructiveness is due to their personality. She points out that each of the heroines fail to attain their goals, or to achieve self-realization. She argues that Edna is an American version of Emma Bovary, and Yoko of *A Certain Woman* is her Japanese equivalent; she uses these characters to point out that human nature is fundamentally the same, regardless of cultural background.

1990

F.44   Fusco, Richard A. "Maupassant and the Turn-of-the-century American Short Story." Diss. Duke U, 1990. *DAI-A* 51.5 (1990): 1612.

Fusco studies seven different short story structures that are present in Maussapant's fiction. He speaks briefly of Kate Chopin, pointing out that she discovered Maupassant in 1889, relatively early in her career. Through Chopin's study of Maupassant, she found literary models to incorporate into her own fiction.

F.45   Rothgery, David Bruce. "Post-Modernism: Ethical Dimensions and 'Competing Chaos' in Pedagogy." Diss. U of Oregon, 1990. *DAI-A* 51.11 (1991): 3758.

Rothgery argues that Post-Modernism and its accompanying theoretical framework presents a new challenge in the classroom. He relates his experience with two groups of undergraduates in a Post-Modernist study of Herman Mellville's "Billy Budd" and Kate

Chopin's *The Awakening*. He concludes that despite the referential problems brought to light by Post-Modernism, literature must remain "ethically meaningful."

F.46   Shumaker, Jeanette Roberts. "Self-Sacrifice in Victorian Fiction." Diss. Claremont Graduate School, 1990. *DAI-A* 51.6 (1990): 2029.
        Shumaker's study addresses a number of texts, including Kate Chopin's *The Awakening*. She argues that in Victorian fiction, sin results from the desires and the aggressiveness of the masculine marketplace. Atonement comes only through self-sacrifice, which is a feminine virtue. Sacrifice is ongoing, however, because avoiding temptation is a constant struggle that becomes self-absorbed. Thus, feminine sacrifice is the counterpart of masculine aggressiveness rather than its opposite, destabilizing notions of gender, along with those of virtue and vice.

F.47   Sparks, Laurel Vivian. "Counterparts: The Fiction of Mary Wilkins Freeman, Sarah Orne Jewett, and Kate Chopin." Diss. U of Iowa, 1990. *DAI-A* 51.12 (1991): 4125.
        In her study of Freeman, Jewett and Chopin, Sparks argues that their short fiction relates character and environment. All three writers used their characters' social places along with these well-known local color environments. They also made use of counterparts and physical and psychological doubles in their character development. Chopin and Jewett used imagery to interrelate characters and settings, but neither surpassed Freeman in this endeavor. The central focus in the fiction of these writers is the questioning of an individual's relationship to society, yet these writers withheld judgement so they could maintain a level of uncertainty about the fictions they created.

1991

F.48   Barker, Deborah Ellen. "Painting Women: The Woman Artist in Nineteenth Century American Fiction." Diss. Princeton U, 1991. *DAI-A* 52.7 (1992): 2549.
        Barker examines female visual artists in American women's fiction of the late 19th century, arguing for that visual artists served as an alter ego for the female writer in terms of artistic, creative and sexual freedom. She discusses Edna in *The Awakening* as an example of women as creators and models. The novel shows how a female painter tries to move beyond representational aesthetics in order to express female desire and ability without appropriating and objectifying the female body.

F.49   Branan, Mary Ellen. "In the Middle." Original feminist poetry. Diss.
        U of Houston, 1991. *DAI-A* 52.6 (1991): 2141.
        In addition to 33 original poems, "In the Middle" includes a critical
        preface which refers briefly to work by numerous women writers,
        including Kate Chopin.

F.50   Castiglia, Christopher Dean. "Captive Subjects: The Captivity
        Narrative and American Women's Writing." Diss. Columbia U,
        1991. *DAI-A* 52.11 (1992): 3926.
        Castiglia's study of the captivity narrative raises issues of audience,
        genre, and women's roles in literature, along with the social
        constraints faced by women. Drawing on the works of Mary
        Rowlandson, Fanny Kelly, Patty Hearst, Ann Eliza Bleecker,
        Susanna Rowson, Harriet Cheney, Catharine Maria Sedgwick, Kate
        Chopin, and Barbara Deming, he places the captivity romance in the
        mainstream of American literature and examines its relationship to
        the more traditional domestic fiction and the sentimental novel.

F.51   Cutter, Martha J. "Revisionary Voices: Language and Feminine
        Subjectivity in the Works of Freeman, Chopin, and Gilman." Diss.
        Brown U, 1991. *DAI-A* 52.9 (1992): 3280.
        Drawing on the revisionary history of Carroll Smith-Rosenburg and
        Barbara Welter along with revisions of Freudian and Lacanian
        theory by Luce Irigaray, Helenè Cixous, and Julia Kristeva, Cutter
        explores female subjectivity and alternative feminine language in the
        fiction of Mary E. Wilkins Freeman, Kate Chopin, and Charlotte
        Perkins Gilman. She argues that these authors make language the
        site of struggle as female characters attempt to construct new
        linguistic systems in which they can speak. Two chapters of the
        dissertation are devoted to a study of Chopin, and she concludes that
        Freeman, Chopin and Gilman move beyond a binary world into one
        in which women can seek full subjectivity.

F.52   Garfield, Deborah Michelle. "Power: Women, Privation and
        Language in American Narrative, 1861-1936." Diss. U of Virginia,
        1991. *DAI-A* 53.1 (1992): 150.
        Garfield addresses the issues of womanhood, deprivation, and power
        in Harriet Jacobs' *Incidents in the Life of a Slave Girl*, Kate Chopin's
        The Awakening, and William Faulkner's *Absalom! Absalom!* The
        author cites the work of Freud, Lacan, and Kristeva, suggesting that
        the heroines of these works seek to construct a language of power
        that subverts the power structure of Southern culture. Edna
        Pontellier is considered a possession by her husband and by society,
        and she attempts a linguistic revolution which amounts to the pursuit

of a voice in which she might express herself above the voices of husband and lover. She and the other female heroes and their authors experiment with the tensions within the narratives.

F.53   Kelley, Annetta Mary Frances. "Kate Chopin's Usage of French and Usage of Subtext in Her Stories and Novels: Two Studies." Diss. U of Toledo, 1991. *DAI-A* 52.7 (1992): 2553.
        This dissertation is divided into two smaller studies, one dealing with Chopin's use of Gallic language and the other addressing her use of subtext. The author argues that English was not Chopin's first language, stating that she achieves clear English, despite her French-Creole background. The study of subtext seeks elements that should be added to Elaine Gardiner's list of Chopin's three most common literary techniques: imagery, contrast, and cyclicalism. The function of subtext is not intended to advance the narrative but to enrich it. She concludes that an author's ability to encode subtext may be the ultimate difference between mediocre writing and works of genius.

F.54   Padlasli, Heidi Marrina. "Freedom and Existentialist Choice in the Fiction of Kate Chopin." Diss. Ball State U, 1991. *DAI-A* 52.3 (1991): 920.
        Padlasli argues that criticism of *The Awakening* silenced Chopin and argues that existentialism provides a useful tool with which to analyze the novel. She argues that previous studies of Chopin and existentialism are either too general or too superficial. She focuses on terms such as anguish, bad faith, and authenticity in Chopin's works. She then argues that Kate Chopin's 'existentialism' placed her ahead of her time in her analysis of social issues.

F.55   Snitzer, Maria Fernandez. "Telling the Lives of Kate Chopin, Edith Wharton, and Willa Cather: The Effects of Social Change and Ideology Upon Literary Biography." Diss. St. Louis U, 1992. *DAI-A* 53.7 (1993): 2374.
        Snitzer argues that literary biography is a cultural product of the era in which it is produced. She compares and contrasts various biographical studies of Kate Chopin, Willa Cather, and Edith Wharton.

F.56   Stayton, Susan Dean. "From Rowson to Chopin: Radical Compromise." Diss. U of Texas at Austin, 1991. *DAI-A* 52.12 (1992): 4334.
        This study searches for strategies that subvert conventional domestic novels to produce radical subtexts. The subtext of each of the six

novels studied focuses on and critiques a particular gender question. The last chapter of the dissertation focuses on Edna Pontellier of *The Awakening* and *Edna Earl of St. Elmo* by Augusta Jane Evans Wilson to demonstrate the failure of compromise.

1992

F.57   Bendel-Simso, Mary Michele. "The Politics of Reproduction: Demystifying Female Gender in Southern Literature." Diss. State U of New York, Binghamton, 1992. *DAI-A* 53.12 (1993): 4318.
        American myth tells young women that they are not fulfilled until they bear children, and that the wish to do so is inborn. Bendel-Simpso argues that women in Southern literature often exhibit the desire *not* to be pregnant. Drawing on the work of Gramsci and Foucault, she examines the effect of asexual motherhood as woman's only acceptable social position. By studying the works of Kate Chopin, Katherine Anne Porter, William Faulkner, Flannery O'Connor, and Alice Walker, she examines the threat that the desire not to be pregnant presents in Southern culture.

F.58   Birnbaum, Michele Amy. "Dark Intimacies: The Racial Politics of Womanhood in the 1890s." Diss. U of Washington, 1992. *DAI-A* 53.6 (1992): 1911.
        Birnbaum's study considers the ideologies of race and gender in late 19th century black- and white-authored texts, focusing on works by William Dean Howells, Frances E. W. Harper, Kate Chopin, and Grace King. She argues that race and femininity are related in the context of conflicting social discourses in the era of Jim Crow. The dissertation is a study of post-bellum race relations and issues of genre, subjectivity, and sexuality.

F.59   Bryant, Sylvia Faye. "Speaking into Being: Spirituality and Community in African-American and Anglo-American Women's Writing." Diss. U of Washington, 1992. *DAI-A* 54.1 (1993): 175.
        Bryant's study attempts to reconcile the intellectual incompatibility between spirituality and mainstream feminism. Using comparative readings of texts to build a critical matrix, Bryant draws on Kate Chopin's *The Awakening* and Rebecca Jackson's *Gifts of Power*; Willa Cather's *My Ántonia*, and Nella Larsen's *Quicksand*; Toni Cade Bambara's *The Salt Eaters* and Alice Walker's *The Temple of My Familiar*; Anne Tyler's *Dinner at the Homesick Restaurant* and Marilynne Robinson's *Housekeeping*. In these texts, spirituality becomes a dimension of the feminist concept of identity.

F.60   Eden, Edward Farrell. "The Work of Women's Desire in
        Turn-of-the-century American Fiction." Diss. U of Virginia, 1992.
        DAI-A 54.2 (1993): 519.
        Eden argues that Jewett, Chopin, Dreiser and Wharton investigate
        women's desires to escape domesticity along with their exclusion
        from professional opportunities. The novels point out the limitations
        of traditional female roles, looking especially at the difficulties of
        middle-class women in the professional arena. He concludes that
        these novels trouble the problem of how women can achieve respect
        in a professional arena that has traditionally sought to exclude them.

F.61   Garvey, Ellen. "Commercial Fiction: Advertising and Fiction in
        American Magazines, 1880s to 1910s." Diss. U of Pennsylvania,
        1992. *DAI-A* 53.11 (1993): 3907.
        Garvey's study places writers such as Kate Chopin, Willa Cather,
        William Dean Howells, and Mary Wilkins Freeman, along with a
        selection of non-canonical writers, in the context of commercial
        writing, rather than literary culture. Arguing that magazines
        appearing around the turn of the century helped to define the middle-
        class reader as a consumer, Garvey states that these fictional worlds
        are consistent with the world as presented in contemporary
        advertising.

F.62   Gentry, Deborah Suiter. "The Art of Dying: Suicide in the Works of
        Kate Chopin and Sylvia Plath." Diss. Middle Tennessee State U,
        1992. *DAI-A* 53.3 (1992): 810.
        Gentry examines the representation of suicide in the works of women
        writers. She argues that Edna's suicide in *The Awakening* breaks
        with the traditional feminine suicide, which is generally the result of
        mental illness because Chopin presents Edna's suicide as an heroic
        gesture, not one that resulted from a psychological breakdown. She
        draws a parallel between Sylvia Plath's last poem, "Edge," and
        Chopin's novel, arguing that both achieve a tone in which the
        suicide of the speaker is presented as a calm and heroic act. She
        concludes that artists such as Chopin and Plath urge that women
        should not have to choose between death and a meaningful life.

F.63   Jones, Susan Agee. "Rethinking American Women's Literary History:
        The Domestic Novel and the Rise of the Short Story." Diss.
        Northwestern U, 1992. *DAI-A* 54.5 (1993): 1804.
        Jones argues that Chopin's work served as the culmination of the
        experience of 19th century American writers. Prior to Chopin's
        work, women's writing had two predominant stages: the domestic
        novel, which was the dominant literary form for women during the

first half of the century, and the effect of the legacy of this domestic novel, which influenced the next generation of American women writers. After examining these phenomena, the dissertation turns to Chopin, arguing that *At Fault* tries to break with the traditions of the domestic genre, but does so unsuccessfully. *The Awakening,* on the other hand, successfully escapes the trappings of the domestic tradition.

F.64   Ma, Yuanxi. "The Myth of Awakening: American and Chinese Women Writers." Diss. State U of New York at Buffalo, 1992. *DAI-A* 53.4 (1992): 1151.

Ma's study looks at the works of Kate Chopin and Edith Wharton, and Chinese writers Zhang Jie and Zhang Xinxin and explores the awakening of consciousness and individuality. The awakening process involves questioning, longing for knowledge, and gaining an understanding of both the outer world and the woman's inner world. Although the writers that Ma studies are separated by several generations, their work shares thematic, structural, and stylistic similarities. The authors share many of the same themes and confront similar problems.

F.65   McCullough, Mary Katherine. "Figuring Gender: British and American Women's Narratives of the 1890s." Diss. U of California, Berkeley, 1992. *DAI-A* 53.10 (1993): 3530.

This dissertation argues that the New Woman novel was defined by its focus on erotic and maternal desire. Both British and American writers of the 1890s used the newly eroticized essentialism as a political strategy. She treats Chopin in the context of the local color school, arguing that she radically addresses race, gender and desire. Other writers studied include Pauline Hopkins, Sarah Orne Jewett, Florence Converse, as well as British novelists Sarah Grand and George Egerton.

1993

F.66   Bauer, Margaret Donovan. "The Fiction of Ellen Gilchrist: An Intertextual Reading with Works by Ernest Hemingway, Katherine Anne Porter, William Faulkner, and Kate Chopin." Diss. U of Tennessee, 1993. *DAI-A* 54.6 (1993): 2147.

This dissertation offers a preliminary, extended analysis of Ellen Gilchrist's fiction. Bauer studies Gilchrist's critical reception and the structure of her canon of work, devoting the rest of the dissertation to comparative studies between Gilchrist and other Southern writers, including Kate Chopin. Gilchrist's *The Anna*

Papers begins where Chopin leaves Edna Pontellier, allowing a triumphant suicide for the protagonist, Anna Hand.

F.67   Berg, Allison Brooke. "Mothering the Race: Women's Narratives of Reproduction, 1899-1928." Diss. Indiana U, 1993. *DAI-A* 54.4 (1993): 1360.
        Berg's study looks at maternity in novels by Pauline Hopkins, Kate Chopin, Edith Wharton, Edith Summers Kelley, and Nella Larsen. She places these writers in the context of early 20ᵗʰ century constructions of the feminist, birth control, and eugenics movements. The study demonstrates the way these writers were influenced by and how they transcended contemporary theories of race and reproduction. She further argues that these writers offered the first realistic depictions of motherhood in American literature and illustrated the personal and social costs of woman's lack of control over her life. She argues that the struggles for reproductive freedom and racial equality were intimately related.

F.68   Den Tandt, Christophe. "The Urban Sublime in American Literary Naturalism." 2 vols. Diss. Yale U, 1993. *DAI-A* 54.7 (1994): 2577. Den Tandt argues that the Naturalists' use of the sublime tropes of terror and wonder amount to a "literary response to social breakdown caused by the rapid growth of cities." The Naturalist text "acknowledges the irremediable fragmentation of the city" but "uses the discourse of sublimity as a rhetorical strategy of retotalization" to synthesize the urban world. The author draws on a variety of Naturalist writers, including Chopin.

F.69   Dickson, Rebecca Joanne. "Ladies Out of Touch: Kate Chopin's Voiceless and Disembodied Women." Diss. U of Colorado, Boulder, 1993. *DAI-A* 55.4 (1994): 962.
        Dickson points out that Chopin's critics often do not base their analyses of her work on historical data of the 19ᵗʰ century or the products of its female writers. She argues that Chopin wrote about women's silence, and their inability, because of cultural restrictions, to write about the experience of the body. She examines Chopin's efforts to develop a language through which white middle-class women could address their bodies, a language that Chopin could not develop because she was silenced by the critical reception of *The Awakening*. The dissertation also discusses Chopin's depiction of issues of race and class structure.

F.70   Di Pierro, Marianne Elizabeth. "The Utopian Vision in the Works of Wollstonecraft, Gilman, and Chopin." Diss. U of South Florida, 1993.

DAI-A 54.1 (1994): 3737.

This dissertation argues that the works of Mary Wollstonecraft, Charlotte Perkins Gilman, and Kate Chopin each attempt to achieve a utopian feminist expression and that their works explicate multiple aspects of the female experience. Chopin uses universal human experience to illustrate female Realism not present in other late 19th century literature. The works of these writers attempt to give women a voice heretofore silenced.

F.71   Dressler, Mylene Caroline. "Unmasking the Female Spectator: Sighting Feminist Strategies in Chopin, Glasgow, and Larsen." Diss. Rice U, 1993. *DAI-A* 54.10 (1994): 3747.

This study takes a feminist psychoanalytic approach, focusing on the theory of the "female spectator," and attempts to answer the question of who she is and what she represents. The author draws on the work of Mary Ann Doane, Tania Modleski, and Teresa de Lauretis, and the first chapter offers a Lacanian analysis of *The Awakening*.

F.72   Harris, Judith L. "The Darkness of Encounter: The Figure of Psyche in Romantic Literature." Diss. George Washington U, 1993. *DAI-A* 54.3 (1993): 923.

Harris argues that the Cupid and Psyche myth is often replayed in the Romantic writing of John Keats, Percy Shelley, Mary Shelley, and Kate Chopin. She argues that the myth gives the reader insight into the writer's mental processes. She points to Chopin's use of the Psyche myth, arguing that Chopin's work traces the journey of the female hero and presents the female artist's quest for individuality.

F.73   Scholz, Anne-Marie Wilhelmina. "Domesticating Female Mastery: Reading Jane Austen in America, 1826-1926." Diss. U of California, Irvine, 1993. *DAI-A* 54.4 (1993): 1432.

Scholz's dissertation is largely a study of Jane Austen, but points out that male writers such as Henry James and William Dean Howells, by designating Austen as a Realist, limited the ways in which 19th century women writers could define themselves in the literary profession. The study addresses Chopin, Wharton, Gilman, and Jewett.

F.74   Shuchter, Lisa. "Contradictory Images of the Housewife as Depicted in Victorian American Women's Fiction and Some Sister Arts." Diss. Columbia U, Teacher's College, 1993. *DAI-A* 54.8 (1994): 3035.

This dissertation deals with works of art and literature that illustrate the tension created by the status of the middle-class housewife in Victorian America. Shuchter studies Harriet Beecher Stowe, Rose

Terry Cooke, Elizabeth Stuart Phelps, Sarah Orne Jewett, Kate Chopin, Mary Wilkins Freeman, Charlotte Perkins Gilman, Edith Wharton, and Willa Cather, along with artists Eunice Pinney, Maryan Smith, Anne Whitney, Harriet Hosmer, Lida Clarkson, Mary Cassatt, Theresea Bernstein, Dorothea Tanning, as well as anonymous needle artists because they represent housewives. Each chapter of the dissertation approaches the housewife's experience from a different perspective in order to reveal the patterns and themes in the artist's treatments of housewives.

F.75   Steele, Phyllis Eileen. "Hungry Hearts, Idle Wives, and New Women: The American Novel Re-examines Nineteenth Century Domestic Ideology, 1890-1917." Diss. U of Iowa, 1993. *DAI-A* 54.9 (1994): 3615.

Steele examines a group of American novels published at the turn of the century that focused on the sex problem. These novels were part of a literary debate that foreshadowed a larger, public debate on gender roles, domesticity, and separate spheres. The author argues that these writers saw the institution of the family threatened by social change. The effect of the increased attention brought to bear by these writers was a reevaluation of the following items: (1) the identity, autonomy, and equality of women; (2) an increased awareness of the sexuality of both sexes, especially women; (3) the changing nature and meaning of work and its effect on gender roles; (4) the nature of marriage and divorce.

F.76   Strysick, Michael Parrish. "The Malady of Community." Diss. State U of New York, Binghamton, 1993. *DAI-A* 55.2 (1994): 273.

Drawing on French post-structural theory and a 1937 lecture by Georges Bataille, Strysick studies the works of various American and Continental novelists, including Chopin. His third chapter, "Madness and the Rites of Awakening" includes a discussion of Kate Chopin's *The Awakening* and Charlotte Perkins Gilman's "The Yellow Wallpaper."

1994

F.77   Bucher, Christina Gloria. "Transgressive Triangles: Desire, Gender, and the Text in Five American Novels, 1852-1905." Diss. U of Tennessee, 1994. *DAI-A* 56.2 (1995): 548.

Bucher argues that "transgressive" love triangles – those "which contain both heterosexual and homosexual desire" – are often overlooked. The existence of these triangles in *The Blithedale Romance*, *The Bostonians*, *The Awakening*, *The House of Mirth*, and

Q.E.D. "destabilizes gender and causes a disruption in the structure of the text or the reader's response" to it. Mlle. Reisz, in Chopin's novel, is portrayed as a sexless woman, who has traded sexual passion for independence. This trade does not erase her desire, however, but intrudes into the narrative as she becomes involved in a triangle with Edna and Robert. Bucher draws similar parallels in the other works that she studies.

F.78   Chelte, Judith Segzdowicz. "Philomela's Tapestry: Empowering Voice Through Text, Texture, and Silence." Diss. U of Massachusetts, 1994. *DAI-A* 55.11 (1995): 3510.
        This dissertation argues that the work of American writers Harriet Jacobs, Kate Chopin, Zora Neale Hurston, Alice Walker, and Maxine Hong Kingston are predicated on Ovid's version of the Philomela myth. This influence offers a definition of voice that includes text, texture, and silence.

F.79   Emery, Mary Ann. "The Sea Has Many Voices." Original Short Fiction. Diss. U of Wisconsin, Milwaukee, 1994. *DAI-A* 55.7 (1995): 1948.
        This dissertation is a collection of six short stories which feature female protagonists of different ages. The images and metaphors of the sea are drawn from the writing of T.S. Eliot, Virginia Woolf, and Kate Chopin.

F.80   Monda, Kimberly Ann. "Resisting Self-sacrifice: Subjectivity and Sexuality in Six American Women's Novels from Chopin to Hurston." Diss. U of California, Los Angeles, 1994. *DAI-A* 55.11 (1995): 3513.
        This dissertation looks at attempts of early 20th century American women novelists to deal with female self-sacrifice. Late 19th century expectations of ideal womanhood deemed women who submitted to subordination of their own needs in favor of the family to be morally superior. In her study of Chopin, Hopkins, Wharton, Austin, Larsen and Hurston's novels, she examines the issues of the societal expectations that the female would sacrifice herself. She also studies the means of resistance to social pressure and the ways the author relates her "heroine's inability to experience herself." She also investigates the consequences of female self-sacrifice.

F.81   Waldron, Karen E. "Coming to Consciousness, Coming to Voice: The Reinvention of Eve in American Women's Writings." Diss. Brandeis U, 1994. *DAI-A* 55.3 (1994): 569.
        This dissertation uses Harriet Beecher Stowe's "sinless child" to create a feminist phenomenology of the novel. Women writers tried

to develop scripts that allowed their maternal voices to be heard as they moved from sentimentality toward Realism. Chopin's *The Awakening* highlights the theme in women's literature of the virgin/whore opposition. Developments in religion, politics and the novel allowed the subversive synthesis of this classic opposition.

F.82   Wright, Charlotte Megan. "Plain and Ugly Janes: The Rise of the Ugly Woman in Contemporary American Fiction." Diss. U of North Texas, 1994. *DAI-A* 55.9 (1995): 2837.

Traditionally, literature has been the domain of the beautiful woman. Plain women have generally been relegated to the role of undesirable old maid, regardless of their success outside of the sphere of marriage and family. Wright argues that homely women have become downright ugly in late 20th century fiction, to the point that important parts of certain narratives could not take place if the character were physically attractive. These "ugly women" stories cause readers to question the high societal value placed on physical beauty and to examine the narrow definition of American beauty. The ugly woman in literature is able to achieve a status close to that of hero because she is not so feminine that she can't be masculinized. Wright's study touches on in excess of 30 authors, with Chopin being one of those discussed.

1995

F.83   Bonifer, M. Susan Elizabeth. "Like a Motherless Child: The Orphan Figure in the Novels of Nineteenth Century American Women Writers, 1850-1899." Diss. Indiana U of Pennsylvania, 1995. *DAI-A* 56.5 (1995): 1773.

Bonifer's study explores the evolution of orphans' tales in novels by Susan Warner, Maria Susanna Cummins, Augusta J. Evans, Elizabeth Stuart Phelps, and Kate Chopin. She examines the evolution of 19th century women in their treatment of their state as social, political and artistic orphans. She concludes that the female orphan's story grows out of a quest for the individual freedom and identity of traditional male heroes.

F.84   Novak, Terry D. "Writing from the Spirit, Writing from the Soul: Five Nineteenth Century American Women Writers as Purveyors of Spirituality and Feminism." Diss. U of Nevada, Las Vegas, 1995. *DAI-A* 56.7 (1996): 2684.

Novak explores the novels of Fanny Fern, Harriet Wilson, Rebecca Harding Davis, Frances E.W. Harper, and Kate Chopin. The study focuses on the concept of "writing from the spirit and writing from the soul" of *l'ecriture feminine* in an effort to explore the uniqueness and validity of 19th century women's writing.

F.85   Palumbo-de Simone, Christine M. "Sharing Secrets: Encoded Meanings in Nineteenth-century Women's Relationship Stories." Diss. Temple U, 1995. *DAI-A* 56.6 (1995): 2240.
This dissertation explores how 19th century middle-class women's relationships produced a shared body of knowledge. The study then focuses on the short story genre, drawing on the feminist scholarship of Annette Kolodny, Lillian Faderman, Nancy Chodorow, and Carroll Smith-Rosenberg, among others, to demonstrate how the unstated aspects of women's relationships served as a structural device in their works. Authors studied include Mary E. Wilkins Freeman, Susan Pettigru King Bowen, Elizabeth Stuart Phelps, Edith Wharton, Sarah Orne Jewett, Kate Chopin, and Lydia Maria Child. The study closes with suggested strategies for reading the "unsaid" in the context of writing by 19th century African-American, immigrant, and working-class women.

F.86   Russell, Kate Esary. "The Hidden Darkness: Landscape as Psychological Symbol in Kate Chopin's Fiction." Diss. Emory U, 1995. *DAI-A* 56.7 (1996): 2686.
Russell argues that the landscape imagery in *At Fault* and the Cane River fiction falls into two categories: the plantation, which symbolizes controlled environments, and the bayous and woods, which symbolize the wilderness that extends beyond the plantation borders. The landscape influences and reflects her characters' attitudes, emotions, and behaviors. Further, the plantation represents the past as well as the future as it attempts to disavow itself from the legacy of enslavement. The bayous and woods represent sources of escape from civilization, but characters take serious psychological risks if they retreat too far from civilization. New Orleans serves much the same purpose as the plantations, and Grand Isle provides an environment much like the bayous and woods. Russell concludes that an understanding of Chopin's use of natural settings is necessary for an accurate reading of her work.

F.87   Wiedmann, Lorna Ruth. "Suicide in American Fiction, 1798-1909." Diss. U of Wisconsin, Madison, 1995. *DAI-A* 56.5 (1995): 1783.
Weidmann identifies five core patterns of suicide that occur in 19th century novels, drawing on historical, cultural, sociological, scientific, and medical sources to prove her argument. She addresses Chopin's *The Awakening* in the last chapter of the study, in the context of gender-specific features in the suicides of artists.

1996

F.88   Dahlberg, Mary Margaret. "'Now She Understood': Free Indirect Discourse and Its Effects." Diss. U of North Dakota, 1996. *DAI-A* 58.1 (1996): 155.
      Dahlberg argues that free indirect discourse is a useful tool with which to analyze literature from a variety of eras, not just works produced during the 20th century. The effect of the discourse varies, based on the narrative voice, and whether that voice represents speech or thought. She surveys works from Antiquity, the Middle Ages, and the turn of the century. Modern authors studied include Joyce, Woolf, Eliot, and Chopin.

F.89   Jasin, Soledad Herrero-Ducloux. "Sex and Suicide in *Madame Bovary*, *Anna Karenina*, *The Awakening* and *The House of Mirth*." Diss. U of Texas, Dallas, 1996. *DAI-A* 57.6 (1996): 2467.
      Jasin argues that critics have practiced discrimination against Emma Bovary, Edna Pontellier, Anna Karenina, and Lily Bart because of their gender and their suicides. She argues that the gender-biased nature of criticism is a result of the devaluation of female agency. Jasin argues that the deaths of these women are crucial in this devaluation and that the Western cultural taboo against suicide causes readers to perceive them as weak and mentally ill. Jasin concludes that the suicides of these characters are courageous, serving as a protection of their own identities.

F.90   Kramb, Marie Annette. "Maternal Responsibility in Turn-of-the-Century Novels by American Women: Power, Resistance, Revision." Diss. U of Notre Dame, 1996. *DAI-A* 57.10 (1996): 4369.
      Kramb's study focuses on the maternal ideals of medicine, commerce, marriage, and art. Chopin, Glasgow, and Cather reveal "idealistic definitions of maternal responsibility" that lead to a moral code that make women's self sacrifice obligatory. She investigates the potential of a 20th century dilemma related to the possibility of women's "ethical subjectivity" again becoming socially acceptable.

F.91   Mathews, Carolyn Louise. "Fabricating Identities: Dress in American Realist Novels, 1880-1925." Diss. U of North Carolina, Greensboro, 1996. *DAI-A* 57.12 (1996): 5152.
      This study examines the basis of clothing as a representation of the self in representative American Realist novels from 1875 to 1925. She notes the expansion of the middle class and consumer culture in this period, along with the rise of the image of the "good life" for all. She argues that as women leave the domestic sphere in response to

these changes, a new model of social evolution emerges. The author examines descriptions of clothing in Henry James' *The Portrait of a Lady*, Kate Chopin's *The Awakening*, Edith Wharton's *The House of Mirth*, Theodore Dreiser's *Sister Carrie*, Willa Cather's *My Ántonia*, and Ellen Glasgow's *Barren Ground.* She applies Mikhail Bakhtin's socio-linguistic theory of the novel to the analysis of how choice of dress represents cultural choice as well. She also presents the study as a model for using images of dress in literary interpretation.

F.92   McGowan, Todd Robert. "The Empty Subject: The New Canon and the Politics of Existence." Diss. Ohio State U, 1996. *DAI-A* 57.2 (1996): 683.

McGowan argues that recent changes in the American literary canon can be linked to the emergence of global capitalism. He focuses on four prominent, recently recovered works: Charlotte Perkins Gilman's "The Yellow Wallpaper," Kate Chopin's *The Awakening*, Charles W. Chesnutt's *The Marrow of Tradition*, and Zora Neale Hurston's *Their Eyes Were Watching God.* His argument presents variations on the theme that political action is derived from human loss. Each novel represents an example of existential awareness resulting in political action. He concludes that only in recognizing the inevitability of death can we challenge ideologies that hold sway over us.

F.93   Seay, Geraldine Hord. "The Literature of Jim Crow: Call and Response." Diss. U of Florida, 1996. *DAI-A* 58.7 (1996): 2659.

Seay investigates turn-of-the-century literature that draws on the realities of Jim Crow for its major themes. These literary texts cross the "color line" repeatedly in attempts to give equal attention to both proponents and opponents of Jim Crow. Using the African-American musical tradition of call and response, she argues that the "call" is pro-Jim-Crow, and the response is the opposition. As each is a part of the whole entity, neither is complete standing alone. The last chapter of the study discusses Chopin's ambivalence toward racial issues and argues that she moves from the role of the caller to the role of the respondent.

1997

F.94   Adamowicz, Catherine. "Indicated Silences in American Novels." Diss. U of Rhode Island, 1997. *DAI-A* 58.8 (1997): 3128.

Adamowicz's dissertation argues that silence is an aspect of speech and analyses the significance of such silences. She attempts to illustrate that an author's uses of silence reflect her position in the moment and tend to evolve gradually and predictably. She uses a variety of authors, including Chopin, to illustrate her theory. In Chopin's writing, the author equates silence with the extent to which the protagonist conforms to the image of the "Southern lady."

F.95   Green, Suzanne Disheroon. "Knowing Is Seaing: Conceptual Metaphor in the Fiction of Kate Chopin." Diss. U of North Texas, 1997. *DAI-A* 58.3 (1997): 870.

The author applies the tools of cognitive linguistics to *The Awakening* and Kate Chopin's short fiction, with an emphasis on the theory of conceptual metaphor (CM). Drawing on the work of Mark Turner, George Lakoff, and Mark Johnson to show that CM's structure words, thoughts, and experiences, she argues that CM's provide one of the structures of literary texts. She notes that CM's are especially evident at the turning points in a text.

F.96   Lem, Ellyn Andrea. "Pioneers and Martyrs: Realism and the "Woman Question" in Turn-of-the-century American Fiction." Diss. New York U, 1997. *DAI-A* 58.9 (1997): 3524.

Lem's dissertation argues that the divergence, in the eyes of critics, of male and female authors at the turn of the century fails to note their equal contribution to the shifts in women's representation in fiction. The author notes the "woman question," and how all of the novelists present progressive-minded females in their texts, along with their challenge to the Victorian American status quo. Lem pairs Chopin and Sinclair Lewis to illustrate the tension between the institution of marriage and the urge to reform it.

F.97   Rippon, Maria Rose. "Whose Crime and Whose Punishment? Adultery in the Nineteenth-century Novel." Diss. U of North Carolina at Chapel Hill, 1997. *DAI-A* 58.8 (1997): 3122.

Rippon makes a comparative study of the Realistic novels of adultery of Tolstoy, Clarin, Chopin, Quieros and Flaubert. She argues that while adultery is always censured, the adulteress often escapes such censure. Wives, however, are more harshly judged and punished, illustrating the hypocrisy of society. She argues that *The Awakening* shows a greater concern with the search for self and a sense of place than with adultery.

F.98   Ruotolo, Cristina Lucia. "Resounding Fictions: Music, Literature and Audience in Early Twentieth-Century America." Diss. Yale U, 1997. *DAI-A* 58.4 (1997): 1284.

Ruotolo discusses the significance of music to turn-of-the-century American writers and to an opera audience. She proposes that music

is crucial to the daily experience of modern Americans, pointing out
the connections between Chopin and the American musical tradition.
She also draws on American authors Theodore Dreiser, Weldon
Johnson, Gertrude Stein, and Virgil Thompson. She further reviews
memoirs, letters, reviews, and criticism to illustrate music's impact
on social relations. She draws on research relating music to gender,
sexuality, and constructions of Black music.

F.99   Sempreora, Margot Sahrbeck. "Translating Women: The Short
        Fiction of Kate Chopin and Alice Dunbar-Nelson and the Films of
        Julie Dash." Diss. Tufts U, 1997. *DAI-A* 58.3 (1997): 875.
        Sempreora's discussion predominately concerns Dunbar-Nelson and
        Dash, dealing with Chopin as a translator of Maupassant's fiction.

Author Index

Reference numbers following author's names refer to entry numbers in the text. Alpha-numeric notations refer to entries in the body of the book. Roman numerals refer to items found in the front matter of this volume.

Adamowicz, Catherine, F.94
Aherne, John R., D.113
Allen, Priscilla, D.23
Amin, Amina, E.4.1
Ammons, Elizabeth, D.184, D.185
Anastasopoulou, Maria, D.188
Apthorp, Elaine Sargent, D.204
Arner, Robert D., E.8.1

Bair, Barbara, F.24
Baker, Christopher, D.241
Ballenger, Grady, D.159, E.1
Bande, Usha, E.4.2
Bardot, Jean, D.123, E.1.1, E.3.1
Barker, Deborah E., E.3.2, F.48
Barrett, Phyllis W., D.72
Battawala, Zareen, E.4.3
Batten, Wayne, D.117
Bauer, Dale Marie, D.146, E.6.1
Bauer, Margaret D., E.8.2, F.66
Beer, Janet, D.296
Bell, Pearl K., D.154
Bendel-Simpso, Mary M., D.205,

F.57
Bender, Bert, D.189, D.206, E.8.3, E.8.4
Benfey, Christopher, D.297, D.304
Berg, Allison Brooke, F.67
Berggren, Paula S., D.24
Berke, Jacqueline, D.1, D.5
Berkove, Lawrence I., E.8.5
Bharathi, V., E.4.4
Birnbaum, Michele A., D.242, D.268, F.58
Black, Martha Fodaski, E.3.3
Block, Tina, E.4.5
Bloom, Harold, D.136, D.232, E.2
Blythe, Anne M., E.3.4
Bogarad, Carley Rees, D.25
Bonifer, M. Susan, D.207, F.83
Bonner, Judith H., D.309
Bonner, Thomas, Jr., A.1, D.26, D.27, D.81, D.88, D.89, D.147, D.309, E.6.2
Boren, Lynda S., D.197, E.3, E.3.5
Borish, Elaine, D.6

Branan, Mary Ellen, F.49
Branscomb, Jack, D.243
Brightwell, Gerri, D.274
Brown, Pearl L., D.190
Bryan, Violet Harrington, D.213
Bryant, Sylvia Faye, F.59
Bucher, Christina Gloria, F.77
Buckman, Jacqueline, D.275
Burchard, Gina M., D.103
Butler, Harry Scott, F.5

Camfield, Gregg, D.276
Candela, Gregory L., D.37
Candela, Joseph L., Jr., D.64
Cantarow, Ellen, D.38
Carvill, Caroline, F.36
Casale, Ottavio Mark, D.39
Castiglia, Christopher Dean, F.50
Castro, Ginette, D.220
Chelte, Judith Segzdowicz, F.78
Chopin, Kate, D.28, D.29
Christ, Carol P., D.59
Clatworthy, Joan Mayerson, F.6
Clemmen, Yves, D.244
Cole, Karen, D.159, D.299, E.1
Collins, Robert, D.104
Corum, Carol S., D.277
Cothern, Lynn, D.245
Craft, Brigette Wilds, D.221
Cramer, Timothy R., D.208
Culley, Margo, A.2, F.51
Cutter, Martha J., D.246

Dahlberg, Mary Margaret, F.88
Daigrepont, Lloyd M., D.191
Dash, Irene, D.30
Davidson, Cathy N., D.7
Davis, Doris, E.1.2, E.3.6
Davis, Sara deSaussure, D.197,
    E.3, E.3.7
Dawson, Hugh J., D.247
Dawson, Melanie, D.209
Day, Karen, D.248
Dearbone, Moselle Arnetta

Williams, F.29
DeKoven, Marianne, D.166
Delbanco, Andrew, E.7.1
Den Tandt, Christophe, D.298,
    F.68
Dickey, Imogene, D.31
Dickson, Rebecca Joanne, F.69,
    D.310
Dielman, Dorothy Eloise Reynolds,
    F.32
Dimock, Wai-chee, D.174, D.214
Dingledine, Donald, D.222
Di Pierro, Marianne Elizabeth,
    F.70
Dressler, Mylène, D.210, F.71
Dunn, Margaret M., E.6.12
Dyer, Joyce Coyne, D.73, D.74,
    D.75, D.76, D.77. D.105,
    D.106, D.107, D.118, D.223,
    D.249, E.2.1, E.2.2, E.6.3,
    E.8.6, F.2

Eble, Kenneth, E.2.3
Eden, Edward Farrell, F.60
Elfenbein, Anna Shannon, D.138,
    D.160
Ellis, Nancy S., D.250, E.3.8
Emery, Mary Ann, F.79
Emmitt, Helen V., D.224
Erickson, Jon, D.170
Ewell, Barbara C., D.124, D.251,
    D.300, D.311, E.3.9, E.6.4

Fineman, Jo Ann B., D.294
Fitzgibbons, Dennis, D.20
Fleissner, Jennifer L., D.287
Fluck, Winfried, D.82, D.269,
    D.288
Foata, Anne, D.252
Foster, Shirley, D.125
Fourtina, Herve, D.225
Fox-Genovese, Elizabeth, D.47,
    E.6.5
Foy, Roslyn Reso, D.192
Franklin, Rosemary F., D.108,

D.226, E.6.6
Fryer, Judith, D.2
Fusco, Richard, D.233, F.44

Gaard, Greta Claire, F.37
Gannon, Barbara C., C.8
Gardiner, Elaine, D.83, E.2.4
Garfield, Deborah Michelle, F.52
Garitta, Anthony Paul, F.3
Gartner, Carol B., D.9
Garvey, Ellen, F.61
Gaudet, Marcia, D.129, F.7
Gehman, Mary, D.148
Gentry, Deborah Suiter, F.62
George, E. Laurie, E.6.7
Gilbert, Jan, D.10
Gilbert, Sandra, D.95, D.149,
    D.161, D.234, E.2.5, E.5.1
Giles, Paul, D.198
Gilmore, Michael T., E.7.2
Giorcelli, Cristina, D.301, E.7.3
Girgus, Sam B., D.99, D.171
Glenn, Ellen Walker, F.8
Goldman, Arnold, D.150
Goldman, Dorothy, D.162
Goodwyn, Janet, D.253
Gopalan, Rajalakshmi, E.4.6
Gosh, Nibir K., E.4.7
Green, Suzanne Disheroon, D.254,
    F.95
Greer, John Thomas, E.1.3
Gremillion, Michelle, E.1.4
Griffith, Kelley, D.215
Grover, Dorys Crow, D.109
Gubar, Susan, D.149, D.161,
    D.234
Guidici, Cynthia, D.193
Gunning, Sandra, D.278
Gupta, Linda Roberta, F.22

Hadella, Charlotte Cook, F.38
Hardmeyer, Steven G., D.11
Harris, Judith L., F.72
Harris, Susan L., D.199

Harrison, Antony H., D.200
Heath, Stephen, D.255
Hermes, Liesel, D.289
Heynitz, Benita von, D.235
Hirsch, Marianne, D.90
Hochman, Barbara, D.270
Hoder-Salmon, Marilyn, D.201,
    F.20
Holditch, W. Kenneth, D.216
Hollister, Michael, D.256
Horner, Avril, D.172
Horton, Susan R., D.40
Hotchkiss, Jane, D.257
House, Elizabeth Balkman, D.48
Howell, Elmo, D.49, D.50
Huf, Linda, D.91, F.10
Huh, Joonok, F.21

Inge, Tonette Bond, C.7

Jacob, Susan, E.4.8
Jacobs, Dorothy H., E.3.10
Jacobs, Jo Ellen, E.6.8
Jacobsen, Cheryl L. Rose, E.1.5
Jarred, Ada D., D.236
Jascnas, Elianc, D.12
Jasin, Soledad Herrero-Ducloux,
    F.89
Johnson, Rose M., D.290
Jones, Anne Goodwyn, D.70
Jones, Susan Agee, F.63
Jones, Suzanne W., D.139, E.1.5,
    E.6.9, F.25
Joslin, Katherine, E.3.11
Juneja, Punim, E.4.9
Justus, James H., D.41

Kaur, Iqbal, D.271, E.4
Kearns, Katherine, D.159, D.194,
    E.1
Keesey, Donald, D.237, E.5
Kelley, Annetta Mary Frances,
    F.53
Keyser, Jeanette Parker, F.11

Kimbel, Ellen, F.12
Klemans, Patricia A., D.78
Klinkowitz, Jerome, D.60
Koloski, Bernard, D.151, D.248,
    D.284, E.6, E.6.10
Kouidis, Virginia M., D.163
Kramb, Marie Annette, F.90

Ladenson, Joyce Ruddel, D.13
Lakritz, Andrew M., E.6.1
Lanser, Susan Sniader, D.71
Lant, Kathleen Margaret, D.110,
    E.2.6, F.16
Lattin, Patricia Hopkins, D.42,
    D.65, D.84, E.6.11, F.1
LeBlanc, Elizabeth, D.291
Leder, Priscilla, D.96, E.8.7, F.13
LeFew, Penelope A., E.1.7
Lem, Ellyn Andrea, F.96
Lenarcic, Faye Mertine, F.27
Levine, Robert S., D.85
Levy, Elaine Barbara, F.14
Levy, Helen Fiddyment, F.17
Linkin, Harriet Kramer, D.259
Little, Judy, D.100
Lloyd, Caryl L., D.292
Lohafer, Susan, D.92, D.164
Lundie, Catherine, D.260
Lupton, Mary Jane, D.114
Lyons, Mary E., D.272

Ma, Yuanxi, F.64
MacCurdy, Carol, D.119
MacDonald, Alan, F.39
Macpike, Loralee, D.66
Mahlendorf, Ursula, D.152
Mahon, Robert Lee, D.306
Malzahn, Manfred, D.195
Manders, Eunice, E.1.8
Manning, Carol S., D.217
Martin, Wendy, D.153, E.7
Matchie, Thomas, D.155
Mathews, Carolyn Louise, F.91
May, John R., E.5.2

Mayer, Charles W., D.51
McCoy, Thorunn Ruga, D.302
McCullough, Mary Katherine,
    F.65
McGowan, Todd Robert, F.92
McIlvaine, Robert, D.52
McMahan, Elizabeth, D.120
Menke, Pamela Glenn, D.261,
    D.279, D.312
Merideth, Eunice Mae, F.33
Merrill, Carol, D.32
Michaels, Walter Benn, D.175
Miller, James E., Jr., D.238
Mills, Elizabeth S., D.14
Miner, Madonne M., D.86
Mitchell, Angelyn, D.211
Mitsutani, Margaret, D.130
Mizrahi, Joan Berman, F.40
Mochizuki, Kaeko, D.131
Moers, Ellen, D.3
Monda, Kimberly Ann, F.80
Morris, Ann R., E.6.12
Morris, Paula J.K., F.41
Moseley, Merritt, D.132
Moss, Rose, D.218

Newman, Judie, D.126
Novak, Terry D., F.84
Nye, Lorraine M., D.133

O'Brien, Sharon, D.33
Oriard, Michael, D.186

Padgett, Jacqueline Olson, D.262
Padlasli, Heidi Marrina, F.54
Palmer, Janet Larsen, D.143
Palumbo-de Simone, Christine M.,
    F.85
Panaro, Lydia Adriana, F.15
Papke, Mary E., D.173, E.6.13,
    F.23
Parker, Pamela Lorraine, F.18
Paul, Premila, E.4.10
Paulsen, Anne-Lise Strømness,

D.53
Payerle, Margaret Jane, F.26
Peel, Ellen, D.176, D.202
Petry, Alice Hall, D.54, D.285, E.9
Pitavy-Souques, Danièle, D.167,
    D.227
Platizky, Roger, D.280
Pontuale, Francesco, D.293
Poovalingam, N., E.4.11
Portales, Marco A., D.79

Radcliff-Umstead, Douglas, D.156,
    D.177
Ramamoorthi, Parasuram, E.4.12
Rankin, Daniel, B.1
Rankin, Elizabeth, E.6.14
Ridgley, Jo, D.61
Ries, Nancy, D.148
Ringe, Donald A., E.2.7
Rippon, Maria Rose, F.97
Rogers, Nancy E., D.97, E.6.15
Roscher, Marina L., D.111
Rosowski, Susan J., D.55, D.93,
    E.2.8, E.6.16
Rothgery, David Bruce, F.45
Roumm, Phillis G., F.4
Rowe, Anne, D.115, D.203
Rowe, John Carlos, E.1.9, E.3.12
Ruland, Richard, D.137
Ruotolo, Cristina Lucia, F.98
Russell, Kate Esary, F.86
Ryu, Chung-Eun, D.168, D.178

Saar, Doreen Alvarez, D.263
Sacken, Jeanee P., D.121
St. Andrews, Bonnie, D.127, F.9
St. Pierre, Ronald, D.281
Samet, Tom, D.159, E.1
Scholz, Anne-Marie Wilhelmina,
    F.73
Schulz, Dieter, D.228
Schweitzer, Ivy, D.179
Scott, Anne Firor, D.219
Seay, Geraldine Hord, F.93

Seidel, Kathryn, D.229, E.1.10,
    E.8.8
Sempreora, Margot, D.264, F.99
Seyersted, Per, A.3, A.4, A.6, B.2,
    D.44, D.140, D.307
Shapiro, Ann R., F.28
Shaw, Pat, D.180, E.5.3
Shaw, Patrick W., D.181
Shillingsburg, Miriam J., D.94
Showalter, Elaine, D.45, D.187,
    E.7.4, E.9.1
Shuchter, Lisa, F.74
Shumaker, Jeanette Roberts, F.46
Shurbutt, Sylvia Bailey, D.230
Silver, Lola, D.1
Simpson, Martin, D.134
Skaggs, Peggy, D.56, D.116,
    E.6.17, E.8.9
Skredsvig, Keri Meyers, D.231
Smith, Stewart, E.8.10
Snitzer, Maria Fernandez, F.55
Solomon, Barbara H., E.6.18
Sparks, Laurel Vivian, F.47
Springer, Marlene, C.1, C.6
Stange, Margit, D.169, D.305,
    E.1.11, E.4.13, E.5.4, E.9.2.,
    F.42
Stayton, Susan Dean, F.56
Steele, Phyllis Eileen, F.75
Steiling, David, D.265
Stein, Allen F., D.62, D.101
Stepenoff, Bonnie, D.141
Stone, Carole, D.135
Strysick, Michael Parrish, F.76
Suárez-Lafuente, María S., D.157
Sullivan, Ruth, E.8.10
Sweet-Hurd, Evelyn, E.6.19
Swigart, Margaret Jane Bugas,
    F.30

Tarpley, Philip, D.128
Taylor, Helen, D.165, D.313
Taylor, Walter, D.294
Thomas, Heather Kirk, C.9, D.182,

D.282, E.3.13, E.8.11, F.35
Thornton, Lawrence, D.67, E.6.20,
E.8.12
Tompkins, Jane P., D.16
Toth, Emily, A.4, A.5, A.6, B.3,
B.4, D.17, D.18, D.19, D.20,
D.34, D.35, D.36, D.44,
D.80, D.102, D.122, D.158,
D.183, D.196, D.266, D.307,
D.308, D.314, E.3.14, E.6.21
Treichler, Paula A., D.63, E.9.3
Trikha, Manorama, E.4.14
Tuttleton, James W., D.286

Urgo, Joseph R., D.142

Valentine, Kristin B., D.143
Vanlandingham, Phyllis, E.1.12
Vevaina, Coomi S., E.4.15
Viswanath, Ganga, E.4.16
Vlasopolos, Anca, D.239

Wagner-Martin, Linda, E.8.13
Waldron, Karen E., F.81
Walker, Nancy A., A.7, D.57,
D.98, D.273, E.5.5, E.6.22,
E.8.14, E.9
Wasson, Leslie, E.4.17
Weatherford, K. J., D.267
Webb, Bernice Larson, D.21, D.87
Wershoven, C. J., D.144
Wheeler, Kathleen, D.240
White, Robert, D.112
Wiedmann, Lorna Ruth, F.87
Williams, Patricia Ann Owens,
F.19
Wilson, Mary Helen, D.22
Winn, Harbour, D.212
Wolff, Cynthia Griffin, D.43,
D.58, D.295, D.303, E.2.9,
E.5.6, E.9.4
Wolstenholme, Susan, D.68
Woodland, James Randal, F.34
Wright, Charlotte Megan, F.82

Wymard, Eleanor B., D.69

Yaeger, Patricia S., D.145, E.5.7,
E.9.5
Yonogi, Reiko, D.283, F.43
Young, Margaret Mary, F.31

Ziff, Larzer, D.46, E.2.10
Zlosnik, Sue, D.172

Title Index

Reference numbers following author's names refer to entry numbers in the text. Alpha-numeric notations refer to entries in the body of the book. Roman numerals refer to items found in the front matter of this volume. Articles appear in normal type and book-length studies appear in italic type.

"Abyss of Inequality, An," D.46, E.2.10

"'Acting Like Fools': The Ill-Fated Romances of 'At the 'Cadian Ball' and 'The Storm,'" E.8.5

After the Vows Were Spoken: Marriage in American Literary Realism, D.101

"'Alien Hands:' Kate Chopin and the Colonization of Race," D.242, D.268

American Catholic Arts and Fictions: Culture, Ideology, Aesthetics, D.198

American City: Literary and Cultural Perspectives, The, D.151

"American Dilemma: Cultural Conflict in Kate Chopin's *The Awakening*, An," D.96

"'American Romance' and the Changing Functions of the Imaginary, The," D.288

"Anthologized Chopin: Kate Chopin's Short Stories in Yesterday's and Today's Anthologies, The," D.258

"Aphrodite Redux: Edna Pontellier's Dilemma in *The Awakening* by Kate Chopin," D.252

Approaches To Teaching Chopin's The Awakening, D.152, E.6

"Armand Aubigny, Still Passing After all These Years: The Narrative Voice and Historical Context of 'Désirée's Baby,'" E.8.2

"Art is an Unnatural Act: Homoeroticism, Art and Mademoiselle Reisz in *The Awakening*," E.1.10

"Art Is an Unnatural Act: Mademoiselle Reisz in *The*

Awakening," D.229

"Artist's Unrest and Arrested
Growth: Edna Pontellier in *The
Awakening*," E.4.11

"Ascent of Woman, Southern
Style: Hentz, King, Chopin,
The," D.94

"'Awakened' Woman in
Literature and Real Life, The,"
D.1

Awakening, The, A.1, A.7, E.9

*Awakening: A Novel of
Beginnings, The,* D.223

"*Awakening*: A Political Romance,
The," D.67, E.8.12

"*Awakening*: A Recognition of
Confinement, *The*," E.3.10

"*Awakening*: A Refusal to
Compromise, *The*," D.25

"*Awakening*: An Evaluation, *The*,"
D.16

"*Awakening* as a Prototype of the
Novel of Awakening, *The*,"
E.6.16

"Awakening of Female Artistry,
The," E.3.2

"*Awakening*: The Economics of
Tension, *The*," E.1.2, E.3.6

"*Awakening* and the Failure of
Psyche, *The*," D.108

"*Awakening* and *The House of
Mirth*: Plotting Experience and
Experiencing Plot, *The*," D.270

"*Awakening* and *The House of
Mirth*: Studies of Arrested
Development, *The*," D.144

"*Awakening* and the Woman
Question, *The*," E.6.1

"*Awakening* and 'The Yellow
Wallpaper': Misunderstood and
Rediscovered, *The*," E.4.17

"*Awakening* Awakens England,
The," D.6

"*Awakening*: Chopin's

Metaphorical Use of Clothes,
The," D.119

"*Awakening* in a Course on
Philosophical Ideas in
Literature, *The*," E.6.8

"*Awakening* in a Course on
Women in Literature, *The*,"
E.6.4

"*Awakening* in a Research and
Composition Course, *The*,"
E.6.19

"*Awakening* in an American
Literature Survey Course, *The*,"
E.6.2

"*Awakening* in an Introductory
Literature Course, *The*," E.6.12

"*Awakening* in the Context of the
Experience, Culture, and
Values of Southern Women,
The," E.6.5

"*Awakening*: Kate Chopin's
'Endlessly Rocking' Cycle,
The," D.48

"*Awakening*: Struggles Toward
l'Ecriture Feminine, The,"
D.293

"*Awakening's* Relationship with
American Regionalism,
Romanticism, Realism, and
Naturalism, *The*," E.6.17

"Barriers of Reticence and
Reserve," D.218

"Bayou Folk Museum, The," D.4

"Beyond the Love Triangle: Trios
in *The Awakening*," D.306

"Beyond Sex: The Dark
Romanticism of Kate Chopin's
The Awakening," D.39

"Boy's Quest in Kate Chopin's 'A
Vocation and a Voice,' The,'"
D.56, E.8.9

"Broken World: Romanticism,
Realism, Naturalism in *A*

Streetcar Named Desire, The,"
D.216

"'Call the Roller of Big Cigars':
Smoking Out the Patriarchy in
The Awakening," D.259
"Cane River Characters and
Revisionist Mythmaking in the
Work of Kate Chopin, The,"
D.230
"Cane River World: Kate Chopin's
At Fault and Related Stories,"
E.2.7
"Catalyst of Color and Women's
Regional Writing : *At Fault*,
Pembroke, and *The Awakening*,
The," D.312
"Characters as Foils to Edna,"
E.6.18
"Characterization of Edna
Pontellier and the Conclusion
of Kate Chopin's *The
Awakening*, The," D.79
"'Charlie': *Travestimento e
Potere*," D.301
"Charting the Nebula: Gender,
Language and Power in Kate
Chopin's *The Awakening*,"
D.274
"Childbirth and Motherhood in
Kate Chopin's Fiction," D.42
"Childbirth and Motherhood in
The Awakening and in
"Athénaïse," E.6.11
"Chopin and Atwood: Woman
Drowning, Woman Surfacing,"
D.7
"Chopin and Mysticism," D.132
"Chopin's 'A Shameful Affair,'"
D.134
"Chopin's 'Désirée's Baby,'"
D.192
"Chopin's Choices and
Challenges: Language and

Limits in 'A Point at Issue,'"
D.231
"Chopin's Movement Toward
Universal Myth," E.3.7
"Chopin's Parrot," D.255
"Chopin's 'Ripe Figs,'" D.243
"Chopin's Sensual Sea and Cable's
Ravished Land: Sexts, Signs,
and Gender Narrative," D.279
"Chopin's Stories of Awakening,"
E.6.13
"Chopin's *The Awakening*," D.256,
D.280, D.302
"Chopin's *The Awakening*: The
Discovery of Eternity," D.156
"Chopin's 'The Storm,'" D.241
"Christianity and Catholicism in
the Fiction of Kate Chopin,"
D.81, D.88
"Circadian Rhythms and Rebellion
in Kate Chopin's *The
Awakening*," D.85
"Circular Structure of Kate
Chopin's Life and Writing,
The," D.21
"Colorful Characters from Kate's
Past," D.14
*Coming to Terms with the Short
Story*, D.92
"Comment on Barbara Bellow
Watson's 'On Power and the
Literary Text,'" D.17
*Complete Works of Kate Chopin,
The*, A.3
*Conflicting Stories: American
Women Writers at the Turn into
the Twentieth Century*, D.184
"Confusing the Issue: Who's *At
Fault*?," D.257
"Construction of Ambiguity in *The
Awakening*: A Linguistic
Analysis, The," D.63, E.9.3
Contexts for Criticism, D.237, E.5
"Contracted Heart, The," D.175

"Courageous Soul: Woman as
Artist in American Literature,
The," D.78
"Courageous Souls: Kate Chopin's
Women Artists," D.267
"Crisis Alert: Kate Chopin House
in St. Louis," D.122
Critical Essays on Kate Chopin,
D.285, E.8

"'Dah you is, settin' down, lookin'
jis' like w'ite folks!': Ethnicity
Enacted in Kate Chopin's Short
Fiction," D.253
*"De G. Flaubert à K. Chopin, du
Paraître à l'être: Notes sur
Emma Bovary, Thérèse
Lafirme, Edna Pontellier dans
The Awakening*," D.227
*Degas in New Orleans: Encounters
in the Creole World of Kate
Chopin and George
Washington Cable*, D.297,
D.304
"Der Weisse Rabe Fliegt: Zum
Kunstlerinnenroman im 20.
Jahrhundert," D.152
"Desire and Depression in
Women's Fiction: The
Problematics and the
Economics of Desire," D.40
*Desire and the Political
Unconscious in American
Literature: Eros and Ideology*,
D.171
"'Development of the Literary
West': An Undiscovered Kate
Chopin Essay," D.182
"Dialogue Across the Pacific: Kate
Chopin's *Awakening* and the
Short Fiction of Zhang Jie"
E.1.3
"Dismantling of Edna
Pontellier: Garment Imagery in

Kate Chopin's *The Awakening*,
The," D.104
*Disobedient Writer: Women
and Narrative Tradition, The*,
D.273
*Diving Deep and Surfacing:
Women Writers on a Spiritual
Quest*, D.59
"Domestic Orientation of
American Novels, 1893-1913,"
D.64
"Dominant Discourse and the
Female Imaginary: A Study of
the Tensions Between
Disparate Discursive Registers
in Chopin's *The Awakening*,"
D.275
"Doubly Dispossessed: Kate
Chopin's Women of Color,"
D.260
"Dr. Mandelet's Real Life
Counterparts and Their Advice
Books: Setting a Context for
Edna's Revolt," E.1.5
"'Drowned in a Willing Sea:'
Freedom and Drowning in
Eliot, Chopin and Drabble,"
D.224

"Echoes of George Sand in Kate
Chopin," D.97
"Echoes of Literary Sisterhood:
Louisa May Alcott and Kate
Chopin," D.212
"Economics of the Body in
Kate Chopin's *The Awakening*,
The," E.1.9, E.3.12
*Edith Wharton and Kate Chopin: A
Reference Guide*, C.1
"Edna and the Tradition of
Listening: The Role of
Romantic Music in *The
Awakening*," D.209
"Edna as Icarus: A Mythic Issue,"

E.6.20

"Edna as Psyche: The Self and the Unconscious," E.6.6

"Edna Pontellier and the Myth of Passion," D.191

"Edna Pontellier's Art and Will: The Aesthetics of Schopenhauer in Kate Chopin's *The Awakening*," E.1.7

"Edna Under the Sun: Throwing Light on the Subject of *The Awakening*," D.210

"Edna's Awakening: A Return to Childhood," E.1.4

"Edna's Wisdom: A Transitional and Numinous Merging," E.7.3

"'Elsewhere' of Female Sexuality and Desire in Kate Chopin's 'A Vocation and a Voice, The,'" D.248

"Epiphanies Through Nature in the Stories of Kate Chopin," D.105

"Existential Dilemma of Edna Pontellier in Kate Chopin's *The Awakening*, The," E.4.4

Faces of Eve: Women in the Nineteenth Century American Novel, The, D.2

"Failure and Triumph of 'The Maid of Saint Phillippe'': Chopin Rewrites American Literature for American Women, The," D.263

"Fairytale Features in Kate Chopin's 'Désirée's Baby': A Case Study in Genre Cross-Reference," D.170

"Fate and Feminism in Kate Chopin's *The Awakening*," E.4.8

"Fear, Freedom, and the Perils of Ethnicity: Otherness in Kate Chopin's 'Beyond the Bayou'

and Zora Neale Hurston's 'Sweat,'" D.254

"Female Artist in Kate Chopin's *The Awakening*: Birth and Creativity, The," D.135

Female Tradition in Southern Literature, The, D.217

"Feminine Double Consciousness in Kate Chopin's 'The Story of an Hour,'" D.211

Feminist Dialogics: A Theory of Failed Community, D.146

"Feminist or Naturalist: The Social Context of Kate Chopin's *The Awakening*," D.57, E.5.5

"Finding the Self at Home: Chopin's *The Awakening* and Cather's *The Professor's House*," E.3.11

"Fissure as Art in Kate Chopin's *At Fault*," D.261

Forbidden Fruit: On the Relationship Between Women and Knowledge in Doris Lessing, Selma Lagerlof, Kate Chopin, Margaret Atwood, D.127

"Forgotten Novel, A," E.2.3

"Four Birth Dates For Kate Chopin," D.133

"Four Points of Equilibrium in *The Awakening*," D.87

"Frauenbilder in der Amerikanischen Literatur: Kate Chopin, EdithWharton, Carson McCullers," D.289

"Frédéric Pronounced It the Same Way," D.8

Freedom and Regret: The Dilemma of Kate Chopin, D.141

"French Creole Portraits: The Chopin Family from Natchitoches Parish," E.1.1,

E.3.1

"French Influence in Kate
  Chopin's *The Awakening*, The"
  D.12

"From Conflict to Suicide — A
  Feminist Approach to Kate
  Chopin's *The Awakening*,"
  E.4.2

"Gender and Fiction," D.185

*Gender, Race and Region in the
  Writings of Grace King, Ruth
  McEnery Stuart, and Kate
  Chopin*, D.165

"Gendered Doubleness and the
  'Origins' of Modernist Form,"
  D.166

"George Sand, Kate Chopin,
  Margaret Atwood and the
  Redefinition of Self," D.121

"Gouvernail, Kate Chopin's
  Sensitive Bachelor," D.73,
  E.2.1

"Half-Life of Edna Pontellier,
  The," E.7.1

"Hedda and Edna: Writing the
  Future," D.207

"Her Own Story: The Woman of
  Letters in Kate Chopin's Short
  Fiction," E.8.14.

"Historical and Cultural Setting,
  The," E.6.22

"'House of Sylvie' in Kate
  Chopin's 'Athénaïse,' The,"
  E.8.11

"'Il etait une fois un moi': *The
  Awakening* de Kate Chopin,"
  D.225

"Illusion and Archetype: The
  Curious Story of Edna
  Pontellier," D.117

"Imaginative Limits: Ideology and

The Awakening," D.221

"Imagining Marriage," D.100

"Impressionism in Kate Chopin's
  The Awakening," D.32

"Inner and Outer Space in *The
  Awakening*," D.112

"Insistent Refrains and Self-
  Discovery: Accompanied
  Awakenings in Three Stories
  by Kate Chopin," E.3.8

"Isabel Archer, Edna Pontellier,
  and the Romantic Self," D.51

"Joy of Spring, The," D.29

"Kate Chopin," C.7, D.58, D.115,
  D.116, D.124, D.214

*Kate Chopin: A Critical
  Biography*, B.2

*Kate Chopin: A Life of the Author
  of The Awakening*, B.3

"Kate Chopin: A Primary
  Bibliography, Alphabetically
  Arranged," C.9

"Kate Chopin: A Reference Guide
  Updated," C.6

"Kate Chopin: A Secondary
  Bibliography," C.8

*Kate Chopin: A Study of the Short
  Fiction*, D.284

*Kate Chopin: A Woman of
  Yesterday, Today and
  Tomorrow: A Manual*, D.236

"Kate Chopin: An American de
  Maupassant," D.113

"Kate Chopin and Editors: 'A
  Singular Class of Men," E.1.12

*Kate Chopin and Her Creole
  Stories*, B.1

"Kate Chopin and Literary
  Convention: 'Désirée's Baby,'"
  D.80

"Kate Chopin and Sarah Orne
  Jewett," D.154

"Kate Chopin and *The Awakening*," D.137

"Kate Chopin and *The Awakening* of Eve," E.4.7

"Kate Chopin and the Bayou Country," D.109

"Kate Chopin and the Creole Country," D.49

"Kate Chopin and the Dream of Female Selfhood," E.3.9

"Kate Chopin and the Fiction of Limits: 'Désirée's Baby,'" D.43, E.2.9

"Kate Chopin and the Literature of the Annunciation, with a Reading of 'Lilacs,'" D.262

"Kate Chopin and the Lore of Cane River's Creoles of Color," D.129

"Kate Chopin and the Pull of Faith: A Note on 'Lilacs,'" D.50

"Kate Chopin as Translator: A Paradoxical Liberation," D.264

"Kate Chopin Bibliography," C.2, C.3, C.4, C.5,

Kate Chopin Companion, The, A.1, D.147

Kate Chopin, Edith Wharton and Charlotte Perkins Gilman: Studies in Short Fiction, D.296

"Kate Chopin-hauer: Or, Can Metaphysics Be Feminized?," D.276

"Kate Chopin: Her Existential Imagination," D.69

"Kate Chopin: Her Serious Literary Ambition," D.31

"Kate Chopin Meets *The Harvard Lampoon*," D.20

Kate Chopin Miscellany, A, A.4, D.44

Kate Chopin: Modern Critical Views, D.136, E.2

"Kate Chopin, Mrs. Pontellier, and Narrative Control," D.310

"*Kate Chopin Newsletter*: History, Future, Apologies and Grovels," D.34

"Kate Chopin on Divine Love and Suicide: Two Rediscovered Articles," D.196

"Kate Chopin: Pre-Freudian Freudian," D.294

Kate Chopin Reconsidered: Beyond the Bayou, D.197, E.3

"Kate Chopin Remembered," D.18

"Kate Chopin: Short Fiction and the Arts of Subversion," D.126

"Kate Chopin Thinks Back Through Her Mothers: Three Stories by Kate Chopin," E.3.14

"Kate Chopin: Tradition and the Moment," D.89

"Kate Chopin Up Against the Wall," D.10

"Kate Chopin's *At Fault* and *The Awakening*: A Study in Structure," D.27

"Kate Chopin's *At Fault*: The Usefulness of Louisiana French for the Imagination," D.269

"Kate Chopin's Awakening," D.47

"Kate Chopin's Awakening to Naturalism," D.60

"Kate Chopin's *Bayou Folk* Revisited," D.26

"Kate Chopin's Call to a Larger 'Awakening,'" D.5

"Kate Chopin's 'Charlie,'" E.3.4

"Kate Chopin's Family: Fallacies and Facts, Including Kate's True Birthdate," D.22

"Kate Chopin's Fascination with Young Men," E.8.13

"Kate Chopin's Fiction: Order and Disorder in a Stratified Society," D.190

"Kate Chopin's Local Color
   Fiction and the Politics of
   White Supremacy," D.278
"Kate Chopin's Music," D.35
"Kate Chopin's New Orleans: A
   Visual Essay," D.309
"Kate Chopin's New Orleans
   Years," D.158
"Kate Chopin's 'Occasional'
   Women," D.193
Kate Chopin's Private Papers,
   A.6, D.307
"Kate Chopin's Problematic
   Womanliness: The Frontier of
   American Feminism," D.103
"Kate Chopin's Quarrel with
   Darwin before The
   Awakening," D.206, E.8.3
"Kate Chopin's Repeating
   Characters," D.65
"Kate Chopin's Sawmill:
   Technology and Change in At
   Fault," D.128
"Kate Chopin's Scribbling Women
   and the American Literary
   Marketplace," D.282
"Kate Chopin's Secret, Slippery
   Life Story," D.314
"Kate Chopin's Sleeping Bruties,"
   D.74, E.2.2
"Kate Chopin's Sources for 'Mrs.
   Mobry's Reason,'" D.68
"Kate Chopin's The Awakening: A
   Dissenting Opinion," D.247
"Kate Chopin's The Awakening: A
   Quest of 'Sybil,'" E.4.14
"Kate Chopin's The Awakening:
   An Assault on American Racial
   and Sexual Mythology," D.138
"Kate Chopin's The Awakening
   and American Literary
   Tradition," D.281
"Kate Chopin's The Awakening
   and the Limits of Moral

Judgement," D.62
"Kate Chopin's The Awakening as
   Feminist Criticism," D.19
"Kate Chopin's The Awakening:
   'Casting Aside that Fictitious
   Self,'" D.162
Kate Chopin's The Awakening:
   Critical Essays, D.272, E.4
Kate Chopin's The Awakening:
   Screenplay as Interpretation,
   D.201
"Kate Chopin's The Awakening:
   Sex-role Liberation or Sexual
   Liberation?," E.4.1
"Kate Chopin's The Awakening:
   The Complexity of Edna
   Pontellier," E.4.6
"Kate Chopin's The Awakening:
   The Narcissism of Edna
   Pontellier," D.130
"Kate Chopin's Wound: Two New
   Letters," D.140
Keeping Secrets: The Girlhood
   Diaries of Seven Women,
   D.272

"La Mere absente et/ou le manque
   a etre d'Edna Pontellier,"
   D.220
"Lafcadio Hearn's Chita and Kate
   Chopin's The Awakening: Two
   Naturalistic Tales of the Gulf
   Islands," D.106
"Land of the Free: Or, The
   Home of the Brave, The,"
   D.155
"Land's End: The Awakening and
   19th Century Literary
   Tradition," E.8.7
Landscapes of Desire: Metaphors
   in Modern Women's Fiction,
   D.172
"'Language Which Nobody
   Understood:' Emancipatory

Strategies in *The Awakening*, The," D.145, E.5.7, E.9.5

"Last Phase of Kate Chopin's Life - from 1900 to 1904, The," D.131

"Laughter of Their Own: Women's Humor in the United States, A," D.102

"Lilia Polka for Piano," D.28

"L'influence Francaise dans la vie et l'oeuvre de Kate Chopin," D.123

Literarische Kontexte von Kate Chopin's The Awakening, D.235

Literary Women, D.3

"Literature of Birth and Abortion, The," D.30

"Literature of Deliverance: Images of Nature in *The Awakening*," D.177

"Local Color in *The Awakening*," E.5.2

"Long and Winding Road: An Analysis of Kate Chopin's *The Awakening*, The," E.4.3

"Losing the Battle but Winning the War: Resistance to Patriarchal Discourse in Kate Chopin's Short Fiction," D.246

"'Lost Soul:' Work Without Hope in *The Awakening*, A," D.24

"Making Places: Kate Chopin and the Art of Fiction," D.251

"Masculine Dilemma in Kate Chopin's *The Awakening*, The," D.53

"Materials, Including Editions, Further Reading for Students, Further Reading for Teachers, and Aids to Teaching," E.6.10

"Maternal Discourse and the Romance of Self-Possession in

Kate Chopin's *The Awakening*," D.179

Maupassant and the American Short Story: The Influence of Form and the Turn of the Century, D.233

"Message from the Pine Woods of Central Louisiana: The Garden in Northrup, Chopin, and Dormon, The," D.299

"Metaphorical Lesbian: Edna Pontellier in *The Awakening*, The," D.291

Modernist Women Writers and Narrative Art, D.240

"More American Adams: Women Heroes in American Fiction," D.72

"Mothers, Women and Creole Mother-Women in Kate Chopin's South," D.205

"Multi-Cultural Aesthetic in Kate Chopin's 'A Gentleman of Bayou Teche,'" D.265

"Music in *The Awakening*," D.277

Myth of New Orleans in Literature: Dialogues of Race and Gender, The, D.213

Narrative Act: Point of View in Prose Fiction, The, D.71

"Narrative Stance in Kate Chopin's *The Awakening*," E.8.10

"Nature and Sexuality in the Fiction of Kate Chopin," D.168

"'Nature's Decoy': Kate Chopin's Presentation of Women and Marriage in Her Short Fiction," D.120

"Negro as a Serious Subject in Kate Chopin's Fiction, The," D.178

"New Biographical Approach, A,"

E.6.21

New Essays on the Awakening,
    D.148, E.8

"New Generation Reads Kate
    Chopin, A," D.266

"New Orleans as Metaphor: Kate
    Chopin," D.203

"Night Images in the Work of Kate
    Chopin," D.75

*Nineteenth Century American
    Women's Novels: Interpretive
    Strategies*, D.199

*Nineteenth Century Southern
    Literature*, D.61

*No Man's Land: The Place of the
    Woman Writer in the Twentieth
    Century.*
        *Vol 1: The War of the
            Words*, D.150
        Vol 2: Sexchanges, D.161
        *Vol 3: Letters from the
            Front*, D.234

"Note on Kate Chopin's 'The
    White Eagle,' A," D.107

"Notes Toward a *fin-de-siècle*
    Reading of Kate Chopin's *The
    Awakening*," D.228

"Novel of Awakening, The," D.55,
    D.93, E.2.8

"Nullification of Edna
    Pontellier, The," D.194

"Oceanic Discourse,
    Empowerment and Social
    Accommodation in Kate
    Chopin's *The Awakening* and
    Henrik Ibsen's *The Lady from
    the Sea*," D.298

"Old Critics and New: The
    Treatment of Chopin's *The
    Awakening*," D.23

"Open Cage: Freedom, Marriage
    and the Heroine in Early
    Twentieth-Century American

Women's Novels, The," D.125

"Paysage langage ou l'impossible
    acces à la parole: une relecture
    de *The Awakening* de Kate
    Chopin," D.167

"Personal Property: Exchange
    Value and the Female Self in
    The Awakening," D.169, D.305
    E.1.11, E.4.13, E.5.4, E.9.2

*Personal Property: Exchange
    Value and the Female Self in
    The Awakening*, D.305

*Perspectives on Kate Chopin:
    Proceedings of the Kate
    Chopin International
    Conference*, D.159, E.1

"Photographic Politics: The Text
    and Its Readings in Kate
    Chopin's *The Awakening*,"
    D.244

"Picture Perfect: Painting in *The
    Awakening*," E.8.8

"Place, Perception and Identity in
    The Awakening," D.139, E.1.5

"Poe and *The Awakening*," D.226

*Portrait of the Artist as a Young
    Woman: The Writer as Heroine
    in American Literature, A*,
    D.91

"Practical Side of Oscar
    Chopin's Death, The," D.15

"Preclosure and Story Processing,"
    D.164

"Presupposition of
    Intertextuality in Clarin's *La
    Regenta* and Chopin's *The
    Awakening*, A," D.157

"Pride in Prejudice: Kate Chopin's
    'Désirée's Baby,'" E.8.1

"Prison into Prism: Emerson's
    'Many-Colored Lenses' and the
    Woman Writer of Early
    Modernism," D.163

"Prologue to Rebellion: *The Awakening* and the Habit of Self-Expression, A," D.142

"Puppets Must Perform or Perish: A Feminist Archetypal Analysis of Kate Chopin's *The Awakening*," E.4.15

"Putting Audience in Its Place: Psychosexuality and Perspective Shifts in *The Awakening*," D.180, E.5.3

"Quintessence of Chopinism, The," E.3.3

"R.D. Laing and Literature: Readings of Poe, Hawthorne, and Kate Chopin," D.99

"Ratio-nal Pedagogy for Kate Chopin's Passional Fiction: Using Burke's Scene-Act Ratio to Teach 'Story' and 'Storm,' A," D.290

"Reader-Response Approach, A," E.6.14

"Regions of the Spirit: Nature vs. Dogma in Chopin's Religious Vision," D.300

"Restive Brute: The Symbolic Presentation of Repression and Sublimation in Kate Chopin's 'Fedora, The,'" D.76, E.8.6

"Return of St. Louis' Prodigal Daughter: Kate Chopin After Seventy Years, The," D.13

"Re-Visioning Creativity: Cather, Chopin, Jewett," D.204

"Revolt Against Nature: The Problematic Modernism of *The Awakening*," E.7.2

"Rhetoric of Nineteenth-Century Feminism in Kate Chopin's 'A Pair of Silk Stockings,' The," D.143

"Rightful Subjectivity," D.174

"'Ripe Figs': Kate Chopin in Miniature," D.83, E.2.4

"Rites of Passage in Kate Chopin's *The Awakening*," D.188

"Sea Holds No Terrors: Search and Beyond in *the Awakening*, The," E.4.10

"Search for Self in Kate Chopin's Fiction: Simple Versus Complex Vision, The," D.84

"Second Coming of Aphrodite: Kate Chopin's Fantasy of Desire, The," D.95, E.2.5, E.5.1

"Self-Reflexive and Impressionistic Feminism of Edna Pontellier in Kate Chopin's *The Awakening*," E.4.5

"Self that Dares and Defies: A Study of Kate Chopin's *The Awakening*, The," E.4.12

"Semiotic Subversion in 'Désirée's Baby,'" D.176, D.202

"Sentiment, Local Color, and the New Woman Writer: Kate Chopin and Willa Cather," D.33

"Sex, Race and Criticism: Thoughts of a White Feminist on Kate Chopin and Zora Neale Hurston," D.38

"Shadow of the First Biographer: The Case of Kate Chopin, The," D.183

"Shifting Focus in Kate Chopin's *The Awakening*," D.181

"Siren of Grand Isle: Adèle's Role in *The Awakening*, The," D.110, E.2.6

Sister's Choice: Tradition and Change in American Women's Writing, D.187

"Social Values of Childbirth in the Nineteenth-Century Novel, The," D.66

"Sonata No. 1 in Prose, the "Von Stoltz": Music Structure in an Early Work by Kate Chopin," D.250

"Speech and Authorship in Kate Chopin's 'La Belle Zoraïde,'" D.245

"Spiritual Bildung: The Beautiful Soul as Paradigm," D.90

Sporting with the Gods: The Rhetoric of Play and Game in American Culture, D.186

"Staking Claims for No Territory: The Sea as Woman's Space," D.239

"Strange Demise of Edna Pontellier, The," D.195

"Struggle Toward Self-Realization: Gustave Flaubert's *Madame Bovary*, Kate Chopin's *The Awakening*, and Arishima Takeo's *Aru onna*, The," D.283

"Student's Response to *The Awakening*, A," D.11

"Stylistic Categories in *The Awakening*," E.6.15

"Suicide as Metaphor: Edna's Search for Identity," E.4.9

"Suicide of Edna Pontellier: An Ambiguous Ending?, The," D.111

"Swinburne and the Critique of Ideology in *The Awakening*," D.200

"Symbolic Setting in Kate Chopin's 'A Shameful Affair,'" D.77

"Symbolism and Imagery in *The Awakening*," E.6.3

"Taming the Sirens: Self-

Possession and the Strategies of Art in Kate Chopin's *The Awakening*," E.3.5

"Techniques of Distancing in the Fiction of Kate Chopin," D.118

"Teeth of Desire: *The Awakening* and *The Descent of Man*, The," D.189, E.8.4

"Tentative Transgressions: Kate Chopin's Fiction as a Mode of Symbolic Action," D.82

"Testing the Waters: Contemplating the Sea in ED's Poem 520 and Kate Chopin's *The Awakening*," D.208

"Timely and Timeless: The Treatment of Time in *The Awakening* and *Sister Carrie*," D.36

"Thanatos and Eros: Kate Chopin's *The Awakening*," E.5.6, E.9.4

"Three Ednas," D.9

"To Your Own Self Be True: A Study of Edna Pontellier in *The Awakening*," E.4.16

Tomorrow is Another Day: The Woman Writer in the South, 1859-1936, D.70

"Towards a Feminist Poetics," D.45

"Tradition and the Female Talent: *The Awakening* as a Solitary Book*," E.7.4, E.9.1

"Two Awakenings: Edna Pontellier and Helena Richie," D.52

"Two Settings: The Islands and the City," E.6.9

"The Unawakening of Edna Pontellier," D.41

"Universal and Particular: The Local-Color Phenomenon Reconsidered," D.54

"Unlinking Race and Gender: *The Awakening* as a Southern Novel," D.311
"Un-Utterable Longing: The Discourse of Feminine Sexuality in *The Awakening*," D.295, D.303
Unveiling Kate Chopin, B.4, D.306

"'Vagabonds': A Story Without a Home," D.249
"Veiled Hints: An Affective Stylist's Reading of Kate Chopin's 'Story of an Hour,'" D.86
Verging on the Abyss: The Social Fiction of Kate Chopin and Edith Wharton, D.173
Vital Signs: Essays on American Literature and Criticism, D.286
Vocation and a Voice, A, A.5
"Voix Étrangères/Voix Féminines," D.292

"Wagnerian Romanticism in Kate Chopin's *The Awakening*," D.215
"Walking through New Orleans: Kate Chopin and the Female Flâneur," D.313
"Walt Whitman and Kate Chopin: A Further Connection," D.37
Western Canon: The Books and School of the Ages, The, D.232
"'What Are the Prospects for the Book?': Rewriting a Woman's Life," E.3.13
"Whitman's Multitudinous Poetic Progeny: Particular and Puzzling Instances," D.238
"Woman Can Walk on Water: Island, Myth, and Community in Kate Chopin's *The Awakening* and Paul Marshall's

Praisesong for the Widow," D.222
Women and New Orleans: A History, D.149
"Women Drifting: Drabble's *The Waterfall* and Chopin's *The Awakening*," D.98
"Women in the South: History as Fiction, Fiction as History," D.219
Women on the Color Line: Evolving Stereotypes and the Writings of George Washington Cable, Grace King, Kate Chopin, D.160
"Women Writers and Death by Drowning," D.114
"Women's Language in *The Awakening*," E.6.7
"Work of Womanhood in American Naturalism, The," D.287
"Wretched Freeman, The," E.1.8

Subject Index

Reference numbers following author's names refer to entry numbers in the text. Alpha-numeric notations refer to entries in the body of the book. Roman numerals refer to items found in the front matter of this volume.

Abortion, D.30

Adamic woman, D.72

Adèle Ratignolle, D.99, D.130, D.135, D.167, D.172, D.201, D.294, E.2.6, E.3.2

"After the Winter," D.297, E.3.8

Alcée Arobin, D.108, D.195, D.247, D.259, E.3.12

Alcott, Louisa May, D.212

Ammons, Elizabeth, D.260

Anthony, Susan B., D.143

Aphrodite, D.95, D.161, D.252, E.2.5

Archetypes, D.117, D.161

Art and Artist, D.135, D.184, D.186, D.267, D.271, E.3.2, E.8.8

"At Chênière Caminada," E.3.8

At Fault, D.27, D.61, D.88, D.89, D.109, D.128, D.213, D.257, D.261, D.269, D.278, D.279, D.285, D.297, D.299, D.312, E.1.7, E.2.7, E.3.1, E.3.6,

E.8.4

"Athénaïse," D.42, D.92, D.120, E.8.11, E.8.14

"At the 'Cadian Ball," D.54, D.160, D.246, D.264, E.8.5

Atwood, Margaret, D.7, D.121

"Aunt Lympy's Interference," D.164

Austen, Jane, D.239, D.310

Awakening, D.1, D.5, D.41, D.55, D.103, D.105, D.120, D.130, D.142, D.157, D.184, D.188, D.194, D.199, D.203, D.210, D.221, D.240, E.1.3, E.2.2, E.2.6, E.2.8, E.3.2, E.3.8, E.5.2

"Awakening of Helena Richie, The," D.52

Awakening, The, D.11, D.12, D.16, D.19, D.23, D.24, D.25, D.27, D.32, D.40, D.42, D.47, D.49, D.51, D.52, D.53, D.54, D.57, D.60,

D.62, D.63, D.64, D.66,
D.67, D.70, D.72, D.79,
D.82, D.84, D.85, D.87,
D.88, D.89, D.90, D.91,
D.96, D.98, D.100, D.104,
D.105, D.107, D.108, D.111,
D.112, D.114, D.117, D.118,
D.120, D.125, D.127, D.130,
D.135, D.136, D.137, D.138,
D.140, D.142, D.144, D.148,
D.150, D.152, D.156, D.157,
D.160, D.162, D.163, D.165,
D.166, D.167, D.168, D.171,
D.174, D.177, D.181, D.182,
D.184, D.186, D.187, D.188,
D.190, D.191, D.193, D.195,
D.199, D.200, D.201, D.203,
D.204, D.205, D.208, D.209,
D.210, D.212, D.213, D.215,
D.216, D.222, D.223, D.226,
D.227, D.228, D.229, D.232,
D.233, D.235, D.239, D.240,
D.242, D.244, D.247, D.249,
D.252, D.255, D.256, D.259,
D.262, D.263, D.267, D.269,
D.270, D.271, D.274, D.276,
D.279, D.280, D.281, D.285,
D.286, D.288, D.291, D.293,
D.294, D.297, D.302, D.303,
D.304, D.305, D.306, D.307,
D.308, D.311, D.312, D.313,
E.1.2, E.1.3, E.1.4, E.1.5,
E.1.6, E.1.7, E.1.12, E.2.1,
E.2.2, E.2.3, E.2.6, E.2.7,
E.2.8, E.3.2, E.3.3, E.3.5,
E.3.6, E.3.7, E.3.8, E.3.9,
E.3.10, E.3.11, E.3.12,
E.3.13, E.5.2, E.5.3, E.5.5,
E.5.6, E.5.7, E.7, E.8.1,
E.8.3, E.8.4, E.8.7, E.8.8,
E.8.9, E.8.10, E.8.11, E.8.12,
E.8.13, E.9.3
    in England, D.6
    and *Sister Carrie*, D.36

Bakhtin, Mikhail, D.146, D.245
Barren Ground, D.40
Bayou Folk, D.26, D.113, D.285
Bayou Folk Museum, D.5
"Bedquilt, The," D.78
"Bênitou's Slave, The," E.1.8
"Beyond the Bayou," D.254
Bibliography, Primary, C.7, C.9,
    D.116, D.124, D.223, D.258,
    D.284
Biological Determinism, D.168,
    D.211
Bildungsroman, D.90, D.121,
    D.135, D.155, D.221, E.2.8
Bierce, Ambrose, D.233
Bi-sexuality, D.293
Brown, Starling, E.1.8
Burke, Kenneth, D.290

Cable, George Washington, D.89,
    D.109, D.160, D.178, D.213,
    D.279, D.297, E.1.8
Cajun, D.129
Cather, Willa, D.33, D.40, D.78,
    D.204, E.3.11
Catholicism, D.50, D.81, D.88,
    D.113, D.198, D.262, D.300
"Cavanelle," D.24
"Charlie," D.120, D.126, D.212,
    D.246, E.3.4, E.8.14
Chestnut, Charles W., D.213,
    E.7.1
Childbirth, D.30, D.42, D.66
Chinese Literature, E.1.3
Chodorow, Nancy, D.204
Chopin, Frédéric, D.8
Chopin, Kate:
    and ambition, D.31
    autobiographical fiction
        elements, D.14
    biographical data, B.1, B,2,
        B.3, B.4, D.58, D.82,
        D.91, D.97, D.105,
        D.115, D.120, D.122,

D.124, D.136, D.137,
D.140, D.141, D.146,
D.154, D.158, D.165,
D.173, D.182, D.196,
D.205, D.214, D.223,
D.249, D.251, D.266,
D.272, D.284, D.285,
D.286, D.308, D.314,
E.1.12, E.3.1, E.3.13,
E.3.14
and birthdate, D.22, D.133
and Cloutierville, D.122
and French influence, D.12,
D.269, D.292, D.297
and graffiti, D.10
and music, D.35
musical compositions, D.28,
D.29
narrative structure, D.27,
D.91
and New Orleans, D.88,
D.122, D.148, D.158,
D.203, D.308, D.313
repeating characters, D.65
and St. Louis, D.13, D.88,
D.122
sources, D.68
Chopin, Oscar, D.15
Christianity, D.81, D.88
Cixous, Hélène, D.248, D.261,
D.279
Clothing, D.104, D.119, D.302
Crane, Stephen, D.287
Creole Communities, D.109,
D.292
Creole Country, D.49
Creoles of Color, D.129
Creole Society, D.57, D.96, D.108,
D.138, D.146, D.148, D.178,
D.198, D.205, D.259, D.297,
E.1.6, E.5.5

Darwin, Charles, D.125, D.255,
E.8.3, E.8.4

Death, D.90, D.101, D.106, D.114,
D.167, D.193, D.208, D.218
Deconstruction, D.265, E.5.7
Degas, Edgar, D.297, D.304
Deland, Margaret, D.52
Depression, D.40
Desire, D.40
"Désirée's Baby," D.42, D.43,
D.80, D.120, D.160, D.170,
D.192, D.202, D.213, D.260,
D.297, E.2.9, E.7.1, E.8.1,
E.8.2,
Deutsch, Helenè, E.5.6
Dickinson, Emily, D.208
Dobson, Joanne, D.279
Domestic Novel, D.64, D.121,
D.153, D.257, D.269
Dormon, Carolyn, D.299
Dr. Mandelet, D.86, D.117, D.172,
D.247, D.256, E.1.5
Drabble, Margaret, D.98, D.100,
D.224
Dreiser, Theodore, D.168, D.287,
E.3.6
Drowning: D.7, D.98, D.100,
D.114, D.224
Dunbar-Nelson, Alice, D.213

Economics, D.165, E.1.2, E.3.6,
E.3.12
"Egyptian Cigarette, An," D.246,
D.248
Elfenbein, Anna S., D.260
Eliot, George, D.114, D.224
"Elizabeth Stock's One Story,"
D.78, D.246, D.273, D.282,
E.8.14
"Emancipation. A Life Fable,"
D.112, D.297
Emerson, Ralph Waldo, D.39,
D.89, D.163, D.212, E.3.9,
E.7.3
Ewell, Barbara, D.257
Existentialism, D.69

Fairy Tales, D.170, D.271, D.288
Family, D.153
Faulkner, William, D.216, E.5.3
"Fedora," D.76, D.248, E.8.6
Female Hero, D.72, D.108,
    D.125, D.156, E.3.3, E.3.10
Feminism, D.19, D.38, D.45,
    D.57, D.95, D.103, D.127,
    D.136, D.143, D.144, D.146,
    D.166, D.171, D.173, D.177,
    D.184, D.210, D.211, D.217,
    D.219, D.221, D.231, D.239,
    D.240, D.260, D.275, D.276,
    D.286, D.287, D.291, D.292,
    D.293, E.2.5, E.5.5, E.5.6,
    E.5.7, E.8.9
Fish, Stanley, D.86
Fisher, Dorothy Canfield, D.78
Fitzgerald, F. Scott, D.119
Flaubert, Gustave, D.113, D.227,
    D.235, D.255, E.8.12
Folklore, D. 129
Fox, Genovese, Elizabeth, E.3.3
Freeman, Mary E. Wilkins, D.78,
    D.287, D.312
Freud, Sigmund, D.99, D.132,
    D.171, D.255, D.259, D.294,
    E.5.6
Fuller, Margaret, D.143

Garden, D.299
Gender, D.89, D.90, D.94, D.96,
    D.98, D.101, D.102, D.103,
    D.120, D.121, D.126, D.130,
    D.138, D.143, D.144, D.146,
    D.149, D.155, D.162, D.165,
    D.167, D.170, D.171, D.177,
    D.184, D.185, D.188, D.194,
    D.196, D.200, D.202, D.204,
    D.205, D.211, D.212, D.213,
    D.224, D.230, D.239, D.246,
    D.248, D.259, D.260, D.267,
    D.274, D.275, D.278, D.279,
    D.302, D.307, D.311, E.1.6,

    E.3.2, E.3.9, E.8.9, E.8.13
"Gentleman of Bayou Têche, A,"
    D.265
Gilbert, Sandra, D.221, D.240,
    E.3.12
Gilded Age, D.89, E.1.2
Gilligan, Carol, D.204, D.257
Gilman, Charlotte Perkins, D.166,
    D.171, D.172, D.287, D.296
Glasgow, Ellen, D.40
"Godmother, The," D.42
"Gouvernail," D.73, E.2.1

Harvard Lampoon, D.19
Hawthorne, Nathaniel, D.39, D.72,
    D.92, D.99, D.179
Health Manuals, E.1.5
Hearn, Lafcadio, D.106, D.109,
    D.178
Helena Richie, D.52
Henry, O., D.233
Hentz, Caroline Lee, D.94
Hester Prynne, D.72
House of Mirth, The, D.40
Huf, Linda, D.130
Hurston, Zora Neale, D.38, D.211,
    D.254, D.262, E.8.11
Huxley, Thomas, D.255

Ibsen, Henrik, E.3.3, E.3.10
Idealism, German, D.276
Imagery, D.104, D.105, D.157,
    D.162, D.208, D.210, D.226,
    D.241, D.243, D.255, E.1.3,
    E.8.1
Impressionism, D.32, D.127,
    D.167, E.7.2
"In the Confidence of a Story-
    Writer," D.263
Irigaray, Luce, D.248
Isabel Archer, D.51, D.72

James, Henry, D.51, D.72, D.233
James, William, D.132

Jehlen, Myra, D.279
Jewett, Sarah Orne, D.154,
 D.204, D.287, D.310
Jie, Zhang, E.1.3
Joyce, James, D.95, E.2.5, E.5.3

Kate Chopin Newsletter, D.34
King, Grace Elizabeth, D.89,
 D.94, D.109, D.148, D.160,
 D.165, D.178, D.213, E.1.8,
 E.1.12
Kolodny, Annette, D.279
Kristeva, Julia, D.248, D.261
Künstlerroman, D.90

"La Belle Zoraïde," D.118,
 D.160, D.213, D.245, D.260,
 D.278, D.297, E.8.14
Lacan, Jacques, D.210, D.248
"Lady of Bayou St. John, A,"
 D.278
Laing, R.D., D.99, D.111, E.5.6
Lebrun, Robert, D.100, D.106,
 D.108, D.135, D.196, D.215,
 D.247, D.259, E.1.4, E.3.12,
 E.5.3, E.8.13
Lebrun, Victor , D.108, E.8.13
Lesbian, D.291
Lessing, Doris, D.218
"Lilacs," D.50, D.249, D.249,
 D.262
Linguistic Analysis, D.63, D.86,
 D.135, D.146, D.167, D.204,
 D.218, D.231, D.248, D.274,
 D.275, D.293, E.5.7, E.9.3
Local Color, D.33, D.54, D.82,
 D.109, D.113, D.126, D.127,
 D.129, D.160, D.165, D.168,
 D.187, D.190, D.203, D.235,
 D.245, D.265, D.269, D.278,
 E.5.2, E.8.7
"Locket, The," D.297
"Loka," D.105, D.249

"Ma'ame Pélagie," D.42
Mademoiselle Reisz, D.130,
 D.135, D.172, D.209, D.215,
 D.229, D.239, D.240, D.247,
 D.256, D.267, D.294, E.1.7
"Maid of Saint Phillippe, The,"
 D.263, D.297
Marriage, D.94, D.100, D.101,
 D.120, D.125, D.130, D.143,
 D.153, D.174, D.199, D.211,
 D.222, D.230, D.231
Marxism, E.3.12
Matriarchy, D.108
"Matter of Prejudice, A," D.297
Maupassant, Guy de, A.1, D.113,
 D.147, D.187, D.226, D.233,
 D.235, D.264,D.269, E.2.10,
 E.7.4, E.8.13
Melville, Herman, D.39, D.96,
 D.130
Metaphor (poetic), D.107, D.119,
 D.172, D.186, D.198, D.203,
 D.250, D.279
Mill on the Floss, D.184
"Miss McEnders," D.120
"Miss Witherwell's Mistake,"
 D.282, E.8.14
Modernism, D.163, D.166, D.187,
 D.198, D.228, D.256, E.7.2,
 E.7.4
Morality, D.62
"Morning Walk, A," D.105
Motherhood, D.42, D.64, D.98,
 D.112, D.117, D.130, D.143,
 D.172, D.179, D.184, D.267,
 D.275, D.293
"Mrs. Mobry's Reason," D.42,
 D.68, D.246
Multiculturalism, D.265, D.284,
 D.292
Murdoch, Iris, D.100
Music, D.209, D.215, D.250,
 E.3.5, E.3.8
Mysticism, D.132

Mythology, D.95, D.108, D.130,
	D.138, D.157, D.161, D.281,
	E.2.5, E.3.7, E.7.3

Narrative Structure, D.164, D.233,
	D.245, D.296, E.2.4, E.2.10
Narrative Style, D.187
Nature, D.105, D.106, D.168,
	D.177, D.299
Naturalism, D.57, D.60, D.95,
	D.106, D.168, D.191, D.216,
	D.240, D.256, D.271, D.287,
	E.2.5, E.5.5, E.7.3, E.8.7
"Nég Créol," D.213, E.1.8
New Historicism, D.287
New Orleans, D.297
New Woman, D.187, D.235,
	D.269, E.7.2
Nietszche, Friedrich, E.7.3
"Night Came Slowly, The," D.118
Night in Acadie, A, D.285
Nineteenth Century:
	Fiction: D.257, D.261, D.263,
		D.269, E.3.7
	Novel, D.66, D.155, E.8.7
	Short Story: D.126, D.155
	Society: D.227, D.229,
		D.230
	Southern Literature, D.61,
		D.155, D.190, D.311
"No-Account Creole, A," D.278
Norris, Frank, D.287
Northrup, Solomon, D.299

O! Pioneers!, D.40
"Odalie Misses Mass," E.1.8
"Out of the Cradle Endlessly
	Rocking," D.48
"Ozème's Holiday," D.24

"Pair of Silk Stockings, A," D.143
Pedagogy, D.151, D.236, D.237,
	D.287, D.290, E.6
Pembroke, D.312

Philomela, D.281
Phenomenology, D.86, D.271
Piaget, Jean, E.1.4
Plath, Sylvia, D.114
Poe, Edgar Allan, D.99, D.226
"Poetess, The," D.78
"Point at Issue, A," D.231
Political Novel, D.67
Politics, D.174, D.202
Pontellier, Edna, D.9, D.41, D.45,
	D.51, D.70, D.72, D.79,
	D.85, D.87, D.90, D.94,
	D.99, D.100, D.104, D.106,
	D.108, D.111, D.112, D.113,
	D.116, D.117, D.119, D.127,
	D.130, D.132, D.135, D.142,
	D.143, D.146, D.150, D.155,
	D.162, D.163, D.166, D.167,
	D.172, D.174, D.179, D.181,
	D.186, D.188, D.194, D.195,
	D.199, D.201, D.203, D.204,
	D.205, D.209, D.215, D.221,
	D.222, D.224, D.227, D.239,
	D.242, D.244, D.247, D.259,
	D.267, D.281, D.288, D.294,
	D.302, D.304, D.305, D.306,
	D.308, D.310, E.1.2, E.1.4,
	E.1.5, E.1.6, E.1.7, E.2.3,
	E.2.6, E.2.8, E.2.10, E.3.10,
	E.5.2, E.5.3, E.5.6, E.7,
	E.8.7, E.8.10, E.8.12, E.9.3
Pontellier, Léonce, D.86, D.100,
	D.127, D.172, D.174, D.247,
	D.259, E.1.4, E.3.12
Porter, Katherine Anne, D.72
Post-Colonialism, D.242, D.253,
	D.296
Psychoanalytic Analysis, D.99,
	D.111, D.166, D.226, D.294,
	E.3.4, E.5.5
Psychology, D.195

Quest, D.56, D.59

Race, D.38, D.89, D.129, D.138, D.160, D.165, D.178, D.184, D.192, D.202, D.213, D.219, D.242, D.245, D.253, D.254, D.260, D.278, D.296, D.297, D.311, D.312, E.1.8, E.8.1, E.8.11

Rankin, Daniel, D.113, D.158, D.183, D.249, E.1.7, E.2.3, E.3.14

Realism, D.84, D.95, D.101, D.127, D.148, D.153, D.154, D.166, D.216, D.235, D.240, D.245, D.256, D.269, D.288, E.2.5, E.7.2, E.7.3, E.8.7, E.8.10

Regionalism, D.148, D.292, D.312

Religion, D.200, D.243, D.303

"Return of Alcibiade, The," D.297

"Respectable Woman, A," D.238

"Ripe Figs," D.243, E.2.4

Romance, D.67, D.94

Romanticism, D.39, D.51, D.100, D.106, D.135, D.138, D.146, D.153, D.154, D.191, D.200, D.209, D.215, D.216, D.228, D.288, E.1.5, E.7.4, E.8.7, E.8.12

Romanticism, German, D.194

Sand, George, D.97, D.121, D.235, D.310

Scarlet Letter, The, D.39

Schopenhauer, Arthur, D.136, D.276, E.1.7

Seidel, Kathryn, D.291

Self, D.51, D.89, D.101, D.104, D.108, D.111, D.121, D.156, D.162, D.181, D.240, D.242, E.3.9

"Sentimental Soul, A," D.297

Seyersted, Per, D.183, D.226, D.249, D.264, E.1.7, E.3.4, E.3.6, E.3.14

Sex, D.38, D.138, D.242

Sexual Determinism, D.191

Sexuality, D.103, D.106, D.118, D.134, D.153, D.157, D.160, D.162, D.168, D.171, D.184, D.190, D.208, D.209, D.210, D.240, D.241, D.248, D.296, D.300, D.303, E.3.3, E.5.3, E.8.3

"Shameful Affair, A," D.77, D.134

Shaw, George Bernard, E.3.3

Showalter, Elaine, D.130, D.193, D.269, D.291

Social Background, D.253

Social Class, D.160, D.165, D.184, D.190, D.202, D.278

Social Contexts, D.57, D.100, D.102, D.109, D.121, D.146, D.150, D.155, D.160, D.165, D.211, D.213, D.250

Social Values, D.66, D.130, D.138, D.167, D.200, D.205, D.221

"Song of Myself," D.48

Song of the Lark, D.78

Southern literature, D.61, D.89, D.115

Spencer, Herbert, D.255

Spirituality, D.59, D.90

Stanton, Elizabeth Cady, D.143, E.3.3

"Storm, The," D.160, D.165, D.241, D.264, D.290, E.8.5

"Story of an Hour, The," D.71, D.86, D.105, D.120, D.211, D.218, D.248, D.262, D.288, D.290, D.297

Stuart, Ruth McEnery, D.89, D.165, D.178, E.1.8

Suicide, D.59, D.85, D.100, D.103, D.111, D.137, D.138, D.142, D.146, D.155, D.156, D.163, D.174, D.186, D.196, D.199, D.215, D.221, E.1.7, E.3.11,

E.8.7
Swinburne, Algernon, D.200,
    E.2.1
"Sweat," D.254
Symbolism, D.77, D.82, D.87,
    D.95, D.104, D.106, D.107,
    D.119, D.125, D.134, D.167,
    D.188, D.222, D.240, D.299,
    D.302, E.2.3, E.2.5, E.3.2,
    E.3.5, E.7.3, E.8.6

"Tante Cat'rinette," E.1.8
Taylor, Helen, D.260, D.264,
    E.8.11
Thoreau, Henry David, D.39, D.89
Toth, Emily, D.153, D.226, D.249,
    D.264, D.286
Tragic Octaroon, D.160
Transcendentalism, D.84, D.130,
    D.136, D.235, D.247, E.8.7
Translation, D.264
Twain, Mark, D.150, D.179
"Two Portraits," D.248, D.249

"Unexpected, The," D.105

"Vagabonds," D.249
Venus, D.95, D.161
"Very Fine Fiddle, A," D.250
"Village Stranger, A," D.78
"Vocation and a Voice, A," D.56,
    E.8.9
Vocation and a Voice, A, E.3.7

Wagner, Richard, D.215, D.235
Walden, D.39
Watson, Barbara Bellow, D.17
Wharton, Edith, D.40, D.144,
    D.172, D.173, D.271, D.296
"White Eagle, The," D.107, D.248
Whitman, Walt, D.37, D.38, D.48,
    D.106, D.130, D.136, D.156,
    D.238, E.8.4
Williams, Tennessee, D.216

"Wiser Than a God," D.246,
    D.267
"With the Violin," D.250, E.3.8
"Wizard From Gettysburg, A,"
    D.297
Wolff, Cynthia Griffin, D.99,
    D.135
Women:
    as artist: D.78
    in 19th century novel: D.2,
        D.185
    literary: D.3
    Southern Writers: D.70,
        D.197, D.205, D.217,
        D.219
    writers: D.102, D.125, D.161,
        D.163, D.166, D.172,
        D.184, D.190, D.199,
        D.234, D.240, D.263,
        D.269, D.273, D.278,
        D.282, E.7.4, E.8.14
"Wood Choppers, The," D.107
Woolf, Virginia, D.100, D.239,
    D.255, E.2.5

Yaeger, Patricia, D.279

Zampa, D.62

About the Authors

SUZANNE DISHEROON GREEN is Assistant Professor of American Literature at Northwestern State University in Natchitoches, Louisiana. She has published numerous articles on Kate Chopin, which have appeared in such journals as *Southern Studies* and the *CEA Critic*.

DAVID J. CAUDLE is a Ph.D. candidate at the University of North Texas, where he is studying literature and linguistics. He has published and presented papers on the American regional novel, Kate Chopin and her works, and the linguistic analysis of literature.